The Letters of
Thomas Merton and
Victor and Carolyn Hammer

for the Sintonis
with esteem
& appreciation !

Paul

The Letters of
THOMAS
MERTON
and

VICTOR *and*
CAROLYN
HAMMER

Ad Majorem Dei Gloriam

Edited by F. Douglas Scutchfield
and Paul Evans Holbrook Jr.

With the editorial assistance
of Leah Casanave

Foreword by Paul M. Pearson

UNIVERSITY PRESS OF KENTUCKY

Scholarly publisher for the Commonwealth,
serving Bellarmine University, Berea College, Centre College of Kentucky,
Eastern Kentucky University, The Filson Historical Society, Georgetown
College, Kentucky Historical Society, Kentucky State University, Morehead
State University, Murray State University, Northern Kentucky University,
Transylvania University, University of Kentucky, University of Louisville,
and Western Kentucky University.
All rights reserved.

Editorial and Sales Offices: The University Press of Kentucky
663 South Limestone Street, Lexington, Kentucky 40508-4008
www.kentuckypress.com

Library of Congress Cataloging-in-Publication Data

The Letters of Thomas Merton and Victor and Carolyn Hammer : Ad
Majorem Dei Gloriam / edited by F. Douglas Scutchfield and Paul Evans
Holbrook Jr. ; with the editorial assistance of Leah Casanave ; foreword by
Paul M. Pearson.
    pages cm
  Includes bibliographical references and index.
  ISBN 978-0-8131-5352-0 (hardcover : acid-free paper) —
  ISBN 978-0-8131-5565-4 (pdf) — ISBN 978-0-8131-5564-7 (epub) —
  ISBN 978-0-8131-5570-8 (leatherbound : acid-free paper)
  1. Merton, Thomas, 1915-1968—Correspondence. 2. Hammer, Victor,
1882-1967—Correspondence. 3. Hammer, Carolyn Reading—Correspondence.
4. Trappists—United States—Correspondence. 5. Catholics—
Correspondence. I. Scutchfield, F. Douglas, editor. II. Holbrook, Paul Evans,
1949- editor.
  BX4705.M542A4 2014
  271'.12502—dc23
  [B]   2014030783

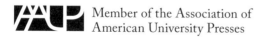

Contents

Illustrations follow page 174

Foreword

Over the years, along with five volumes of Thomas Merton's selected letters, a growing library has been published of Merton's complete extant correspondence with a wide variety of friends and contacts—lifelong friends such as Robert Lax; publishing contacts such as James Laughlin and, soon, I hope, Robert Giroux and Naomi Burton Stone; literary correspondents such as Czeslaw Milosz; cultural ones such as Ad Reinhardt and Edward Deming Andrews; theological correspondents such as Jean Leclercq, D. T. Suzuki, and Rosemary Radford Reuther; and Kentucky friends such as Jonathan Greene and Ralph Eugene Meatyard.

The volume of correspondence you are currently holding could easily fit into a number of those categories—cultural, literary, publishing, theological; however, it seems to fit best into the category of Kentucky friends. Readers familiar with Merton's journals and correspondence are well acquainted with many of Thomas Merton's local friends—Tommie O'Callaghan, Mary Luke Tobin, Dan Walsh, Ron Seitz, Jonathan Greene, John Loftus, Ralph Eugene Meatyard, Jim Wygal, and numerous others. While contemplating Thomas Merton's various visitors at Gethsemani overs the years, I found myself asking the question, "Who were his most frequent visitors?" The answer may well surprise many of Merton's readers. Between 1955 and 1968 Merton records in his journals and correspondence well over thirty visits with Carolyn and Victor Hammer, a couple who, over the years, would become some of his closest and dearest local friends.[1] But, besides those visits, Thomas Merton and the Hammers kept up an extensive correspondence, as witnessed to here—though, as you begin to read these pages, you'll also get an insight, frustrating at times, into the number of letters that either Merton or the Hammers failed to save for one reason or another. Before the establishment of the Thomas Merton Collection at Bellarmine College (now University) in 1963, Merton kept only a small fraction of the letters he received, and he rarely kept carbon copies of the letters he wrote. From the establishment of the collection at Bellarmine until his death in December 1968, Merton was much more conscientious about preserving the letters he received and carbons of the letters he sent. This can be clearly seen in these pages: before November 1963, only occasional letters from the Hammers were saved by Merton and have survived for publication.

Merton's correspondence with Victor and Carolyn Hammer remained much more formal than that with many other friends, and for a much longer time. After the first few letters to most of his correspondents, Merton would quickly drop the more formal "Fr. Louis" and begin signing simply "Tom," and then he and his correspondent would generally be on first-name terms. It was almost seven years, however, before that change took place in Merton's correspondence with the Hammers. This reflects partly the respect in which they held each other, and also the more old-fashioned, and therefore more formal, nature of their friendship.

Initially Thomas Merton's contact with Victor Hammer came about through Merton's sensitivity to the poor quality of the religious artwork in the Abbey Church and Monastery at Gethsemani during his early years there in the 1940s and 1950s. With his own artistic and cultural background, Merton was appalled by some of the Catholic artwork of this period, and his criticisms would often appear in his journals and correspondence. His abbot during this period, James Fox, certainly respected Merton's views on this matter and gave Merton considerable leeway, both artistically and financially, in commissioning artwork for the monastery.[2] Merton, working with Brother Giles, commissioned the British sculptor Peter Watts, working in the tradition of Eric Gill and Aristide Maillol, to sculpt numerous pieces for the abbey, including statues of the Sacred Heart, Saint Benedict, Saint Bernard, Saint Robert of Molesme, a crucifix and a Madonna and child, along with the fourteen Stations of the Cross in the abbey cloister. Then, later in the 1950s, when he was novice master,

Merton commissioned an Ecuadorian sculptor, Jaime Andrade, to carve a statue of the Virgin Mary and child Jesus in mahogany for the novitiate.

It is not entirely clear from the extant correspondence when Merton's first contact with Victor Hammer occurred. Certainly the first surviving letter, from October 1955, which also includes a reference to Peter Watts, suggests that this was not their first contact, as Merton asks, "Have you given any further thought to our text?" A slightly earlier letter from Brother Giles to Victor Hammer also makes reference to Merton's interest in having Hammer print a book for him. Quickly their correspondence developed from this initial contact into a deeper exchange about the aesthetics of art that led to Merton's discussing with Hammer the possibility of his creating various pieces of artwork for the monastery, including a crucifix, tabernacle and candles, altar cards and other religious cards, along with his publishing, over the years, a number of limited-edition fine press books based on texts written by, or translated by, Merton. Also, Victor's wife, Carolyn, through her work at the University of Kentucky Library, became one of a number of sources, along with his publishers, other friends, and other libraries, that supplied Merton with the books that he was so voraciously reading and that he required for his writing and teaching.

A much deeper friendship, however, soon developed between Thomas Merton and both Victor and his wife, Carolyn. The couple frequently visited Merton at Gethsemani for conversations and, not infrequently, picnics; less often, Merton would visit the Hammers in their home in Lexington, Kentucky. Victor, with his classical, highly civilized, European background and his work as an artist and printer, was one of the few people of his own intellectual prowess whom Merton could meet with and converse with reasonably frequently.

In contrast to Merton's friendship with Victor Hammer is his lifelong friendship, begun in his premonastic days at Columbia University, with the abstract artist Ad Reinhardt, referred to by both Merton and Hammer in this volume. Although Merton shared much in common with both men, it becomes clear through his correspondence with Victor Hammer, and some of Merton's own journal entries, that Hammer found it next to impossible to understand Reinhardt's work or that of other abstract artists of this period. In contrast, Merton would call Reinhardt "possibly the best artist in America" and describe his work as "pure and religious. It flies away from all naturalism, from all representation to pure formal and intellectual values. . . . Reinhardt's abstract art is completely chaste, and full of love of form and very good indeed."[3]

When Reinhardt and another of Merton's Columbia friends, Robert Lax, visited Merton at Gethsemani in April 1959, Merton tried, unsuccessfully, to arrange to take them to Lexington to meet with Victor and Carolyn. Victor, in a subsequent letter, while noting that he was sorry to have missed them, left no doubt in writing to Merton, in one of the few letters of this period that Merton saved, of his views on abstract art. Victor labels it "pure perversion" and, in describing Reinhardt in his work "as an abstractionist," writes of him as "a sinner against the Holy Ghost"—a view supported by Carolyn, he adds, who described abstract art as "a travesty on creation."[4] In response, Merton replied to the Hammers, defending Reinhardt's work and describing his approach as "very austere and ascetic. It is a kind of exaggerated reticence, a kind of fear of self expression. All his paintings are very formal and black. I certainly do not think he is a quack like so many others, on the contrary he is in strong reaction against them."[5]

As Thomas Merton himself turned to abstract art in the 1960s, he reflected in his journal, no doubt in trepidation after the exchanges of 1959, on how Victor Hammer would react to his calligraphies, especially when he began exhibiting them, at a show that opened at Catherine Spalding College in Louisville on November 13, 1964. So Merton wrote in his personal journal on November 4, 1964, as he prepared for that show: "One thing that saddens and embarrasses me—that he [Victor Hammer] will be shocked at my exhibition of drawings or calligraphies or what you will. There is no way to explain this to him, and in a way I am on his side, on principle. And yet they have a meaning, and there is a reason for them: an unreasoned reason perhaps." He continues, with a note of humor: "I feel like writing to him and saying: if you heard I had taken a mistress you would be sad but you would understand. These drawings are perhaps worse than that. But regard them as a human folly. Allow me at least, like everyone else, at least one abominable vice, etc."[6] And in a letter to Victor Hammer, written the same week, Merton warns him: "If you should hear news of my exhibiting strange blobs of ink in Louisville, ignore the information: it is not worthy of your notice. As always my feelings about it are very mixed. . . . I think I have made it plain to all concerned that I do not regard it as 'art' and that they are not supposed to either."[7]

Victor Hammer's responses to Merton's experiments in abstract art, and to his exhibit, remain unknown. If he did put them in writing to Merton, Merton did not keep the letter. But from the intensity of his comments about Reinhardt, one can imagine his reaction, and, perhaps, Victor thought it best just to remain silent. There is also no indication that Merton ever showed Victor and Carolyn his abstract work or gave them any, as he was certainly accustomed to do with nearly all his other visitors. Students of Thomas Merton have frequently noted that Merton possessed a unique ability to hold many of the paradoxes in his life in a creative tension—so too in his friendships with Ad Reinhardt and Victor Hammer. Thomas Merton could unite the paradoxical views of these two close friends in himself and would, all too soon, mourn deeply their passing, dying as they both did just a few weeks apart in the summer of 1967.[8]

The protean nature of Thomas Merton has often been noted both by his friends and by the scholars and readers of his work. This collection of correspondence reveals further facets of Thomas Merton as well as the frequently paradoxical nature of Merton's friendships, especially in the contrast that is so evident between Merton and such friends as Ad Reinhardt and Robert Lax on the one hand, and Victor and Carolyn Hammer on the other. Merton had that very rare ability to make almost everyone he met feel that he was his or her best friend. Victor and Carolyn Hammer were certainly among some of Merton's closest friends, and we are indebted to F. Douglas Scutchfield, Paul E. Holbrook, and the University Press of Kentucky for this volume, which sheds further light on that unique friendship and on that exceptional, multifaceted diamond, Thomas Merton.

Paul M. Pearson

Preface

For many of us Thomas Merton, Father Louis, is a Kentucky writer. Though the early part of his life, chronicled in his autobiographical search for himself, *The Seven Storey Mountain*, was spent in Europe and New York City, the time that he actually spent in productive writing was in the Abbey of Gethsemani. The abbey, a monastery outside Bardstown, Kentucky, founded in 1848, was where he became a Trappist monk and spent the majority of his life. Thus, Merton holds special interest to those of us in Kentucky and those interested in Kentucky writers, even of a spiritual nature, though many would hold that much of Kentucky literature is spiritual, even if not written in a monastery.

Bound as he was to the monastic life, he had little time for contact with those outside the walls of his chosen abode. This did not deter him from engaging those outside the monastery. His correspondence with all nature of individuals is well known and, in fact, chronicled in several publications of his correspondence with those of a variety of faiths, political leaders, and those who influenced his "turning to the world" and its pressing social problems of racism, nuclear weapons, and social justice.

There were, however, rare occasions when physical proximity and friendship were possible, which allowed for a deeper interaction than that which could occur only through correspondence and rare visits to the monastery. The subjects of this book formed such a relationship, one that prospered through proximity and a confluence of interest, thought, and convenience.

Victor and Carolyn Reading Hammer lived in Lexington, Kentucky, a reasonable distance by car, so they could on occasion drive to the monastery for a picnic prepared by Carolyn Hammer and consumed in the Hammers' car, in a tobacco barn, or, in the best of times, on the grounds of the monastery, perhaps by a lake. In addition, Merton, on some pretext, was sometimes able to travel to Lexington—to accompany a sick novice or to visit a publisher—for furtive meetings and lunches with the Hammers. This proximity allowed for an ongoing dialogue in person, not just on the written page.

It was apparent that there was a confluence of interest. Victor was an artist; he was an accomplished painter, sculptor, printer, and architect. Merton had a love and appreciation for art. He was raised by two artists, his mother and father, and he spent time with his father while his father was painting after his mother's death. He was a bit of an artist at Oakham, his English boarding school, and again at Columbia, drawing for publications at both institutions. There is little doubt that he loved Byzantine art and, in fact, one of the prompts for his religious conversion was his experience with Byzantine art in Rome. He took up calligraphy, following his love of D. T. Suzuki's words and art; later in life he was given a camera by John Howard Griffin and encouraged in his photographic efforts by Griffin and other photographers, such as Ralph Eugene Meatyard. In addition, Paul Pearson, from the Merton Center at Bellarmine, has created an exhibit of his photos that reflects the "hidden wholeness" of Merton's Zen photography.

He obviously loved the hand-printed books produced by the Hammers on their presses in Lexington and provided much material—as Victor Hammer and Merton would say, "a pretext for printing." The beautiful books, altar cards, broadsides, and ephemera reflect the love they shared for fine printing. These friends clearly enjoyed several intellectual interests in common and undoubtedly spent many hours discussing those interests and collaborating on them.

Merton's reading habits were prodigious. The volume and breadth of his reading is truly remarkable. His notion of *Lectio Divina* was obviously quite broad, though he points out that occasionally in his work as master of novices he had to read scripture and religious history books, in many cases to his delight. But he also read about different religious experiences, particularly Buddhism and especially Zen, though he also studied and wrote about mysticism in Judaism and Islam. He read about issues that concerned him broadly, in addition to becoming familiar with such popular writers as Camus, Pasternak, and other Russian writers. As there was an influx of Latin American novices and invitations to establish new foundations in Latin America, he read extensively about that region and its literature, poetry, and history. Many of these books were not available at the abbey and he needed to borrow them from friendly libraries, and certainly the University of Kentucky Library was such a place.

Thus, for Merton and the Hammers, there was proximity, community of interest, and, certainly in his needs for reading material, the convenience of the access to a library and a librarian who was a friend and colleague. So it is no wonder that their relationship grew and prospered over twelve years, until the deaths of Hammer and Merton, and, in fact, continued with Carolyn's publishing, after both their deaths, a copy of *Hagia Sophia* in 1978; a brass engraving of Hagia Sophia constitutes the frontispiece of the hand-printed book.

This friendship produced a remarkable correspondence of great interest to those of us who enjoy the relationship between polymaths like the Hammers and Merton. The archives at the University of Kentucky contain substantial Merton material, given to the library by Merton in response to requests by Dr. Lawrence Thompson, who was the librarian for the University of Kentucky (UK) following Margaret I. King's term as director. Thompson initiated a correspondence with Merton in 1950 and attempted to obtain as much of Merton's materials as Merton would part with, which resulted in a not inconsequential collection of Merton memorabilia at the UK archives. In addition, given the Hammers' close relationship to the library and its presses, the material from their estate passed to the UK Library and contains substantial amounts of correspondence from Merton.

One can only assume that there was the hope that UK would become the repository and perhaps the center for Merton studies that Bellarmine University has become, with its Thomas Merton Center. Nevertheless, Merton decided to give the bulk of his work to Bellarmine, which has curated it and added to it the materials that continue to be produced about Merton and new items as they are uncovered. As a result, a substantial portion of his correspondence with the Hammers is at the Merton Center at Bellarmine. This interesting juxtaposition of Hammer-Merton materials was not lost on the editors of this book and became the impetus for pulling together this correspondence and reflecting on its nature.

We are well aware that this correspondence is incomplete; no doubt some of the letters from Victor and Carolyn Hammer to Merton were not retained, and Merton only later in his life began to copy his letters, recognizing that posterity would have an interest in what he had written. Included in this volume are 250 letters from Thomas Merton to the Hammers, 48 from Victor to Merton, 26 from Carolyn, and 14 that both of them signed to Merton. Of the total Merton letters, 17 were included in William Shannon's collection of letters, *Witness to Freedom*. There is a prior article that reflects the relationship between the Hammers and Merton: "Victor Hammer and Thomas Merton: A Friendship Ad Maiorem Dei Gloriam," written by David Cooper and published in 1987 by the *Kentucky Review*. We make no apologies for what we lack, and we of course wish that the entire corpus of their correspondence could be reproduced. We also were not privy to the conversations that were held either on the shores of Monks Pond or at the small house in Gratz Park where the Hammers lived.

We believe this to be the full extent of the correspondence between the Hammers and Merton. We have explored other potential sites for their correspondence and discussed the possibility of other materials with the executor of the Hammer estate, Gay Reading, Carolyn Hammer's nephew, and with Paul M. Pearson, the director of the Merton Center, and neither knows of any other correspondence that exists.

We have reproduced the entire corpus of work that we have found, fragments, postcards, and quick notes on dates to meet and the like. Some of the correspondence is profound, such as their exchange regarding the nature of art, whereas some is mundane and reflects only meeting times and dates. As is the case in most publications of correspondence, we have made silent edits on the narrative of the letters.

There were typos, dropped words, and instances where the letters were clearly not edited before they were sent; there were more of these in the case of Merton, who was writing or typing quickly. Victor's letters were mostly handwritten in an almost calligraphic style, beautifully composed and put on paper, much as an artist would be expected to do. If there are questions and concerns about these silent edits, the reader is encouraged to return to the originals, readily available in both the Merton and Hammer archives at either the University of Kentucky or Bellarmine University.

We enjoyed creating this book. The ideas and sparks that flew from the correspondence generated in us a feeling of envy at not being present at the conversations they had. We missed the letters that we know were lost and that probably contained even deeper exchanges about the issues that these extremely bright and thoughtful people penned. Nevertheless, we are pleased with the results and believe that you will enjoy, as we did, the interplay of thoughts and ideas of these individuals.

This book, like so many others, would not have been published without the help of so many people. We wish to express our deep appreciation to Leah Casanave, our faithful companion in this journey, and recognize her editorial role in this effort. Paul Pearson, the director of the Merton Center, is a wonderful, knowledgeable, brilliant scholar who seemed to have a solution to every question we raised. The staff members at the University of Kentucky Library and the archives of that library were incredibly helpful and kind in their efforts to help us bring this set of letters together. Our publisher, Steve Wrinn, has been waiting for years for us to bring this book on board, and his encouragement and advice have been invaluable to us. We thank the University Press of Kentucky for publishing the final copy that is in your hands.

A special thanks goes to the trustees of the Merton Legacy Trust, Peggy Fox, Anne McCormick, and Mary Somerville, for their support and encouragement. We also wish to thank Gay Reading for his assistance and encouragement. We hope that they are as proud of this product as we are. So we leave you, dear reader, with the motto of the book, for it is to us, as it was to the Hammers and Merton, *ad majorem Dei gloriam.*[1]

Introduction

This one is somehow different, because there was no one like Victor. Just no one. And for such a loss there are no compensations. . . . Of course he is with us, and we with him, . . . through the medium of the book. So significant, too, the fact that all this really was ad majorem Dei gloriam.

—Thomas Merton to Carolyn Hammer,
July 11 and 27, 1967

When Thomas Merton entered the gates of the Abbey of Gethsemani in 1941 as a postulant to a monastic vocation, he did not abandon his earlier vocation as a writer. Indeed, each of these dual vocations enlarged and informed the other throughout his life. Thomas Merton became the monk, the hermit—and later the social critic and humanist he was—precisely because of this dual tension, creative within him. Merton was born with the instincts of a writer, and he nurtured his talent as a youth. He read widely and voraciously. His public school education in England and both his undergraduate and graduate education at Columbia University were literary ones. Merton's brief teaching career at St. Bonaventure (1940–1941) focused on literature and creative writing. Dom Frederic Dunne, his abbot, recognized his orphic gift and encouraged and supported his literary efforts. When Thomas Merton's autobiographical account of his monastic vocation, *The Seven Storey Mountain,* was published in 1948, he became overnight a literary success; sixteen printings and several foreign editions were published by 1952. The book, which chronicled his youth and conversion to Catholicism, was a beacon for many young men who returned from the Second World War confused, depressed, and victims of what we now know as post-traumatic stress syndrome. The book became an incredible recruiting tool for monastic vocations, and Merton was inter-

1

nationally famous. Dom Frederic provided continued encouragement, and served as an emotional shelter amid Merton's increasing self-doubt fueled by the ever-present tension between a writing career and the contemplative life.

Thomas Merton came to Gethsemani—to the contemplative life—fleeing from what he saw as the nihilistic aimlessness of secular life. Writing and the poetic arts were connected in his mind with the secular life he had left behind. Dom Frederic asked him to write a text for a commentated volume celebrating the abbey's centenary, as well as a full history of the Cistercian Order, insisting to Merton that writing need not be an impediment to contemplation. Thomas Merton continued to write: poetry (the psalms serving as his poetic paradigm), essays dealing with the tension between art and spirituality, between the sacred and the profane, and always his journal entries. And he continued to question: "It is obvious then, that contemplation has much to offer poetry. But can poetry offer anything in return to contemplation?"[1]

Throughout his life Thomas Merton also engaged in a voluminous correspondence with numerous individuals. He responded to many who wrote to him, answering their questions about the monastic life. The range of topics within the corpus of his correspondence is vast, and it only enlarged over the years. His correspondence often paralleled his own writings, reflecting his concerns, and ranged from religious topics of the Eastern and Western traditions, contemporary theological developments, monasticism, aesthetics, and the contemplative life to the social issues of the day, poverty, the cold war, nuclear threats, civil rights, and finally the Vietnam War.

Among those with whom Merton corresponded from the mid-1950s to the end of his life were Victor Hammer and his wife, Carolyn, the friendship among them being the subject of this volume of letters. Much of Thomas Merton's correspondence has been published. William Shannon (as general editor and editor of the first and fifth volumes) edited a five-volume set of letters Merton wrote to a variety of colleagues and friends. *When Prophecy Still Had a Voice* is the correspondence between Merton and his great friend Robert Lax.[2] And yet some valuable material has not yet been made available to the interested reader. This volume of letters is an attempt to address one such lacuna, one that provides insights into Merton and the creative tensions he embodied, as well as into the esteemed friendship with a couple quite close to him for over a decade.

The correspondence between Thomas Merton and the Hammers is rich, and although some of the letters Merton wrote to them have been previously published, there has been no comprehensive compilation of the letters among these friends.[3] They collaborated on several projects, notably the printing of several pieces of Merton's work, and the letters exchanged are remarkable in volume and in the breadth of the subjects they chose to discuss, most notably the question of art and spirituality. In addition to this written record, we know that Merton and the Hammers often met at the abbey for picnics and, when Merton was allowed to leave the abbey, at the Hammers' home on Gratz Park in Lexington.

Thomas Merton is internationally well known, while Victor and Carolyn Hammer are less familiar, even to those who are students of Merton's writing and his monastic life in Kentucky. A brief biography of each will provide a necessary background for the exchange of correspondence that makes up this volume and will clarify the depth of their friendship, as evidenced by the note Thomas Merton wrote to Carolyn Hammer that begins this introduction.

Thomas Merton was born in Prades, in the south of France, in 1915. His mother, Ruth Jenkins, from New York, and his father, Owen Merton, from Christchurch, New Zealand, were artists. They met at an atelier in Paris, where they both studied. Merton had a younger brother, John Paul. Their mother died when Merton was six years old. Thomas and John Paul lived with their maternal grandparents after her death. Thomas traveled intermittently with his father to Provincetown, to Bermuda, and then at eleven years of age to France, where he continued his schooling. In 1929 Thomas Merton was enrolled in an English boarding school, Oakham, where he excelled. From there he was able to travel through Europe. After a period of ill health, his father succumbed to a brain tumor. In 1933, a little more than a year after his father's death, the eighteen-year-old Merton was in Rome when, at the church of Sts. Cosmas and Damian, the Byzantine mosaic of Christ in the apse "descended upon him with such power that it triggered a religious conversion episode and established one of the first felt links between aesthetics and spirituality in Merton's life."[4] He records this experience vividly in *The Seven Storey Mountain*. "What a thing it was to come upon the genius of an art," he wrote, about those artists who created a "subservience to higher ends, architectural, liturgical and spiritual ends which I could not even begin to understand, but which I could not avoid . . . since the nature of the mosaics themselves and their position and everything about them proclaimed it aloud."[5] This was a first episode in a process that ultimately resulted in his religious conversion, and this dramatic discovery of the Byzantine aesthetic, with its stress on otherworldliness, informed his interior dialogue regarding art and spirituality. It convinced him that art can only be a vehicle to higher spiritual ends and aims. And for Merton, the Byzantine aesthetic trumped all others, including Renaissance classicism.

At Oakham, Merton obtained a scholarship to Clare College, Cambridge. A trust fund was created for him by his grandfather Jenkins, who even during the Depression continued to do reasonably well financially, publishing movie industry–related books at Grosset and Dunlap. Thomas I. Bennett, a physician and Merton's godfather, was given the responsibility for managing the trust. Unfortunately, Thomas Merton's first year at Cambridge was a disaster. His behavior evidenced a spoiled, self-indulgent young man, by his own admission. After a year of poor grades and behavioral problems, he was advised to return to America and his grandparents, which he did. Beginning in 1935 he was at Columbia University, where he participated fully in college life. A member of a number of organizations and literary societies, he made many friends, including several lifelong ones: Robert Lax, Ed Rice, Seymour Freedgood, Robert Gibney, and others. Supported and encouraged by his teacher Mark Van Doren, Merton completed his A.B. degree in February 1938 and began his master's thesis, working on the writings of William Blake. His Blake studies drew him further into

Eastern religions. He made a study of Jacques Maritain's *Art and Scholasticism* and became interested in Meister Eckhart and D. T. Suzuki.

The Hindu monk Brahmachari visited Columbia in the spring of 1938. Merton asked him what he should read to gain a proper understanding of mysticism and the spiritual life. Brahmachari suggested he return to his Christian roots and read Christian classics such as Saint Augustine's *Confessions* and Thomas à Kempis's *Imitation of Christ*. This brought Merton to a reevaluation of Catholicism. He also during this period began to take classes with Dan Walsh, an adjunct professor at Columbia from Sacred Heart College, who became a good friend. Thomas Merton had not been in a Catholic church since his visit to Rome, but he decided to go to the Church of Corpus Christi on 114th Street, just to be there. Later in the fall he told the parish priest, Father Ford, that he wanted to become a Catholic. He was received into the church on November 16, Ed Rice serving as his sponsor and godfather.

In February 1939 Merton received his M.A. in English. That spring he and Dan Walsh went to hear a lecture by Jacques Maritain, whom Walsh already knew. They both admired Maritain's "innocence of heart"—a quality most valued by Merton. Merton opened up to Walsh about the possibility of a priestly or monastic vocation, and Walsh confirmed that he had expected it of Merton, which was of great significance to Merton.

In June 1940 Merton began teaching at St. Bonaventure College in upstate New York. He continued to write and to make submissions to publishers. He visited Cuba, making a pilgrimage to Our Lady of Cobre, which resulted in a poem. He attempted to join the Franciscan Order, but he was rejected by the Friars Minor, owing to his disappointing behavior at Cambridge. He did, however, become a member of the Franciscan Third Order in February 1941. At the suggestion of his teacher and friend Dan Walsh, who himself had visited Gethsemani, Thomas Merton made a retreat at the Cistercian Abbey near Bardstown, Kentucky, in April 1941. The overriding questions that arose from that visit continued afterward to obsess Merton and remained at the center of everything: "What do you mean by contemplation, anyway?" "What is the effective peaceful alternative to violence?" "How can we represent social injustice?" "What can we learn from other religious traditions?"[6]

In December of that year Thomas Merton presented himself at the gates of the monastery and expressed his desire to become part of the monastic community. He remained at Gethsemani for the rest of his life. He became a choir monk and was ordained to the priesthood in 1949. He served as master of scholastics in 1951 and, for a more protracted period (1955–1965), as master of novices. Over time Merton began to feel an eremitic calling—a call to live in solitude. He thought about joining an eremitic order like the Carthusians or Camaldolese, and he requested the opportunity to do so. This was denied by the order, but eventually, in 1965, he was allowed to live apart from the monastic community in a hermitage on the grounds of Gethsemani.

Thomas Merton's interest in mysticism, Eastern monastic traditions, Buddhism—especially Zen Buddhism—continued and expanded. In 1966 the Vietnamese monk Thich Nhat Hanh visited Gethsemani and dispelled for the monks any idea of nihilism as the basis of Buddhist thought. His visit underscored the ideas of reverence for all life and a love of all living things that was comparable to Saint Francis's. Because of his desire to learn more about Buddhist teaching and Eastern monastic vocations, in 1965 Merton was allowed by his new abbot, Dom Flavian Burns, to travel to seek potential sites for future Trappist foundations. He was permitted to visit the Far East, to see Buddhist holy sites and visit with monastics, as well as to attend conferences and an ecumenical meeting on monasticism. He visited India, Thailand, Ceylon, and Singapore.

During his visit to India, Thomas Merton met three times with His Holiness the Dalai Lama, with whom he felt a great personal connection. They discussed differences in Eastern and Western traditions, contemplation and emptiness. Merton asked the Dalai Lama about the role of the contemplative monk in the world: "I said it was important for monks, etc. in the world to be living examples of the freedom and transformation of consciousness which meditation can give."[7] They also spoke of achieving *Samadhi*, in the sense of controlled concentration. After a visit to Ceylon and the Buddha statues of Polonnaruwa, Merton returned to Thailand for the Aide à l'Implantation Monastique (AIM) Conference. It was at this meeting that Thomas Merton died from accidental electrocution on December 10, 1968.

Victor Hammer was an artist and craftsman of exceptional range and abilities, a master of every medium in which he chose to work. Although his primary métier was painting, especially tempera on gesso panels, and chiefly portraiture, Victor Hammer excelled in the arts of metal engraving, woodcut, and mezzotint. As a master artisan, he crafted furniture, including two clavichords (its prototype having been encouraged by Albert Schweitzer) and worked in gold and other metals. Hammer was a master of the book arts—printing, bookbinding, calligraphy, and typography—and created five uncial typefaces. He sculpted the bronze memorial bust and marble inscription for his friend the poet and dramatist Hugo von Hofmannsthal in Salzburg's Festspielhaus. As an architect he built and appointed a small stone chapel for friends in Alsace.

Victor Hammer was born in the oldest quarter of Vienna in 1882 and grew up very close by. As he records in his old age:

> I was born into the eighteenth century, yet I was not consciously aware of this fact for a very long time. I first opened my eyes in, and onto, one of the parts of Vienna, the Vienna of Maria Theresa. . . . I was born in Griechengasse nine, but my earliest recollections, all of them visual, hinge on the place we occupied in the Schöenlaterngasse.
>
> These first few years of my childhood in the last quarter of the nineteenth century have formed my view of the world as an artist and have moulded it in the character of the late seventeenth and early eighteenth centuries. I had no chance, nor had I the capacity (being then a little boy not yet in school) for realizing that all things that surrounded me were already two hundred years old. This world in

which I was born and in which I began to live was a world contemporary with me—I saw no other. . . . Their world of artistic achievements was the only world of which I, at this early age, was aware; it was self-evident and it was beyond all question. I had never heard of art, would not have understood the word nor could I have conceived of quality and achievement. But I looked upon the Jesuit's Church, its ceiling with the fresco by Padre Pozzo, and at Jadot's Aula of the University; I absorbed and accepted—unknowingly. . . . The house in which we lived was separated from the Church by a narrow passageway . . . it opened through no more than a doorway into the Universitätsplatz where the church stood. I liked to play, or just "to be" in this place. Every time I stepped through the small doorway into this room without a ceiling—through these four well ordered walls–the sight of it cleared my breath, made me feel free . . . for me this world still lived and gave nourishment to my vision, my mind.[8]

This well-ordered space was the womb that nurtured the art of Victor Hammer in his youth and set the trajectory for him as an artist. His experience as a child and its importance to his artistic vision is interestingly parallel to Thomas Merton's own encounter in Rome in 1933 with religious art and architecture at the Church of Sts. Cosmas and Damian. Merton's experience was highly dramatic; Hammer's was almost imperceptible, yet both experiences shaped their aesthetics and their worldviews and were crucial to their vocations.

As Thomas Merton knew as a youth that he had a vocation as a writer, so Victor Hammer knew his vocation was as an artist. Despite his father's concerns, he was enrolled in the Vienna Academy of Arts and Crafts in 1897, where he was apprenticed to Camillo Sitte, the famous artist, architect, architectural historian, and city planner. Sitte recognized Hammer's artistic talents and encouraged him to apply to the Vienna Academy of Fine Arts to study painting and sculpture. In 1898 Hammer was accepted as a student and remained at the academy until 1908, studying with Professors Christian Griepenkerl, Edmund von Hellmer, Anton Hanak, and Jan Bitterlich. In 1907 he exhibited his art publicly for the first time. Following his education at the academy, he received a government traveling fellowship for the year 1908–1909, having won the Staatspreis for a portrait of his future wife. He was able to travel to Paris, Berlin, and Munich and to visit Italy for the first time. After his return to Vienna, he married Rosa (Rosl) Leopoldine Rossbach in 1909. The Hammers would have two children, a son, Jacob, born in 1913, and a daughter, Veronica, in 1918. Hammer received the Prix de Rome in 1909, which permitted further traveling. He exhibited on a regular basis, including a show with the Vienna Sezession, into which he was elected a member in 1912. In 1913 the Munich Neue Pinakothek purchased a painting. In 1914 Victor Hammer joined the Austrian army as a war artist, and he served in that capacity for the duration of the war. He had limited experience in combat and spent time in the Urals, Trieste, and Constantinople. Hammer returned to Vienna at the end of the war to establish himself as a portrait painter, maintaining a studio there until 1939. Because of Austria's bad economic situation at the end of the war, the Hammers moved to the countryside, to Obernberg am Inn, in 1918, and thereafter to St. Martin am Inkreis, where they lived on the estate of their friend and patron Count Ferdinand Arco-Valley. In the fall of 1922 Victor Hammer established his atelier in Florence, at first in a villa at Soffiano, then in the Casa di Boccaccio in Settignano, where he was a neighbor of Bernard Berenson at I Tatti. Here Hammer began his efforts as a printer; the title of his first issue was suggested by Berenson: John Milton's *Samson Agonistes*. His first press was constructed with the assistance of Ezio Pratesi by 1927. Hammer's first typeface was cut by a Swiss typecutter. Hammer did not like its appearance, so Paul Koch came from Offenbach am Main to assist him in cutting a second face, the Samson Uncial. Koch was the son of the great German typographer and craftsman Rudolf Koch. Victor Hammer was supported in his typographic endeavors by his American patron, Edgar Kaufmann of Pittsburgh. Edgar Kaufmann was a wealthy businessman who was responsible for the construction of the classic home Fallingwater by Frank Lloyd Wright, in Pennsylvania, and the Kaufmann House, by Richard Neutra, in Palm Springs, California. He was also a patron of the arts and commissioned work by Victor and sent his son, Edgar Kaufmann Jr., to apprentice with Victor in Florence. It was Edgar Junior who owned Victor's classic portrait of Merton, frequently used by individuals to illustrate books and other printed pieces. The painting was lost when Edgar Junior's home burned.

The growing household was joined by Fritz Arnold from the Klingspor Type Foundry and Reinhold Roether from the Bauhaus. Needing more space, the atelier moved to the more spacious villa il Santuccio in the via San Leonardo in 1927. There Hammer's press, the Stamperia del Santuccio, was named in honor of the nameless little saint that stood in a niche beside the doorway. *Samson Agonistes* was issued in 1931 and bore the letters A.M.D.G. in its colophon—emblematic of the carving on the portico of the Jesuits' church in Vienna's Universitätsplatz that sheltered his childhood games and crystallized his artistic vision—because all Victor Hammer's work was done with a spiritual goal in mind.

Victor Hammer's years in Florence were most productive, and he met a broad circle of friends, artists, and intellectuals, including Rudolf Serkin, Adolf Busch, Ulrich Middeldorf, Carlo Placci, Edward Bruce, Aldous Huxley, and his Florentine friend Delfino Cinelli. During these years he executed several important commissions in Austria, Italy, and England, as well as in the United States for the Kaufmanns and their circle. Two more books were issued by the press. In 1931 Hammer moved to London, hoping to find wider public recognition for his work. Despite several shows, there were no commissions, so he left for France, where he painted a number of portraits, including that of Mme. Jacqueline Seydoux de Claussone in 1934. In the background of the painting, partly obscured by the subject, appears—as if carved in stone—the beginning of Dante's *Paradiso:* "All things have an order among themselves, and it is in this way that the universe resembles God."

In 1933 on his way from Paris to Austria he stopped, as he usually did, at the home of his friends Antoinette and Alexandre de Grunelius in Kolbsheim, a small village southwest of Strasbourg, in Alsace. They told him about their plan to build a private chapel on the grounds of their château, adjacent to the parish church, which was used by both Protestants and Catholics of the village. The couple had recently converted to Roman Catholicism and wanted a shelter for the Blessed Sacrament between Masses. They offered Hammer the role of architect, which he accepted without hesitation. Victor Hammer and his family lived at the château with only short interruptions from 1934 to 1936. Into this project he incorporated every facet of his art. He was responsible for all sculptural ornamentation and interior decoration, including the *Crucifixus*, which was not completed and placed until after World War II. It was at Kolbsheim that Hammer became friends with Raïssa and Jacques Maritain—close friends of the Grunelius family. Jacques Maritain suggested the inscription above the chapel doors: "*Redemisti Nos in Sanguine Tuo*" (Redeem us in your blood), and the inscription that Victor Hammer cut into the mantelpiece in the library of the château, stating the three requirements of a work of beauty from Thomas Aquinas, echoing Aristotle: "*Integritas, Consonantia, Claritas*" (Wholeness, harmony, radiance).

In the summer months of 1934–1936, Victor Hammer founded and operated a school in Grundlsee, Austria, at the request of his friend and patron Anna Mautner. The Meisterschule für freie und strenge Kunst (Master School for Independent and Strict Art), operated on a master-apprentice arrangement and offered courses that included painting, book printing and binding, calligraphy, wood carving, and cabinetmaking. His goal was to educate a generation of artists able to create good pieces of art without being spoiled by the negative influence of industry and mechanization.

In September 1937 Victor Hammer was offered a post at the Academy of Fine Arts in Vienna, which he accepted and so became a professor at his alma mater. Germany annexed Austria in March 1938. The Hammers' daughter was married to Hermann Felix, the Baron von Oppenheimer, of an old Viennese Jewish family. Hammer had belonged to a conservative political group. As a result of these facts, and others, Hammer was permitted to retain his studio at the academy but not allowed to teach. In August 1939 he was retired indefinitely from his post. Fearing that he would be co-opted to produce propaganda art for the Nazis, and knowing that he could not let his artistic freedom and human dignity be compromised, he and Rosl left Vienna unobtrusively for Kolbsheim, as if for the weekend. He had been advised to leave Austria by his friend and patron Albrecht Graf von Bernstorff, a Grunelius family friend, the musician Nicolas Nabokov in New York, and the painter Edward Bruce, who at the time was in charge of the WPA at the Treasury Department in Washington. With this advice and the help of Tudor Wilkinson, in Paris, Hammer secured a job teaching in the Art Department at Wells College in Aurora, New York. The Hammers arrived there in September 1939.

At Wells, as professor of art, Victor Hammer was able to establish a printing press, issuing books under the imprints of the Wells College Press and the Hammer Press. Jacob Hammer was able to leave Austria and enter the United States via Mexico, and to join his parents in Aurora, where he served as a pressman. During his stay at Wells, Hammer was able to cut a new uncial typeface, the American Uncial, since his second face, Pindar, cut in 1935–1937, had been left in Vienna. The Hammers also became American citizens and met a number of helpful friends: R. Hunter Middleton, typographer and printer in Chicago; the calligrapher Paul Standard in New York City; publishers Alfred Knopf and James Laughlin, also in New York; poet Wallace Stevens in Connecticut; social critic and missionary Lewis Mumford; and New York City type designer Joseph Blumenthal, who lent Hammer his Spiral type to use at the press at Wells College.

In 1948 Victor Hammer reached mandatory retirement age at Wells, and he was invited to return to Vienna to assume his former post at the Academy of Fine Arts. Being unsure whether the Academy wanted him to return because of his own merits as a painter, or because he was known as an anti-Nazi, Hammer declined the offer. His old friend Ulrich Middeldorf, then in the Art Department of the University of Chicago, and Bob Middleton, the design director at the Ludlow Typograph Company, arranged for an exhibit of Hammer's paintings and books for the Renaissance Society of Chicago at the Newberry Library. Invited to the exhibit were Middleton's friends Joseph Graves, a member of the Board of Curators at Transylvania College in Lexington, Kentucky, and Raymond McLain, its president. Highly impressed by the range and quality of Hammer's work, they invited him to become artist-in-residence and professor of fine art at their college. Hammer accepted, and he and Rosl arrived in Lexington in the fall of 1948. His presence in Lexington resulted in two developments of importance. First, he found himself free from financial worry and in the company of supporters and friends, academics, printers, intellectuals, artists, all truly interested in the arts and human creativity. He was free to follow his artistic vocation as he understood it—not to "build and work for the gratification of human needs, but to build with thought of a future life of the Spirit on this earth."[9] Victor Hammer was finally able to dedicate his work *ad majorem Dei gloriam*. The second result of Hammer's arrival was that he found a group of people who realized what such dedication meant and assisted in its promotion. Lexington became a center of interest in the book arts, a legacy still valued and upheld today. Victor Hammer was important to the Gravesend Press of Joseph Graves; to the Bur Press of Amelia Buckley and Carolyn Reading; to The Anvil Press, established by friends and students of Hammer's to learn directly under his tutelage; and eventually to the King Library Press, providing the inspiration and model for its operation. In all his several media, Hammer felt that his best work was accomplished during his years in Kentucky. It was the most productive time in his life, as he printed a number of books, including those of Thomas Merton, and completed a number of paintings, Merton's portrait among them.

In 1954 Rosl Hammer died of cancer after a protracted illness. Carolyn Reading had been Victor Hammer's student since 1948, and then his apprentice at the Stamperia del Santuccio. She accompanied Rosl on her first visit to Austria after the war and had been a help to them both during Rosl's illness. Victor Hammer asked Carolyn Reading to become his wife in 1955, and they were married that year. They shared the Stamperia del Santuccio imprint after 1958. Carolyn Reading was a native of the Bluegrass. Her mother's Scots-Irish family had lived at Pisgah, in Woodford County, since its settlement, coming from the Shenandoah Valley to the fort at Lexington and then to Pisgah in 1784, a group of interrelated families including the Gays, the Dunlaps, and the Stevensons. Her grandfather and uncles operated saddle-bred horse farms. On her father's side she was a descendant of John Reading (1686–1767), the first native-born colonial governor of New Jersey and a founder and trustee of Princeton University. Carolyn Reading grew up in Paris, Kentucky, graduated from Transylvania College, and went to Columbia University to obtain a graduate degree in library science in 1932–1933. It was at Columbia that she became interested in private press printing through Professor Mary Shaver's course on the history of the book, and a class visit to the Morgan Library, presided over by Belle da Costa Greene. Carolyn Reading's term paper for Dr. Shaver was on John Bradford, Kentucky's first printer, his *Kentucky Gazette* first issuing in 1787.

In 1933 Carolyn Reading secured a job at the Library of Congress. In 1936, longing to be back in Kentucky, she accepted a job as a librarian at a Kentucky mountain school in Blackey, Kentucky, the Stuart Robinson School. There, as she records, from her students and their mining families she "learned so much more than I could ever give to them."[10] Demands of her economic future bore down on her, and she took a job in Frankfort, Kentucky. In 1940 she went to the University of Kentucky Library to work under its first librarian, Margaret I. King, also a Columbia graduate. Carolyn Reading remained at the UK, becoming head of the Acquisitions Department and later curator of rare books.

Carolyn Reading and Amelia Buckley established their Bur Press in 1943, where they printed four Kentucky monographs by their friends and colleagues, as well as calendars featuring photographs from members of the old Lexington Camera Club, as well as other titles. In anticipation of the Hammers' arrival in 1949, she and Amelia planned a class among their friends, who subsequently gathered for their first session with Victor Hammer. By the end of the semester, Amelia wanted to focus on calligraphy, and Joseph Graves and Carolyn Reading wanted to learn to print on the hand press. As Carolyn records: "We had become true friends, Rosl and Victor Hammer, Amelia, Joe Graves and Lucy, his wife, and were often together in the Hammers' home on Gratz Park. One evening, as I left the group, Victor accompanied me to the door, I ventured to ask if I might come one afternoon and look on as he printed, only to be answered, 'My friend, no one learns from looking on; one must do.'"[11] Convinced of her serious determination, Hammer agreed to offer his help when she acquired her own flatbed press and type in 1952. In that same year, The Anvil Press Associates formed to produce books that Victor Hammer would lay out and his son Jacob would print. Jacob completed the fifth Bur Press monograph as well: Clay Lancaster's *Back Streets and Pine Trees* in 1956.

The old Chandler and Price platen jobbing press used by the Bur Press was taken to the King Library in 1956, where Carolyn Hammer established what was then called the High Noon Press, since it was operated by librarians on their lunch hour. One volume was issued. By then hearing of the press, a sympathetic friend—Thomas Merton—sent his *Prometheus, A Meditation* for the group to print. This title called for an imprint not so suggestive as High Noon might be, and so it came about that the King Library Press was chosen as both dignified and practical.

The Hammers had first met Thomas Merton in September 1955. Victor Hammer and Thomas Merton were aware of each other's presence in Kentucky, through their mutual friends Jacques Maritain and James Laughlin. Victor Hammer was invited by Brother Giles, the monk responsible for the architectural quality of the monastery, to advise on the placement of the Stations of the Cross, commissioned of the British sculptor Peter Watts, who was unable to attend to that detail at the time. Hammer was to attend Mass and afterward to meet Brother Giles to discuss the Stations' placement. While Victor Hammer was so occupied, Carolyn Hammer went to the guesthouse to have breakfast and then to the ladies' parlor to sit until Hammer had completed his task. While she was there, Thomas Merton walked in. They introduced themselves and began to get to know each other, and they were soon joined by Victor Hammer himself. Together they all then took a walk and parted that day with a hope of seeing each other again soon. After their departure, Victor Hammer remarked to Carolyn on Merton's "vivid" personality and presence. From this initial conversation grew a friendship that was both deep and long-lasting—one that allowed these remarkable individuals to explore areas of common interest and concern. The correspondence between Merton and the Hammers began in September 1955 and lasted beyond Victor Hammer's death in 1967, until Merton's own death in 1968. Hammer and Merton were simpatico. Both were culturally isolated, in fact, and each was contemplative by nature. Their friendship and the dialogue that evolved from it was of great value to each of them, and to us who, with this volume of letters, may share in its evolution.

the letters

Oct. 24, 1955
Dear Mr. Hammer—

This is to let you know that work is fast progressing on the translation of the Guerric Christmas sermon.[1] I have enlisted the aid of a nun at Seton Hill College, a good Latinist, who has attacked the job with enthusiasm. If in the future you might be looking around for something else interesting to publish, she has one or two translations of the 12th century material, particularly by St. Aelred of Rievaulx. She would be glad to let you have them. I will let you have the translations surely in a few weeks. The Latin text is in Migne vol. 185.[2] I sent her my copy so I cannot check the columns, but they are near the beginning. Probably it would be more convenient for you to set the Latin up from a typewritten copy. In that case, please let me know and I will inform Sister Rose.

Have you given any further thought to our text?

How did you like *Zodiaque* and the book on Autun? The monks who did those books are thinking of publishing some of their work in this country. Do you think that Pantheon, for instance, would be interested in the Autun volume?

Peter Watts, our sculptor of the stations, is now here and the stations with him.[3] But they are still not unpacked. However, the photographs of them seem to me to be exceptionally good.

With best wishes to you and Mrs. Hammer and God bless you both.

Devotedly in Christ

fr Louis

By the way I am on the point of sending Dr. Thompson[4] some more material from my files.

8. XI. 55
Dear Father Louis:

Thank you for your letter of October 24. My wife and I are happy to hear that the translation of the sermons is under way and progressing, for a translation will be necessary in order to bring about a decision of the board of the members of the Anvil Press as to whether to print it or not.

You ask me whether I have given further thought to your text. Yes I have. Your text means a great deal to me, but I wouldn't be surprised to learn that to most people it would mean little more than your famous name. As any great thought, your thought is simple and not new, which makes it difficult to understand. Would I not know you and brother Giles personally, I too would not have understood. Since I have seen you in the monastery and exchanged ideas I realize that your text is largely autobiographical and that it reveals more of your inner self than the facts told in *The Seven Story Mountain*. I am curious to see whether the sermons themselves (in translation) are as intelligible to me as is your exegesis. In the light of your interpretation they probably will.

I may be mistaken but it seems to me that the same thought, that is, silence as a result of understanding is expressed in the last two scenes of Hofmannsthal's play, Der Schwierige, the Difficult One.[5] Here too, humility opens the eyes. So, please let us have the translation and let us hope we will be able to publish the piece.

After a while I shall send you a translation of the three posthumous fragments of Fiedler,[6] a German philosopher of the second half of the nineteenth century.[7] I thought of him when reading the sentence on p. 24 of your Notes on Sacred Art: "What St. Bernard condemns is *attachment to aesthetic pleasure*," . . . Fiedler also emphasizes that aesthetic pleasure is not the key to the understanding of works of art, and that the essence of art, its secret, has nothing to do with aesthetics in its modern sense of a philosophy of the perception of the beautiful. Your notes to the sermons of the Bl. Guerric, and Fiedler's theory have one feature in common: they are only understandable for those who already know. Those who do not yet know, but want to know, will be helped when they genuinely and humbly seek understanding.

It took me almost thirty years of reading Fiedler in order to realize what he was talking about. If now I would try to word Fiedler's theory in my own terms I would, in brief, say: our apparatus of vision, the eyes, can perceive only in the manner of flat or curved planes, that is, in two dimensions. Visual actuality, i.e. three-dimensional seeing can only be realized in and through works of classic art. Primitive art does not go beyond two-dimensional perception; it states its facts on uninterrupted, as it were on unframed, planes. Classic art sees and produces three-dimensionally. In order to achieve this it has turned deliberately away from the uninterrupted planes, from the fields, from the environment of earth and water, setting up a man-made enclosure, the frame of the agora, the market place, the polis. Art becomes spiritual, intellectual, human; classic art is civilized art. Within a definite framework (of inorganic, crystalline, i.e. spiritual character) it creates a foreground that pushed the onlooker somewhat outside the frame, preparing him to realize the depth visually, as a third dimension; then, behind the foreground the main plane rises, acting against a background. These three planes, so interrelated that in the elevation the ground plan can be sensed, permit the onlooker to perceive all three dimensions in a single act of contemplation. This is the visibility of civilized man who turns his eyes toward the dwelling place of the gods. No aesthetic pleasure is involved, he is lifted above animal vision. The secret of art then, to Fiedler, its essence, consists in the creation of three-dimensional space with two-dimensional means.

This applies to sculpture and architecture as well as to painting. The artist who creates classic works of art does not need focused perspective, to him overlapping forms suffice. However, these individual overlapping forms must be so proportioned that one form cannot be confused with the other within the frame. Spiritually active, the artist conceives his work as pure form which is strong enough to hold any content, such as beauty, emotion, and even aesthetic pleasure. Woe to the artist who does not conceive in pure form or neglects it altogether.

If the elements of classic art (or as to that, those of pure form) consist only of the frame, foreground, middle plane, background and overlapping forms, then it is clear that such works of art can be produced according to recipe, i.e. academically. How then is the genuine distinguished from the academic?

The maker of a thing which, when finished, is named a work of art is from the outset fully aware whether he produces according to a recipe or whether an intensified awareness of existence guides him in his activity and makes him create according to inner necessity. Whatever thing, idea, feeling, story, the artist shapes, remains dead material, substratum, until it has taken on that form of being which for vision is three-dimensional space. Yet, not only in painting but also in sculpture and architecture the artist can only produce what he and any other onlooker is compelled to perceive in two-dimensional terms.

While the artist actively shapes the substratum of three-dimensional space, thus striving for artistic truth, the onlooker, the critic, the historian, the patron is merely faced with the substratum, that is, with beautiful, exciting, ugly, soothing, enigmatic and so on forms. Are there criteria to enable him to judge the artistic worth of the work of art in question? In other words how fit is the layman to understand artistic truth? Who are the teachers to open his eyes?

Shall they point to a picture of Chardin where the table on which the boy erects a house of cards, represents the foreground and acts as such; and shall they indicate that the drawer, slightly pulled out of it, pushes the onlooker a little farther away so that he can see the boy better, or for that matter in three-dimensional space?

Or shall the teacher point to a picture of Bingham, the fur traders on the Missouri and show how the stone which stands out of the water creates the foreground with which the spectator can identify himself in place, and thus actually *see* the gliding boat with the beast and the traders. Did the spectator see the stone before it was pointed out to him, or does he believe the stone *was* there when the picture was painted? Does he realize that that branch of a dead tree, sticking out of the water in the background makes the boat float between it and the stone? Does he see now, does he experience the vastness of space?

Is this aesthetic pleasure, or is it visibility created by classic means? Dear Father Louis, it seems that St. Bernard knew what he was talking about. I know, all this could be said with much more grace than I am gifted with but I tried to be as clear as possible.

We finally found the book of Snell: The Discovery of the Mind. It was sitting quietly right in front of our noses while we looked for it everywhere else, my wife will send it tomorrow. You have to wait for the Fiedler, I have to bind your copy.

My friend Grunelius in Kolbsheim[8] writes that Maritain has talked of you several times.[9] He tells me also that three years ago while Maritain was in Kolbsheim you wrote to him about a dream you had, that you would retire to a place near Strasbourg. Both were convinced this place must be Kolbsheim. Alas says my friend, nothing came of it. I wish you were installed in the little house next to my chapel, a two room place where you really could quietly meditate. If you read in my little book what I said about Kolbsheim and its situation you would get a glimpse of what you dreamt.

Please remember me to brother Giles, and my wife wants to be remembered to both of you. As soon as I have finished my triptych, and it should be finished soon, I shall write and find out what would be best to show it in your monastery, at least for a few hours when we are there.

Yours in Christ
Victor Hammer

Nov 26, 1955
Dear Mr. Hammer—

On the Eve of the First Sunday in Advent, I am happy to be able to send you the translation of Bl. Guerric's Christmas sermons. I think Sister Rose has done a good job, and I hope you will like them. Of course, though, it occurs to me that if you print them, the book will be read here and there by erudite Jews who will not understand the references to the rejected synagogue as if all this had something to do

23

with anti-Semitism. That might be another obstacle to printing the book. I had not thought of it, of course, when preparing the material.

As you say, readers will probably find it difficult in spots. It was for that reason that I thought your press would be the logical one to handle it, as Pico is not easy either! What you say about the autobiographical undertones of the piece is probably quite true, but I had not thought of that either. Of course, all that is said objectively about the truths of our faith and of our redemption, has subjective repercussions in the lives of those who have been granted a share in the fruits of that redemption. Whatever we believe we are obliged, in some way or other, to live and even to experience.

I was very interested in your remarks on Fiedler's theory, and they tend to entrench me in my own prejudice *against* classicism. Not as art, but as *sacred* art. It is quite true that primitive and two dimensional art is intellectually poor and limited. Precisely. Less human also—just that! It is the poverty of primitive art that makes it more able to serve as "matter" so to speak for a sacramental and religious form.

It seems to me that the self-assurance with which the classical eye accepts the "man-made enclosure" tends, at least in most cases, to exclude the transcendental in the sense of the "Holy"—das ganz Andere.[10] Precisely, in the polis, everything is familiar. In the agora we trade our own opinions and our own vegetables too: and this is right and fitting. There must be humanism, and Christianity is humanistic. And it certainly speaks up in the market place—where else? But it brings the desert into the market place too, and the desert is vast, empty, and poor, and has no frame . . .

I do not argue that three dimensional art cannot be holy—(Fra Angelico!)—only that it grows up in a context where in fact holiness is not encouraged: the academic context.

How about the spirituality of *line*, of *shape?*

Of course, in all this, there is always the probability that we are talking about two entirely different things: or else that we are seeing the same thing from diametrically opposed viewpoints—or that what seems to be a difference is none at all. In any case I entirely agree with you on the different viewpoints of the artist (who is "in" the space he sees, or at least sees his way into it) and the patron who wants something beautiful and has to be talked into seeing something more than a pleasing subject or a pleasant arrangement of things he likes to look at. Whatever may be the artist's approach, he opens up the doors of spirit: but sometimes it is a spirit that is enclosed in its own reference rather than open to the transcendent.

Talking about art and the sacred: I have moved into a new job as master of novices and find that in the novitiate chapel we have utterly unholy (because vulgar) altar cards. Do you remember that we spoke of that? Is there any hope of getting you to do us three sets of altar cards, for the three small altars of our chapel? At most, the largest card would be twenty four inches long. Your art would then pray for you in Gethsemani by helping the monks to pray better.

Yes, the Snell book is here and I have begun it. I can see its great importance, and therefore I ask you to bear with me if I do not return it in a hurry. My time is rather sparsely portioned out and it takes time to think through such a book. Many thanks for your kindness— and I also look forward to seeing the Fiedler.

Our new Stations of the Cross are installed and look very well. Bro Giles did not dare, after all, to use the plain brick background, but the dark plaster is quite effective behind the light bath stone.[11] When will you be over to see them?

With best advent wishes to both of you and with all blessings and prayers that you may have a holy and happy Christmas—

Devotedly yours in Christ

fr Louis

⁂

December 3. 55

Dear Father Louis:

The translations arrived and we can now more definitely plan for an edition. Yet, I would like to have the Latin text too since I have to order the new type and have to draw up a special foundry list for Latin.

My wife thinks that the Anvil Press can hardly afford to engage on so Catholic a project as these sermons would be. So, my wife and I decided to venture to print and publish this book in an edition of 100 copies at our own risk and expense. Whether we will finally decide to publish it under the Anvil Press imprint, or as a publication of my own Stamperia del Santuccio remains to be seen. As it will take a year or more to see this through there is no rush except for the Latin text because I have to order the type quite soon.

The play[12] is still under consideration though no decision has yet been reached, mostly because two other projects have to be finished before the play could be undertaken. I hope you are not in a hurry to see it published for the Anvil Press would like to spend more time on reaching a decision.

As to your remarks on Fiedler. It would tempt me to argue further but I think I cannot afford to do so, rather spending my time on painting and printing. No doubt I am conditioned by my experiences of childhood. Having grown up in the old part of Vienna amidst baroque and Italian architecture I cannot help being a city man. Besides these years were spent near the church of the Jesuit fathers and though not educated by them I must have inhaled their spirit somehow. So I cling to Rome though Christianity is not only Rome. Enclosed find a few notes jotted down 10 years ago on a special occasion. Basically I have not changed opinion but hope to be more exact in my expressions than at that time.[13]

Instead of carrying on a correspondence on these matters I wonder if it would not be more fruitful if you could live for a week with the triptychon I painted for my wife: Christ King.[14] She is willing to lend it but would not like to miss it longer than a week, say from one weekend to the other, provided it could stay in your room where the monks may see it, though it should not be publicly exposed. Perhaps brother Giles could rig up a stand or something where it would be safe for it is also painted on the back.

You can keep the Snell as long as you want. Next time we come I will bring with me the proofs I made, years ago, for the altar cards. We could then discuss as to how to proceed. Did I ever send you the short introduction to the exhibition of my work in Chicago, written by Professor Middeldorf?[15] If you want it let me know. Please remember us to brother Giles. Kindest wishes and regards from my wife and myself.

Yours in Christ

&

Dec. 17, 1955
Dear Hammer—

I have waited for the typescript of the Sermons to be ready before writing to you. I send it herewith. I forgot to tell the (new) typist to double-space it, and incidentally he did not even make a carbon, so this is the only copy. I hope it is satisfactory.

About the *Tower of Babel* my agent has arranged that this will form part of a volume of poetry which will be published by New Directions in the winter of next year. If Anvil Press were to do it, (which would be a fine thing, I still think) it would have to be as a kind of special edition in conjunction with New Directions. I have no doubt Laughlin would like the idea but no doubt it complicates matters too much.[16]

And now, thank you so much for the Fiedler. It is intensely interesting and thought provoking. As I had suspected, the arguments I tentatively put forth in my last letter had little really to do with Fiedler whom I see to be just as "anti-academic" as I am. However, I do not think I have mastered his thought well enough to discuss it, and as you say it would be far more fruitful simply to live in the light of some concrete embodiment of his doctrine put into effect. I will ask Father Abbot about the triptych. He has just come back from a long trip. Thank you for offering it to us for a week. I shall discuss the whole project with Bro Giles and we will see if it can be done safely and reverently. Then I will let you know.

To return to Fiedler, I am very interested in all that he says about words "creating" our reality for us. I am not too good on the idealism in which he is rooted, but I find many of his intuitions very powerful and right. Actually, modern man uses words as an excuse for *not* entering into contact with the real (however you define it) and talking is also an excuse for not seeing. Hence again the vanity of argument about so deep a subject, until one is first sure that his eyes are open and that he is looking at the object. I think Fiedler has evidently hit upon the heart of the whole question of artistic expression. He clarifies also your characteristic division that separates artist and patron. The patron has not expressed anything and is not going to express anything: he is simply going to look at what the artist has created. But the artist, on the other hand, has a problem of expression and creation—not only as a work of art, but in some sense of reality itself.

As for your notes of 1946 about the Catholic Artist, I entirely agree with you. But how on earth are we ever going to get anyone to see these things? It is enough to reduce one to despair. But the world is being punished for its sins—*all* its sins. The depravation of human nature, even for instance of human techniques of work, is also a sin against God the Author of nature. Is it not part of the natural law that man should work humanly and taste joy in creating, and work for something else besides money?

In this season when Christ comes to us, when the Word is made flesh and God takes to Himself *humanity*, we can lament the fact that we have forgotten to be first of all human in our religion, and we can cry out with tears for a Redeemer Who is perhaps the only one left Who appreciates what it is to be Man and to praise God with a Man's Heart, and with a Man's tongue. And to open upon the world the eyes of human intelligence enlightened by divine wisdom.

I return the notes, and with them I send you both all my best and most fervent Christmas wishes and blessings. God be with you, and may His light fill you, and may His grace guide you and His love possess you.

Devotedly in the Christ Child:

fr Louis

PS I fully understand what you mean about cities. If I had seen more of Vienna and less of London and New York, I would have less prejudice. In fact, I sent to the Ky U. library a page or two I once wrote about Havana[17] which shows that we agree too about the *polis* after all.

I will probably be returning Snell with deep gratitude after the holidays.

Feb 5, 1956

Dear Hammer—

My new life as novice master[18] is a busy one and I am more often in the woods than at the typewriter. However, I finally have a chance to write to you and tell you that I am sending the Snell book back— long after I had promised to do so. It is indeed an important book, and I regret that it is so far from my present context that I was unable to do it full justice. It is so difficult to follow all the avenues that open out before one, and I must of necessity leave the vistas of Greek thought somewhat misty, to my regret. I have no other choice, since my limited time for reading and study is now almost all taken up with scripture and mysticism and monastic history and whatnot—things necessary for myself and the novices. So I did not master all of Snell.

But in any case I warmly thank you for your kindness in sending me this interesting and deep book.

The Benedictines, whose magazines I gave you, have come out with a wonderful volume on Romanesque art in Auvergne— "L'Auvergne Roman."[19] You can get it from La Pierre qui Vire if you are interested.

I am enclosing a note which I am writing at the request of my agent who always wants me to pretend to be business-like even when there is not a matter of business. She wants a black and white agreement about the Guerric book. Namely that I have given you my essay and the Guerric texts in Latin and English, with the understanding that you can print a 300 copy edition at the Stamperia del Santuccio (or the Anvil Press), while I retain the right to further dispose of the text, which I do not at present intend to do anyway. If you will be so kind as to sign and return the attached note I will be able to placate my agent when she comes down here in a week or two to give me a session of spiritual direction. This letter will serve as your copy of the agreement.[20]

I send you both my very best wishes. God bless you always.

Devotedly yours in Christ Our Lord,

fr Louis

PS. New Directions is definitely bringing out the Tower of Babel next fall.

March 28, 1956

Dear Hammer—

I have not forgotten that you asked me the address of the Benedictines who publish *Zodiaque*. I send it along now with my best Easter wishes: Write to

Rev Pere Dom Angelico Surchamp. OSB.

Abbaye de la Pierre qui Vire

S. Leger Vauban

(Yonne) France.

He will be delighted to have some sign of interest in this country, and I think his work is so very good that he deserves all the encouragement possible. I have not been able to help him at all in getting a volume on Burgundy and its Romanesque churches published here. Did I tell you he had a brand new one on the Churches of Auvergne? It is amazing country and the architecture is rugged and primitive to suit the land and the people.

So, I shall be praying for you both especially on Easter Sunday at Mass. Have you ever been here in Holy Week? This year of course there are a lot of changes, but certainly it will be an experience to have the solemn Mass of Maundy Thursday in the evening, at the time of the Last Supper.

I wonder if Mrs. Hammer could track down one of these books for me in the university library? Father Abbot has permitted me to ask for either Series I or II (or both) of Dr. Suzuki's[21] Essays on Zen Buddhism, or the same author's Introduction to Zen, published by pantheon (or is it some other author)? I would be very grateful for any one of these.

Many thanks, and God bless you both.
Sincerely in Our Lord
fr Louis

❀

April 17, 1956
Dear Mrs. Hammer—

Under separate cover I am returning the booklet on Japanese Buddhism, for which many thanks. I found it interesting and a good general picture. If you ever manage to get those books on Zen, I will be eager to borrow them. Meanwhile, I think I will try the Library of Congress. Maybe the Introduction to Zen that I mentioned was published by the Philosophical Library and not Pantheon.

In returning the booklet I also enclose an Italian magazine containing some unpublished material of mine, in Italian. It is the text of two talks given here at Gethsemani to a group of priests of the Louisville diocese, in 1954.

What a wonderful April we are having—or it seems so to me. With so much rain, everything is fresh and green and I have never enjoyed the spring here so much. We have our fire tower on the hill, now, and it commands a wonderful view of the valley of the Rolling Fork River.

Please give my best regards and those of Brother Giles, to Victor. We will always be delightedly looking forward to news about the Christmas Sermons. I have a man here who can translate the

Cassiodorus, if you just give us the references to the passages you want done. I think it sounds like a fascinating little project.[22]

If you want a fascinating picture book for the library I suggest an album or whatever you call it on Hindemith[23]—"Paul Hindemith, Zeugnis in Bildern" published by Schott, at Mainz.

Please give my kind regards also to Dr. Thompson and his good family. With all blessing.

Devotedly in Our Lord

fr Louis

❦

July 19, 1956

Dear Hammer—

Today I am mailing back* to the Kentucky university library the most interesting "Manual of Zen" by Suzuki.[24] I am deeply grateful to Mrs. Hammer for having sent it to me. It contains fascinating texts—and somewhat less fascinating pictures. Popular Buddhism has its ugly streak just like any other religion. Anyway, I am most thankful, as also for the other book on Buddhist meditation she sent a few months ago. I was able to get some interesting volumes of Suzuki from the Library of Congress, and will try them for more.

Did you ever send me the letter she announced, with the passages from Cassiodorus for translation? I never received it. Please let me know. The project sounds fascinating.

Meanwhile, I have another small thing. I have composed a prayer to the Sacred Heart, since the Holy Father is reminding us of this devotion now. I thought it would make a nice little leaflet and can think of no one I would rather have do it for us than you. Can you please look it over and let me have your ideas, and also let me know what it would cost. My idea is a little leaflet, folded double, with the prayer on the inside, and a kind of title page in front, with the imprimatur on the back. Please let me know your reaction.

The monks of La Pierre qui Vire have brought out another marvelous volume on the Romanesque Churches of the Loire

Valley. I should think they would want those things at the university library.

Very best wishes and blessing to you both. When are you coming down again? (I expect to be absent for a couple of weeks, beginning Sunday) I keep you in my prayers.

Devotedly in Our Lord

fr Louis

*I also send a new volume of "monastic orientation."[25]

Aug 31, 1956.

Dear Hammer—

Thank you for your note. I was so glad to hear you would be able to get over soon. It will be a pleasure to talk with you about the prayer, and I will have some things to show you. Also some books Mrs. Hammer can take back to the university library.

Any time between the 5th and 15th would be all right but if you ask me to name a day, why not next Thursday, the 5th, or Friday the 6th? This letter ought to reach you at least by Monday, so you will have time. I would suggest that you come over Thursday morning. Mass is early again, eight o'clock (Tierce begins at 7.45) if you want to attend, or if you can get here that early. I will be free to see you after Mass Thursday morning (about 9) until 11 in the morning and then again in the afternoon, from 1.30 until 3.30.

If I do not hear further from you I shall assume you are coming next Thursday the 5th. If you want to come Friday, or some day the following week, please let me know. Again, Thursday would be the most convenient day.

Probably the most convenient thing for you would be to start out early from Lexington and get here for dinner, and we can have the afternoon to talk. Or else you might do as you did last time, come over to Bardstown and be here for Mass, and we could talk in the morning and even part of the afternoon if you were not in a hurry to start back. I will be on the alert for you any time Thursday, but again, remember if you want to come to Mass perhaps it would be better to send word quickly so that the brother could have the gate open.

Looking forward very much to your visit—with all blessing for both of you.

Devotedly in Our Lord,

fr Louis

P.S. Watts did a fine St. Benedict for the novitiate which I will show you.

Oct. 19, 1956.

Dear Mrs. Hammer—

Here are the extracts from Cassiodorus, and I hope you find them satisfactory. I think our man has translated them well enough and I think they will make up a very interesting little book, except that I suppose you will cut a little of the longish section on grammar. The description of Vivarium has always fascinated me.

I did not go east as I had expected. So I have been here all along. How are the proofs of the little prayer coming along? I am eagerly expecting them. No doubt too things are moving forward with the other work. In the course of my reading I am running across lots of interesting material in the Desert Fathers, but as I am not undertaking any projects at present I do not know if Father Abbot would want me to get the material on paper just now. But it will always serve for later—or I can put the material in the hands of a translator. We shall see.

Meanwhile, it was indeed a pleasure to have you and Victor here again. Everything is as usual, I am busy in the forest, we are cutting some nice walnut logs which I hope someday to use in paneling our novitiate chapel.

Very best wishes and blessings to both of you,

Devotedly in Christ Our Lord

fr Louis

Nov. 3, 1956.
Dear Victor—

Thank you so much for the proof. The prayer[26] looks very fine, and I have had to make a very few changes—the most important one being that a "c" should not be in the name of the good Archbishop. I also evidently forgot a preposition "to" which is necessary for the line to run smoothly. The date is in Latin. I am very excited about the whole project and look forward to seeing the final proof. Father Abbot has gladly confirmed the order for the electrotype and we would be grateful if you would go ahead with that and have the bill sent to us, as arranged.

The fall days are wonderful here. It is a glorious season, with so far no fires because there has been a little blessed rain. We are planting new elms around the house, to have a little shade. Our building is so stark and barren in all the parts that are lived in. Our St. Benedict is finally established on his wall and looks very well indeed. Whatever we do with the chapel will have to wait for some time, I am afraid. There is no likelihood of any quick action. But why should monks hurry?

There are so many wonderful things you could print—from the Patristic age and from the Middle Ages. In my own spiritual reading I am busy with a delightful Benedictine of the 12th century, Pierre de Celle. I have also come across a beautiful little Carthusian text on contemplation. Then, of course, one could always print a few selections from Dom Augustine Baker. Or, above all, how about a page or two of Tauler? For that you would not need me, but how wonderful anyway. The ancient German text could face the English. Isn't it an attractive thought?

May the Spirit Who formed the saints and taught the ancient craftsmen work in us and possess us and fill us and reach others through our lives, Amen. God bless you both.

Devotedly in the Lord
fr Louis

Nov. 19th 1956.
Dear Victor—

Needless to say I feel immensely indebted to both of you for the beautiful work you did on the prayer. The quantity question is of no importance, I was in fact quite delighted at the little extra touch added by the crosses in red. These only make everything all the more perfect. I am very happy about the job. The electrotype will take care of the rest.

Perhaps you do not know that some time ago Father Abbot had decided that it would be best if I undertook to write no prefaces, as so many requests come in which have to be refused, and if we accept one, then the others have reason to feel offended. In addition, I am really writing nothing at all for a year or so, and this too is in accordance with the command of my superiors who feel that too much has been published and that some time should be allowed to pass in which unpublished manuscripts can be printed and so forth. I asked Father Abbot about making an exception in this case, but he felt it would not do. However, he did say that he would be glad to let me provide some texts from the Desert Fathers, after a year and this would include a little piece about them of course. This is something I can be thinking about all along, in my reading. So if you will excuse me for the moment, I will beg off the Cassiodorus project and concentrate instead on the Desert Fathers—I think in particular of a little selection from a very interesting and little known monk called Evagrius who was in fact very important. How about a book of "Sayings of Evagrius"?[27] Besides, I know very little really about Cassiodorus.[28]

Again, I am deeply grateful for the prayer, and I beg Our Lord Himself to reward your kindness. God bless you both—
Devotedly in Christ
fr Louis

Tuesday [March 1957]
Dear Victor

The proofs are very attractive. I have corrected this one set and am
keeping the other. I especially like the idea of the titles and Latin
words in red. It is all right to alter the order of the "words," the only
exception would be the final one—but there again we might come to
an agreement.

I look forward in seeing you both if possible on the 4th. There is a bit
of flu here now, and I have it—but we'll probably be all over it by then.
Meanwhile I'll send a list of books. Easter blessings to both of you.

Faithfully in Christ
fr Louis

July 5, 1957
Dear Mrs. Hammer:
How are you these days? I often think of you and Victor. My
expectations of getting to Lexington have dimmed. I am very busy
here, and have not been out of the monastery all year until yesterday
when I had to go in to Louisville and see one of our postulants who is
ill in the hospital.

When I was in town I was hoping to get some books from the
library, forgetting that it was the 4th of July. Everything was closed.
Hence, I am writing to you. I hope you will be able to lend me some
of the following from the university library. I will give a "first list" and
then name a few alternatives in case the ones on the first list are not to
be had. They are all books about South America.

Clark, Sydney: All the Best in South America, West Coast, N.Y.
1947.
Russell, Wm, The Bolivar Countries, N.Y. 1949.
Means, P.A. Ancient Civilizations of the Andes, N.Y. 1936
Butland, Gilbert, Chile, an outline of geography . . . N.Y. 1951.
And the latest and best things you have on *Colombia* and *Ecuador*.

In any case one or other of the above is not to be had, then as alternatives I would like if possible to see one of the following:

Sandeman, A wanderer in Inca Land, N.Y. 1949.
Clissold, Chilean Scrapbook, N.Y. 1952.
Crow, Carl, Meet the South Americans, N.Y. 1941.

I have not listed anything specific on Colombia and Ecuador but these two countries interest me most at the moment.

Please do not let me be too much of a nuisance with these requests, and if I have asked for too many books in asking for five, then I can take them in smaller batches—twos and threes.

Has anything developed yet with the Guerric sermons?

We have lots of novices and postulants at the moment. I am getting many from South America, and that accounts in part for my interest in the above books.

Please remember me to Dr. Thompson. When Gov. Chandler[29] showed up here a month or so ago I was half hoping Dr. Thompson might be in the group, as I heard there were some people from the university in the party. Especially remember me to Victor. God bless you both, and thanks in advance for anything you can do about these books.

Sincerely yours in Christ
fr Louis

❧

Wednesday Jul. 10 1957
Dear Mrs. Hammer—

I was very glad to get your letter and to hear that you and Victor would be over. I think the best time would be next Thursday, a week from tomorrow, the 18th. Come whenever is convenient for you, I presume you will be over some time in the morning, and I will be expecting you then especially. If for some reason this letter is delayed and does not reach you or if some other hitch comes up, perhaps you could come on the following Saturday. If I don't hear anything I will be expecting you on Thursday the 18th. I can imagine complications about the two colors and the translation of the texts in Guerric.

Meanwhile, many thanks for sending the books which I am expecting eagerly. If many are not available and you can lay hands on something more obvious about the same regions, then you will not make a mistake by bringing it because here I have nothing at all. Looking forward to seeing you both—

God bless you—

Very best wishes, in Our Lord

fr Louis

I will tell Bro Giles you are coming.

Aug. 8, 1957.

Dear Victor—

Immediately after my letter to Mrs. Hammer went out in the mail the other day, your *Dialogue*[30] was handed to me. It is one of the most beautiful books I have seen in a long time: though I must admit that when you boldly call it a "pretext for printing" you almost order the reader to refrain from reading it and just look at it. However, I intend as soon as possible to disobey this implicit order and when I have done so I will share with you the fruits of my disobedience.

Thank you for this beautiful gift, and thank you for the inscription. Brother Giles and I shall treasure the volume.

By now you may perhaps have looked at the meditation I sent along—as another pretext for printing. It is short enough and simple enough not to interfere with any more important plans. But perhaps you might not find the theme important . . . I don't know. In any case, I thought I would send it.

We are now very busy clearing a way through the woods for an electric line to the fire tower, and the marvelous weather of the last few days made it especially agreeable work: except that many of us were bitten by yellow-jackets. It seemed that whenever one went to cut down a tree one found a nest of them somewhere. And there is a huge hornet's nest on the fire-tower.

Well, again, *bon voyage*. I will accompany you spiritually to Kolbsheim. And may Our Lady accompany you everywhere with many graces. All blessings
Devotedly in Christ our Lord,
fr Louis

Aug. 24, 1957.
Dear Victor,

Many thanks for your letter and for the picture and article which accompanied it. I was very interested in the picture—which I had seen before in a magazine which Brother Giles had, but more so in the article about it. I am happy that you want to print Prometheus.[31]

I have asked Father Abbot what we ought to do. The number of copies, seventy five, is fine. But we thought of another way of handling the cost. If you sell copies of the meditation, it will have to be censored. And this is such an inordinate amount of trouble, that for a small thing of this sort, and particularly for a small edition, it is hardly worth while. The censors begin by keeping every manuscript for three or four months if not more. Then, if they don't lose it, they find an excuse for causing all kinds of trouble over the slightest things. Then the Abbot General gets up in the air about it, and in the end we end up where we started, because there is usually nothing wrong anyway. In order not to have to spend the next five months in a teapot tempest over something that is for all practical purposes a manuscript, I think it would just be best for *us* to pay the costs, and distribute the work, leaving you of course as many copies as you want for yourselves.

This I think is the best thing to do and if you want to print fewer than seventy five copies, that is all right with us too. In a word, this is again an "excuse for printing" and not a commercial venture or the dissemination of a message or anything like that. Later on, the thing will probably go into a book, and then it will be another matter.

I was glad to get the new material on Ecuador. It is of high quality and a really serious study. Many thanks. I will send the book back under the label that Mrs. Hammer enclosed.

Once again I close in wishing you a wonderful trip to Europe. I will be with you in spirit, especially at Kolbsheim. And of course please remember me very warmly to the monks and Dom Angelico if you go to see them.

With every blessing,
Devotedly in Our Lord Jesus Christ
fr Louis
I am presuming you want the picture and article returned.

15. X. 57 [Aix-en-Provence]
Our Father Louis, this was a revelation, the perfect Cistercian architecture. Soon it will be restored and then destroyed by the tourists. We just came at the right time. Regards to Brother Giles and we will write to him from England. I cherished the picture of the shroud of Torino.
Yours in Christ, C + V.

January 28, 1958.
Dear Mrs Hammer:

The Cassiodorus was a wonderfully pleasant surprise. It is splendid, and I think the initial is one of the very best things Victor has yet done in a book. It is a very satisfying piece of printing and I compliment you both on it. Thank you very much for this volume. I shamelessly and unhesitatingly ask for two more, one for Fr Augustine, the translator, and the other for the abbey library and scriptorium (this one is for the novitiate). It is a very monastic book indeed, and one which I would like to see as fast as possible in the hands of as many monks as possible. They will be, in the best sense of the word, "edified."

I am very eager to have you go ahead at the library with the

41

Prometheus. I presume this is a different sort of a project than it would have been at the Stamperia, but I am sure it will be as good. And I hope also that it will be more convenient for us all. Is there a convenient number of copies I can ask for? I would myself say we could use a couple of hundred. By all means you can have fifty or as many as you like. Remember I wrote to you before about our paying for the work. The purpose of that was to obviate its being sold, for it would then need an imprimatur and that would take endless time and trouble—which is out of place for so small a job which will not get around very much anyway. So that is the one thing that we are really intent on: and if there is no other way of covering the expenses, then we will cover them. Please let me know.

Surely the best thing would be for you and Victor to come over and we can discuss it all at our leisure, and get everything ironed out smoothly. Any time in February or March would be fine except for February 12th, when I have a forester coming over with a movie about fire fighting in the woods. Also March 19th, 21st and 25th are bad days for us. I would suggest one of the Thursdays in February—the 21st or 27th[32] or even the 6th which would be right soon, and when it comes to a visit from you, then I'd say the sooner the better. Just let us know.

Can I beg a book or two from the library? Here is a list of some of the things I am looking for at the moment: you might send three and bring others when you come, if you have them. I would be glad to know if you have them, though, so that if they are not available I can try elsewhere.

Ciro Alegria, Broad and Alien is the World (even better in
    Spanish, but I don't know the Spanish title)
Leslie B. Simpson Many Mexicos NY, 1941
V.S. Pritchett—The Spanish Temper
J. Icaza Husipungo (Quito, Ecuador, 1934)
Gil Gilbert Nuestro Pan (Guayaquil Ecuador, 1941) (there is an
    Eng. trans)

G. Arcienagas The State of Latin America (N.Y. 1952)
N. Whetten Rural Mexico Chicago 1948.
Moseley—Russia after Stalin
Mehnert—Stalin vs Marx
Orlov—Secret History of Stalin's Crimes.

That is a good sized list but I presume you will not have many of them. Again, many thanks. I am very happy about the printing project. I will send some more things to Dr. Thompson soon. Blessings to you all.

 fr Louis

March 27, 1958.
Dear Victor:

The crucifix[33] is very impressive in its hieratic simplicity. I find the quiet color scheme and the whole design very contemplative. I have shown the transparencies to Father Abbot and he is impressed with them. But when I spoke to him of getting Mrs Froedtert to pay for it, and mentioned the sum he felt that this was too much for a small project like our novitiate and he would not allow me to have it. You see, even though someone else is paying for it, it comes to the same as if we paid for it ourselves in the sense that Mrs F. buys a lot of things for the abbey and Father Abbot does not want to be continually imposing on her for more and more. Besides his feeling is that with my attempts to get one more statue I have already had more than my fair share. (I am still working on one statue project).

My own feeling is though that perhaps later on, when we actually get around to the novitiate chapel project, the matter might be reopened. This is the wrong moment for it as the project as a whole has been unceremoniously put on the shelf. No one in the monastery takes any interest in it except myself, they are all head over heels in other things and we are the last on the list of priorities. I feel the time is just wrong, and nothing can be done. I am so sorry.

I enjoyed the Italian piece[34] and have translated it myself. There are only one or two words you might want to polish up and make more sharply accurate, I leave that to you. If you print this, then, I hope that as translator I may merit two copies? One for the novitiate and one to present to a friend.

How is *Prometheus* coming? I have already finished many of the books and am sending them gradually back. I will soon send another list. Many thanks to you both, and to Dr. Thompson. I will remember you all in a*

*This letter ends here.

Dear Father Louis—we shall appreciate your returning this[35] as soon as possible; please send to us at the library.
CR Hammer
8 April [1958]

Thursday, April 10, '58
Dear Mrs. Hammer—

Many thanks for this first proof. Everything is fine. I like Prometheus better in uncials. The type makes it necessary to slow down and think and gives an extra ruggedness to the thought. This is a very satisfactory effort. I look forward to seeing more. Meanwhile, many thanks for the library books, some of which are particularly good.

With all good wishes to you both—
In our Lord
fr Louis

May 2 [1958]
Dear Victor

When I wrote yesterday I may have given the impression that the only convenient time for you to come next Thursday was in the morning before 11.30. This is of course not the case—you can also see me after 12.15. I remember last time you were here after dinner. That is quite all right. Just drop me a line and let me know whether to expect you before or after noon.

    With all best wishes—in Xt our Lord
    fr Louis

May 9, 1958.
Dear Carolyn—

I greatly enjoyed the visit yesterday,[36] and thank you both for coming. I apologize for rushing off so suddenly, but I did not know it was so late and I was supposed to see Father Abbot at that time.

    The proof is perfect this time. And I am returning it herewith. Naturally I am very satisfied at the conclusion we reached about the cover, I think that is the right decision.

    I looked up my notes and found at least some of the books I had asked for in the previous letter that was lost: there is no rush for them, of course. If you have any of them, I would be glad to get them in due time.

Benitez, Leopold: Ecuador, Drama and Paradox
Hindus, M. Mother Russia.
Bauer, R.A. The New Man in Soviet Psychology.
Kantor, H. The Ideal and Program of the Peruvian Aprista
    Movement.

Here are a couple of other possibilities:

Curtis, J.S. The Russian Church and the Soviet State.
Smith, Lynn Brazil, People and Institutions.
Preston, James Latin America.

Again, many thanks for your visit, the stimulating conversation, and for all your kindness. Among other things, our talk reminded me of the fact that I find it rather hard to formulate exactly what I am thinking these days, as I am trying to reach out into uncharted territory. I think it is certainly true that anyone who thinks must always try to reach out beyond what is simply familiar, and I know both you and Victor would agree.

Very sincerely in Christ
fr Louis

May 22, 1958
Dear Victor

Many thanks for the pictures—they are just the kind of thing I am looking for, and I like St Notburga.[37] I like her intelligent and alert expression (even though I think the most pure tradition of sacred art demands that the saint look a bit gaga and withdrawn) and find it very edifying. It will certainly add to the collection I am trying to get together for the book.[38]

I cannot however let you have the manuscript as yet since all the copies are in the hands of censors. May God preserve me from their worst idiosyncrasies.

The letter that we could not find in the car, turned up, as expected, tucked between the pages of one of the books—I return it herewith.

But now I can't find your own letter, the one I am trying to answer; I remember the main business matter it contained. The price of the covers. This is a little higher than I expected, so let us just cover 50 of the books, and the rest will have to be covered in a simpler manner here at the abbey. I think we can still do something decent. The main thing will be the good fifty.

In haste I go on to a pile of letters I have to write. God bless you both.

Devotedly in Our Lord
fr Louis

I have an idea for another short thing like Prometheus—I can keep it on ice if in the future you would like to print it. It is not yet written out.

June 6, 1958.
Dear Mrs. Hammer:

First of all, my thanks to Victor for the picture of the crucifix which arrived and which I am very glad to have for the book. So far you are the ones who have given me most help in my search of illustrations.

Then many thanks to you for the last batch of books. The magazines, yes, were useful. The ones you sent were a bit general but provided useful background. I have dug up some references which I will list below, of magazine material that I will be glad to look at if I can.

The ms. I mentioned has not yet taken sufficient shape for me to type it but as soon as I do I shall send it to you to look over and I hope it will be suitable for one of your projects. I still have not forgotten the Desert Fathers either: but that will have to wait a little more, as I am immersed in so many other things at the moment. The Russian material is going to bear fruit, I seriously believe.

And, yes, I do want to keep up with the South American stuff also.

May I list a few more titles of books that would be useful if you have them? First I will give you the titles I have dug up, then a few names of authors for whom I have as yet no references but whose work is represented in your library in some form, I hope.

The books:

Spinka, M. Christianity Confronts Communism, N.Y. 1939.
Russell, Bertrand, Theory and Practice of Bolshevism. London, 1949.
Lenin, on Religion and also Materialism and Empirio-Criticism.
Astrov, M. (Ed.) The Winged Serpent (anthol of Indian poetry)
Frank, Waldo America Hispana
Tannenbaum, F. Mexico, Struggle for Peace and Bread.

Some magazine articles that I am interested in—

New Republic, Feb. 26, 1944 (Catholics in Latin America)
"Twice a Year" 1946–47 A. Camus on the "Human Crisis."
Current History, Jan. 1953, (Moslems in Soviet Union).
Christian Century, Sept 6, 1950 (Religious Liberty in Russia)

Some names of authors I am interested in—rather than send the books right away, perhaps you could give me some idea if you have anything by them:

Chestov (or Shestov); Esenin, S.; Camus, A.; Zoshchenko, M.; Blok, A.

I hope that I am not getting too far beyond my limits. Of course I do not ask for all this in one gulp, but as it may be convenient for you. I intend to write to Dr. Thompson to reply to his very kind letter which has gone for a long time without answer.

Again, many thanks and all best wishes, as ever.

Devotedly yours in Christ

fr Louis

Above all, thank Victor for Fustel de Coulanges[39]—he is going to be very interesting.

June 26, 1958
Dear Carolyn:

I have more and more to thank you for each time, and to make sure that I am not ungrateful I am going to enclose, with this letter, a short manuscript[40] of which I spoke vaguely before. It is a kind of exhortation to intellectuals, non-religious, short, I hope pointed, and I also hope universal. If by chance the library wants to print it and send it around, then I want you all to have it first, since the reading which you send is nourishing my "new think."

Thank you for the great batch of material, the copy of the article in Christian Century, the volume of Current History—the most useful periodical for me so far. I have sent some of the titles back, as I have finished with them, and will continue to be businesslike about getting things back.

The New Republic reference I had is obviously wrong, then. The name of the article I am looking for is "Catholics and Latin America" by Inman. It might be in the early issues of 1944 somewhere, but don't hunt too hard for it.

Thanks for looking up the Russian poets. I have run into a few in anthologies of Russian verse (the books by C.M. Bowra I have already had, so do not send them if you come across them in your searches for me.) I think I will manage to find what I am looking for here and there.

Since you have sent me the Camus titles—may I ask for:

Le Malentendu—(Camus) and also—
Almond,—The Appeals of Communism—Princeton 1954 (if you
    have it)
Inman—Latin America N.Y. 1937 (again, if you have it)

I am struggling along with my "Art and Worship" gathering pictures here and there and having some success, gradually. I wonder if you have one or two very nicely done small art books that I could use as an example to show the man in Louisville who is helping me design it. The kind of thing Skira has put out, perhaps—or some book with modern yet traditional design, with plenty of space and nice type. I want the book to be particularly good. I thought you might have something there, from Europe no doubt. I do *not* mean the big heavy expensive art book with color plates tipped in, etc. I think Germany, as far as I know, has done the best in this line so far. If you can send me something like this without too much difficulty, I would be immensely grateful, it will be such a help. At the moment we are floundering a little and my man wants to give us something more like a magazine, which is what I do not want at all.

Father Abbot is not here but I shall ask him permission for you to come again this summer, as soon as he gets home and I see no reason why he should say no. I will look forward very much to seeing you both. Really, you have no idea what a help the books have been. For a long time I have been needing a good solid mouthful to chew on.

I am glad to hear that the crucifix project is going forward nicely and that everything is as it should be again.

I have sent back Vol. xi of Lenin. I am wondering if there is anything of any significance of his on religion in any of the other volumes. Could you have someone glance through the contents, when convenient? I got quite a few things from this volume, the essence of his thought in fact—as far as religion is concerned. Many thanks again for everything and God bless you both.

fr Louis

PS I am sending the library some mimeographed notes on the liturgy.[41] If Victor would be interested in a copy for himself just let me know and I will send one.

July 4, 1958.
Dear Carolyn:

I am celebrating the fourth of July by giving an exam to the novices, and while they are all busy racking their brains, I have time to write to you a note to thank you for *Prometheus*.

The first copy arrived, then the other two, then the unbound ones. It is a very fine job, I am extremely pleased with it. I cannot think of anything else of mine that has been so well printed. Or at least printed in a way so satisfactory to the author. I hope it impresses everyone you send it to, and that many will even *read* it. I should be curious to know some of the places you might possibly be sending it to abroad, especially in Russia, if any. I am thinking of trying to get a copy through to the poet Boris Pasternak,[42] if I can figure out his address correctly from an article I have read about him.

I am grateful also for the art books Victor sent. The Piranesi is very well done, but I do not know if, with the material I have, I will be able to follow that model exactly. For the text, I should like to. Everything is still indefinite. People are beginning to tell me that I am crazy to have it printed in Louisville and that nobody there can do a decent job, etc. Still that is the only way I can keep track of it adequately.

You ask about *nihil obstat* and *imprimatur*. The imprimatur is given by the ordinary of a diocese (usually bishop)—either the diocese in which a book is printed, or the one in which it is published, or the one in which the author lives. The *nihil obstat* is the decision, given by a censor to whom the book has been sent for censorship. He tells the bishop that there is "nothing against" printing the book, (nihil obstat) and the bishop then says "let it be printed" (imprimatur).

Where a religious Order is involved, the Supreme Head of that order also puts in his two cents worth with an *Imprimi potest* ("It can be printed") which does not have the full force of an imprimatur, but is a statement that as far as the Order is concerned the book can be published. Here too, censors of the Order can come in with their *nihil obstats*. That accounts for the complicated censorship notices in my books.

And as I mentioned, the "pro manuscripto" of our Prometheus is a statement that since it is a private printing equivalent to circulation in manuscript, the imprimatur was not asked for.

Sometimes the bishop does not want you to know who gave the *nihil obstat* and withholds the name. Then there is only the *imprimatur*. This is customary at present in Louisville.

I sent back the big Kulski book yesterday and one other. I will be sending the Current History volume as soon as possible. *Inside Russia*[43] is very informative, and so recent. I had not dared ask for it, I thought everyone would be reading it voraciously. It is a great help. I will get it back to you soon.

Finally, Father Abbot has given permission for your visit before you leave for Europe. Any Thursday will be convenient for me, at the usual time—about noon. July 24 would probably be a bad one though. July 17 too. How about July 31, or August 7 or 14th. These would probably be the *best* days. If you can manage better some other time just let me know. In any case, I will be expecting you one of the three days I mentioned, and perhaps you would let me know just which one.

Meanwhile I shall be eager to hear what you think of the "Letter to the Innocent Bystander."[44] Being isolated here my judgment suffers from lack of perspective and it is always very helpful to know what someone outside thinks about what I have to say—particularly when as in this case, I feel it to be important.

With best wishes and gratitude—

Sincerely yours in Christ

fr Louis

P.S.—As soon as I can get something of the Art Book[45] to send to Victor I will do so. Perhaps a set of proofs. But that may be delayed for quite some time as we are still in thick woods with this project.

July 18, 1958
Dear Carolyn:

I have had some luck with the bindings of Prometheus here—I think. A binder who frequently visits the monastery has promised to give our bindery some good material to bind them with. I have not seen it but I trust his taste, so we will bind our copies with them. Of course I received the copies safely—the unbound ones. I know the others may be a little delayed, it is slow work.

By now everything of the U of K. Library that I had borrowed is on its way back. Unless the unbound and unmarked copy of Camus' *La Chute* was from you. It was given to me unpacked and I had no idea where it came from and assumed it was from a friend of mine in France. So in any case I have Camus' *La Chute* and you will not need to send me that. But let me know if it is yours.

Here are a few possibilities. The first two I would like at your earliest convenience and the others could wait until you come.

Berdyaev N. Christianity and Class War
(or else Origin of Russian Communism if you don't have this).

Dallin, D. J. Soviet Russia and the Far East.
And later: Liddell Hart, B.H. The Other Side of the Hill—
   London 1948.
Schapiro L.—Origins of the Communist Autocracy
Almond G. The Appeals of CommunismPrinceton 1954
Gunther, John—Inside Latin America
Hicks, A.C. Blood on the Streets (about Trujillo)

I presume you won't have some of these.

The art book is moving so slowly as to be not moving at all, but I think eventually we will get somewhere with it. I have managed to borrow a lot of fine pictures here and there and am still hoping for more. In the end I hope to have a very unusual set of illustrations, and only hope we can reproduce them properly.

When do you expect to come? I look forward to our next visit, and another pleasant talk with you and Victor before you go to Europe again.

As ever, with all good wishes and blessings,
Sincerely yours in Christ
fr Louis

※

July 29, 1958
Dear Victor

Here is the proof of "The Unquiet Conscience."[46] I have only made one fussy change, moving a phrase to make a sentence sound better.

I will be expecting you both on August 7th, at one o'clock (by which I presume you mean fast time). This will be very good for us.

About the Innocent Bystander: indeed one of the purposes of the piece was to discuss the possibility of his existence at all. What is said toward the end, about the King's New Clothes, is rather a statement of what the bystander ought to do if he were really innocent. And in any case if he did this he would not be a bystander he would be in the fullest sense a participant, and this too was one of the main reasons for writing the piece. That one should not delude himself with the thought that it is possible to be innocent by being a bystander, and that what matters is not to seek to avoid guilt by avoiding participation, but to participate in an innocent way, which is almost impossible, and humanly speaking this is impossible but it has been done by Isaias, Jeremias, Ezechiel, William Blake, St. Francis of Assisi. . . .

Well, I will see you both on the 7th and then we can talk more of all this—perhaps the piece is too ambiguous.

With all blessing and good wishes in Christ

fr Louis

Do they have in the library Palmer, E.E.—Communist Problems in America—New York 1951

14. VIII. 58

Dear Father Louis:

I found your paper to be most stimulating and I hope you will permit me to attach a few notes which will convey my reactions.

1. That you talk about *sacred* art and not about religious or Catholic art seems to me very fortunate. Sacred art must be hieratic, that is, it must recognize the Divine "striking the beholder with deep reverence and with awareness of the divine presence." And it is sacred because it is consecrated "to actual use in divine service." Bachofen points to the contrast of Sanctum and Sacrum, to hieros and hosios, and in your Liddell-Scott you find 'osios (2) as opp. to 'ieros (that which belongs solely to the gods).

2. Intellectual quality of Art: it is the intellect, not merely the apparatus of seeing, which makes us aware of the deepness, the depth of God's world, i.e. its quality. Here belongs the difference between *aesthetic* and *artistic*. A work of art may be beautiful (an undefined and perhaps undefinable term) or ugly—in both cases it can be of artistic worth. If it only

pleases (beauty—id quod visum placet)[47] it is aesthetic. There is also artistic truth (but no aesthetic truth exists)—yet truth is not always *pleasing*. The *knowledge* of a three-dimensional world, conveyed through an imperfect apparatus of seeing, is an intellectual achievement for it is not passively, *aesthetically* experienced, but actively, *artistically* bought about. Even the eyes of a beholder have to be *opened* before he can experience any intellectual satisfaction.

3. You are right: a master is the one who is beyond experimentation, he always knows exactly how to proceed, and knows when to finish. He does not attempt to do things, he does them. However, I would not advise young deacons or talented seminarians to "design" a chalice or a chasuble, rather have them stick to their own business of *using* them when ordained. I must have said all that before, it seems to me.

We enjoyed our recent visit so much and are truly happy to have you so near to us, it is a great consolation.

Yours in Christ

Victor

Dear Mrs. Hammer

On second thoughts, I think I will include a few titles of books in this letter to Victor, as I will probably be finished with the others soon. But there is no rush, as I will be rather busy with liturgy next week anyway. Here are a few names:

Koestler, etc. The God that Failed.
Collier, J. The Indians of the Americas, N.Y. 1947.
Maynard, Sir J. Russia in Flux, N.Y. 1948.
Berdayev, N. The Russian Revolution

And will you please let me know if you have anything by or about

A.S. Khomiakov (no use telling me anything in Russian—but English, French ok.)

Many thanks—I reiterate all the greetings in Victor's letter.
Sincerely in Christ
Fr Louis

❀

14–10–1958

Dear Father Louis, we had to stay longer here than we expected. I had to do a cross much bigger than the one I brought with me. We have a wonderful time with our friends, meeting a number of interesting people from the Council of Europe. Hope to see you in November.

Devotedly in Christ yours. C+V.

❀

Nov. 29, 1958
Dear Carolyn:

Are you back? You must be, it is nearly December. I am writing with good news. You know we spoke about a collection of sayings from the Desert Fathers? I have finished the translations and a short preface. It will make a book of some thirty pages. Is that too big?

I am anxious to discuss it with you. We are typing it and I will hold it until I hear from you—perhaps you and Victor would like to come over and pick it up. Or, if you cannot come, I could send it next week. Please let me know.

Your trip must have been wonderful. The card from Strasbourg was very welcome and the work on the crucifix must have been quite rewarding—I am glad it served as an occasion for more time in Alsace.

Of course, as you know, I am always on the lookout for some book or other, and I hope I didn't make Jim Gribble's life too miserable with my strange requests (for African novels, that's the latest).

One I am looking for now is:

De Riancourt—The Coming Caesars

And two I couldn't get in Louisville—

C.G. Jung—The Undiscovered Self
Gandhi—Non Violence in Peace and War.

I wish you a happy Advent and preparation for Christmas, and am anxious to hear about the trip.

God bless you both.

fr Louis

Could I have a few of the translation from Bargellini[48] to send out at Christmas—just fifty or so? Thanks. I mean the little quote about St Aloysius.

Please thank Jim Gribble for being so helpful. I am sorry he was ill and hope he is better.

❀

Dec. 9th, 1958.

Dear Carolyn:

Many thanks for your letter of last week. It is good to have you both back, and to know that you will be over in January. The best date would be early in the month—Friday the 2nd, Monday the 4th or Thursday the 8th would all be good. I hope I have my days correct, I do not have the calendar here: but the first Monday or Friday and the Thursday *after* New Years' day would all be good. I look forward to hearing which day you pick and to seeing you on it, by the grace of God.

Since you are going to have a little time between now and then, I thought it would be a good idea to send the Desert Fathers' manuscript so that you may both look it over. One of the questions I would like to ask would be: is it too long, or not long enough? And: would you like me to add some more to make it an even hundred paragraphs. (You will see I have numbered each saying, and at present there are only 82. I was afraid of being too long.)

Thanks for the books which have arrived safely. I also have a volume of Zoshchenko which Jim Gribble sent, and this I will keep until you come unless you want it back at once. I also find I have two volumes of your Lenin selected works, which I have been promising myself to read in parts, and yet I cannot get around to it. Lenin can be tedious—though not half as tedious as Stalin. If I haven't got anywhere with him by the time you get here I will give these volumes to you also and not hold them up any longer although I don't suppose there is much of a run on them in the library.

Work on the book about Religion in Russia has bogged down and I have decided that I need to know Russian, so I am laboriously started on *that*. I hope to persevere.

A lot of things have happened since you were last here and I am sure your stay in Europe must have been wonderful, so that we will have lots to discuss.

The Art Book has finally become too complicated for us to produce ourselves and I am turning it over to a New York publisher.

The Bargellini pages have been received, and I am very grateful. They are handsome indeed, and some of the novices have already asked for them. I will send some out at Christmas. Now all that I need to do is put into practice what I have translated and you have printed.

I close with all my very best wishes and blessings for a Holy and Happy Christmas and for all graces in the New Year. Brother Giles joins me in this greeting of the season. And of course I will especially remember you in my Masses on Christmas morning.

Faithfully in Christ Our Lord

fr Louis

&

Jan 2. '59

Dear Victor,

The 17th will be fine. We will be expecting you two weeks from today. Meanwhile I shall return some of the books to the library

Happy New Year
fr Louis

❀

Jan 10, 1959
Dear Carolyn:

Thanks for your card—I will expect you and Victor next Saturday,
a week from today. I will be waiting in one of the rooms of the
gatehouse about noon, so the brother will not have to run all over the
monastery looking for me.

If you have the Suzuki Manual by then, I will be glad to get it. I
cannot place the list of Suzuki books Jim sent, but any other one or
two of his that is available will be welcome.

Here are one or two others I have on the list—I am about finished
with the others you sent and will return them Saturday:

Dallin—Soviet Espionage.
Berdyaev Solitude and Society
Kalme, A. Total Terror
Farson, Negley—Mirror for Narcissus
Wolfe, B.D. Khrushchev and Stalin's Ghost
Wilson Ed. Red Black and Olive. (?)

I realize you probably won't have them all.

Everybody is commenting favorably still on Prometheus and on the
little Unquiet Conscience too.

Well, I look forward to seeing you Saturday.

Until then, God bless you.

Faithfully in Christ
fr Louis

❀

Feb 10, 1959
My Dear Victor:

After reading over the Fiedler ms. I find myself in a difficult position. The material is extremely interesting. The translation seems to me to be inadequate. At least it reads very heavily, and at times is almost impossible to understand. There is a wealth of mixed metaphors, and very often one runs up against expressions that are not English, but hang in a sort of no man's land between English and German. I can see where the translator has worked nobly at a very difficult job, but I really think it requires a lot more work and some more heads need to get together on it.

I wish I could offer something more constructive myself but I do not want to rush in with my own inadequate knowledge of German, and the Italian is not enough to go on.

I think you ought to edit the work quite a lot, as the translator suggests. But above all it should be reduced to fluent, readable English. Technical if you like, but without too great a burden of jargon, and with greater precision all along the line. This may be demanding a lot—perhaps only a really first class translator, an extraordinary translator, would be able to manage it, and such people are rare.

I am enclosing the sheet on which I started to jot down observations as I went along, but I stopped doing so since they were so largely negative. It would be ungracious to find fault without having anything constructive to offer to balance it. I am very sorry I cannot be of more help to you.

Tomorrow is Lent, and in order to clear the decks I am getting the manuscript back to you now so that you can go further with it. I look forward with interest to the notes on classical art which you announce.

And now as for the Desert Fathers—how can anyone argue with a Santuccio? Certainly the manuscript belongs to the Santuccio. Print it as you please. The conditions mentioned in your letter are quite acceptable: namely 50 copies for the Santuccio to sell and 12 for me to give away. This letter will serve as a contract and I will keep yours for the same purpose.

May Lent be a *ver sacrum*[49] full of light and joy for both of you, a season of renewal in preparation for the great renewal of Easter.

Faithfully in Christ

fr Louis

I have the Zen book and it is marvelous. Do you mind if I hold on to it for a few weeks more?

March 6, 1959

Dear Victor:

Here is the proof. I need not say that as usual I am very pleased with it. The uncial will be suitable for the material. I have filled in the number of the volume (73) and approve your change of the title. So here is the proof with no corrections except the ones already anticipated.

I am especially happy with the beautiful appearances of the pages of your classical art.[50] Perhaps some day you can do something of mine along those lines too. As for the thesis I may say that I am really in agreement with all that you say, and that I heartily approve of your distinction between city art and cave art: but then at last we come to my incorrigible preference for cave art. I cannot do otherwise, because I think that city art is in itself less capable of being sacred. Or maybe I am just a Lascaux man at heart, having lived so long, or rather at such an important period, in the midst of the country where those works existed under the ground. When you come over again we can talk about problems of style though I find none. And when would you be coming? The Saturday after Easter is a good time for me. (April 4th I think). After that I would hardly be free until early in May. What say you?

Best wishes and blessings—

fr Louis

March 16, 1959
Dear Victor:

Perfectly all right about the copyright. I think it is safe to let it go, and of course that will help the printing I am sure. I am sorry I forgot about your ten extra copies. By all means, as many as you like.

I hope the weather will be nice April 4th.[51] Sometime before then I'll have some more books listed. I had more or less given that up for Lent, otherwise I would have a list right now. I have also put aside the Russian for the time being, so maybe the Russian professor could come some other time. Looking forward to more proof.

Affectionately in Christ

fr Louis

I salute you from my spiritual cave in the desert.

April 28, 1959.
My Dear Victor:

It is already a week since the "all-memorable day" of my visit to Lexington and to the Stamperia del Santuccio.[52] The happiness of it has not faded. I still think with pleasure and edification on your very monastic house and all the things in it which give glory to God by their workmanship.

I have not written because I have been waiting for a moment to look up some Latin texts for your silver plates.[53] I have looked only in the Vulgate, though perhaps the texts more appropriately might come from Virgil, but I am too much out of touch with him now. That is to say I would not know where to begin to look. But at any rate here are a few from the Vulgate. I put the one which seems to me most appropriate in first place. The others . . . well.

Argentum electum lingua justi. (Proverbs 10:20)
(This seems to me best for dinner plates—a social text, referring to conversation.)

Habet argentum venarum suarum principia (Job 28:1)[54]
(A mysterious text, in a chapter on wisdom.)

You might also check Exodus 35:31–32, about Beseleel, who had
the Spirit of God in him to work in gold and silver, and finally
I Kings 10:22 the famous text about the ships coming from Tharsis
with gold, silver, ivory, apes and peacocks. I still think the first one is
appropriate. The others don't seem to fit, except perhaps the one from
Job.

I am also enclosing some Latin from the *Verba Seniorum* which will
I hope serve for your cover project. Is there enough of it?

Lax and Reinhardt were down over the weekend but I could not
find a way for them to get over to Lexington.[55] They would have liked
to come very much. They brought two interesting Jewish records, texts
from the Canticle of Canticles and the Psalms etc. sung in Hebrew
by a singer called Magdalith. Very impressive. (Very *primitive*).
Though Reinhardt is a very abstract painter, he is perhaps the most
severe painter in the world and I am sure you would agree basically on
classicism—though his painting is very two dimensional. I don't know
why. But austere.

We drove home last week through Shelbyville and Frankfort. I
found Frankfort quite interesting. A rare town with character. The sun
came out and the country was very charming in the evening light.

Carolyn—thank you for Marco Pallis which arrived today. I shall
be sending back the others, or at least some of them, this afternoon.
Did Berdyaev's "Destiny of Man" and Mayer's "Madison Avenue"
come in yet? I have received the new Suzuki from Pantheon as a gift
and it is a splendid book. About the broadside—I thought I would
sign each copy, as there will hardly be too many. It is after all a
"signed confession."[56] When will there be another chance to come to
Lexington? I still do not know how our patient is over there. Perhaps
I will be back. Meanwhile, God bless you both.

Faithfully in Christ

fr Louis

2. V. 1959[57]
Dear Father Louis:

Ever since you, looking at the triptych, have asked me who is the
figure crowning Christ (which I couldn't tell you exactly) I am
thinking about your interpretation: she being Hagia Sophia and also
the mother of Christ. We were much intrigued by what you said
but do not remember clearly what it was. Carolyn got the photostat
from the catholic encyclopedia, which I enclose. The painting from
Novgorod bears a certain similarity with my own painting but I
cannot understand its relation to the Russian writers.

My triptych has a story or rather a happening behind it. Carolyn,
after coming back from Europe, where she was in 1951 for the first
time, commissioned me to do a triptych of a Madonna with the child.
At that time we were not married and only after she insisted and
said she actually wanted the thing, I began to work. My first attempt
showed a landscape reaching from one wing over the center panel
to the other wing. This was the background and in front of it there
was the mother sitting with the child on her lap—ruins around and
at the left wing an eagle looking at the child. On the right wing the
calvary in the background. But that didn't work and in the course of
changing the child grew bigger and stood in front of the mother. By
that time I had scrapped the eagle and the calvary, working only on
the center panel. Part of the landscape remained and also the stones
standing and lying around. All the time we wondered why the child
had changed so much and where I got the idea that She crowns
Him.—Between the town in the background and the waste land in
the foreground is that golden river that separates both. But the huge,
chipped gravestone on the left hand side of the foreground, leaning
sideways and only partly seen, overlaps the river and part of the town
wall in the background. And for months to come I could find no
ways and means of separating this stone from the town wall which it
overlaps. I grew a bush behind the stone, set a snake on its top, but

as there are no shadows in the picture, nothing worked. We used to fancy all kinds of things which would do the trick. One evening when we again were sitting on the bench in front of it, looking at the unfinished painting, Carolyn said: you haven't put a halo on either of them—I immediately realized that a halo of rays around His blessing hand would certainly separate the gravestone in the foreground from the town wall it overlaps. It did so when I had put the rays in.—This IS and IS NOT part of the artist's technique, but it is something out of the reach of incompetent daubers and abstractionists.

I am very sorry we missed your friends Lax and Reinhardt. I would have liked to talk to Reinhardt as I am still unable to see anything in abstract art or understand it. These triangles, squares, dashes and moving lines ought to *underlie* a work of art (as it is the case in all classic art), they ought to be hidden and *not to be shown*. They are the hard core, the skeleton of a work of art.—If we were insects with the hard crust outside, abstract art would be appropriate. Characteristically enough we depict death as a skeleton. To me abstract art is pure perversion. Reinhardt may be sincere, but as an abstractionist he is a sinner against the Holy Ghost. It is a travesty on creation Carolyn said.

I had Carolyn as a patron (she even paid a nice sum for the painting; this was before we married) and she herself is also in the picture. And now you should come in too, telling us more about hagia sophia and christen the triptych giving it a title. So far we have not been able to find one.—I am reading seven story mountain again. Why I had forgotten everything except Dr Brahmachari[58] I cannot imagine. Obviously I was not ripe for the message, or because my own experiences at that age were so completely different from yours. Anyhow, you see so clearly what is wrong and will remain wrong in this world of ours which can be kept going only through the intercession of the few saints unknown and unheralded, among us. When we sit at our little table, we often think of you; perhaps you will sit with us once more, or we will see each other in Gethsemani. The red ink finally arrived and we are back on your book. Carolyn does the printing now and she is very good. I suspect the cataract on my left eye impairs my judgment as to whether the inking is right or wrong.—Meantime we thank you for the Latin quotations.

Carolyn prefers that from Job. greetings.

In Christ Yours

Victor + Carolyn

❧

May 14, 1959

Dear Victor:

I have not rushed to reply to your letter first because I have been a little busy, and second because it is most difficult to write anything that really makes sense about this most mysterious reality in the mystery of God—Hagia Sophia.

The first thing to be said of course is that Hagia Sophia is God Himself. God is not only a Father but a Mother. He is both at the same time, and it is the "feminine aspect" or "feminine principle" in the divinity that is the Hagia Sophia. But of course as soon as you say this the whole thing becomes misleading: a division of an "abstract" divinity into two abstract principles. Nevertheless, to ignore this distinction is to lose touch with the fullness of God. This is a very ancient intuition of reality which goes back to the oldest Oriental thought (there is something about it in Carolyn's wonderful book *Peaks and Lamas,* incidentally). For the "masculine-feminine" relationship is basic in *all* reality—simply because all reality mirrors the reality of God.

In its most primitive aspect, Hagia Sophia is the dark, nameless *Ousia* of the Father, the Son and the Holy Ghost, the incomprehensible, "primordial" darkness which is infinite light. The Three Divine Persons each at the same time are Sophia and manifest her. But where the Sophia or your picture comes in, is this: the wisdom of God, "reaching from end to end mightily" is also the Tao, the nameless pivot of all being and nature, the center and meaning of all, that which is the smallest and poorest and most humble in all:

the "feminine child" playing before God the Creator in His universe "playing before Him at all times, playing in the world" (Proverbs 8) (This is the Epistle of the F. of the Immaculate Conception.) This feminine principle in the universe is the inexhaustible source of creative realizations of the Father's glory in the world and is in fact the manifestation of His glory. Pushing it further, Sophia in ourselves is the *mercy* of God, the tenderness which by infinitely mysterious power of pardon turns the darkness of our sins into the light of God's love.

Hence, Sophia is the feminine, dark yielding, tender counterpart of the power, justice, creative dynamism of the Father.

Now the Blessed Virgin is the one created being who in herself realizes perfectly all that is hidden in Sophia. She is a kind of personal manifestation of Sophia. She crowns the second Person of the Trinity with His Human nature (with what is weak, able to suffer, able to be defeated) and sends Him forth with His mission of inexpressible mercy, to die for man on the cross, and this death, followed by the Resurrection, is the greatest expression of the "manifold wisdom of God" which unites us all in the mystery of Christ—the Church. Finally, it is the Church herself, properly understood as the great manifestation of the mercy of God, who is the revelation of Sophia in the sight of the angels.

The key to the whole thing is of course *mercy and love*. In the sense that God is Love, is Mercy, is Humility, is Hiddenness, He shows Himself to us within ourselves as our own poverty, our own nothingness (which Christ took upon Himself, ordained for this by the Incarnation in the womb of the Virgin) (the crowning in your picture) and if we receive the humility of God into our hearts, we become able to accept and embrace and love this very poverty, which is Himself and His Sophia. And then the darkness of wisdom becomes to us inexpressible light. We pass through the center of our own nothingness into the light of God.

I wrote that first page without keeping a carbon, but I am getting someone to copy it because I am going to want to know what I said.

I say these things and forget them, and then someone refers to them again and I can no longer remember what is being talked about. I cannot remember what it was I said when I was there in Lexington and we were looking at the triptych.

The beauty of all creation is a reflection of Sophia living and hidden in creation. But it is only a reflection. And the misleading thing about beauty, created beauty, is that we expect Sophia to be simply a more intense and more perfect and more brilliant, unspoiled, spiritual revelation of the same beauty. Whereas to arrive at her beauty we must pass through an apparent negation of created beauty, and to reach her light we must realize that in comparison with created light it is a darkness. But this is only because created beauty, and light, are ugliness and darkness compared with her. Again the whole thing is in the question of mercy, which cuts across the divisions and passes beyond every philosophical and religious ideal. For Sophia is not an ideal, not an abstraction, but the highest reality, and the highest reality must manifest herself to us not only in power but also in poverty, otherwise we never see it. Sophia is the Lady Poverty to whom St. Francis was married. And of course she dwelt with the Desert Fathers in their solitude, for it was she who had brought them there and she whom they knew there. It was with her that they conversed all the time in their silence.

I wish I had a fuller remembrance of your picture. I just remember the general idea. The story you tell of its growth is very interesting and revealing and I am sure Hagia Sophia herself was guiding you in the process, for it is she who guides all true artists, and without her they are nothing.

When Reinhardt was here he was discussing art too. His approach is very austere and ascetic. It is a kind of exaggerated reticence, a kind of fear of self expression. All his paintings are very formal and black. I certainly do not think he is a quack like so many others, on the contrary he is in strong reaction against them. I think you and he would be in fundamental agreement. It is a pity he was not able to get over there. He is certainly not a brilliant success (like so many of the others who are making fortunes with their stuff.)

Now J. Laughlin, whom you know, is coming down in June. He wants very much to see you, and will write to you about it. My novice who was in the hospital came out but is going back, and it is possible that perhaps it might be necessary for me to make one trip more. I do not know what the future will bring, but until I know more about it let us wait and expect the possibility at any rate. If nothing comes up, then we could plan on you both coming over here later in June. I could write about that. I think often of the Desert Fathers, and the work progressing. And how is the broadside? Maybe we could make a little broadsheet on Sophia, with the material begun here????

I am really enjoying Peaks and Lamas, and also the Athos book[59] has been very fine—and the Hesiod. When you have thought about this material on Sophia perhaps we could make a further step toward thinking of a title. I am so happy to be involved in what is clearly a very significant work, spiritually as well as artistically.

Thank you for the photostats from the encyclopedia. I looked them over and they just begin to touch on the mysterious doctrine. Carolyn should try to get for the library a book by Sergius Boulgakov, called the "Wisdom of God" published in London in the thirties. It would cover very well the Sophia theme. I have notes on it, but the book is very technical in its way.

Is Berdyaev's *Destiny of Man* available at the library yet, I wonder?

All the best to both of you. I will let you know what comes up. Meanwhile, God bless you. And especially this Whitsunday, for we are entering into the great feast of wisdom and creativity. May the Holy Spirit be with us and bless us.

Faithfully yours in Christ

fr Louis

Does the library have anything new or especially good on Mexico— travel book type, or anything to do with one way of life, mentality of the people etc. Have they any other book by Laurens Van der Post besides the "Dark Eye in Africa"?

May 29, 1959
Dear Carolyn,

Many thanks for your letter and for the slips. I thought the easiest thing would be simply to mail back the slips for the books I'd like to get first—so here they are. Thanks for all the trouble.

I have the Berdyaev + Bauelt. Again thanks.

I may be over next week, but cannot be sure yet.

Faithfully in Christ

fr Louis

❧

June 1, 1959
Dear Victor:

Thanks for your letter and the proofs—I am returning these with a couple of corrections.

J. Laughlin is not yet here, he was to have arrived this afternoon but probably will not get here until Wednesday. I think we can plan on being over in Lexington on Thursday or Friday. I will call you up Wednesday sometime and tell you definitely. Can we invite ourselves to lunch at your delightful place? I can think of nothing more pleasant. I do hope everything will work out nicely.

You must have had an active weekend. I hope you enjoyed it, and will have fully recovered by the time we descend on you. I am sure there will be many interesting things to talk about, but do not expect me to be wise about Sophia. Such lights as I have on that subject come most unaccountably, and at the moment I feel I have no lights on anything at all, which is a very solid kind of situation to be in. I ought to be in it more often.

Carolyn: a very good friend of mine[60] who has connections at the Marquette University library, wonders about borrowing some of my material (the mss.) from the U. of K. library and arranging a joint exhibit of such things with the collection they have there. I forget what on earth you might have there. Perhaps you could let me know in a general way. We'll talk about it; I do not know if we will have much time to spend in the library this trip however.

Looking forward to seeing you both—with all blessings.

Faithfully in Christ

fr Louis

※

June 12, 1959

Dear Carolyn:

Here it is already more than a week since Laughlin and I were over there. The lunch in the shady garden was wonderful, and everything about the day will be a treasured memory, except the fact that we were so late. J. has written a letter to say how wonderful a time he had.

I dare say it will be a long time before such a chance comes again. Our novice is returning home, I mean to his people outside. His health is not adequate for our life. So unless someone else gets sick and is sent to Lexington, I don't think there will be much chance of my coming over. So I will be looking forward to a visit from you and Victor in July! Almost any weekday is good, if you come at noontime. The 16th is a bad day though. Though it doesn't matter, I am always free for a while after dinner. I wish I could invite you to venison!

Here are a couple of slips for books—and do you have these others:

Nevada, American guide series.

Something descriptive on the Virgin Islands?

Hoping to hear from you soon—with blessings to you both.

Faithfully in Christ

fr Louis

※

June 13, 1959

Dear Victor:

Your letter reached me this morning. I think it is a very good idea to include the story about the mummies, and here it is. Unfortunately it is the original rough copy, and not very tidy. But I know you won't mind that. By all means use it anywhere and in any way you like. Incidentally, I notice that the one directly above it is rather good too (John the Dwarf at it again!) and perhaps you might want to exchange it for another of the short ones that are rather non-committal. Do as you like. I believe the fragments of stories on this page are going to make you insatiably curious. Perhaps I shall have to send you the rest of the additions. Let me know.

I wrote to Carolyn yesterday asking for some books and took the occasion to tell her how much J. and I enjoyed our visit. It is so rare to find things, even for an hour or so, so perfect. I only regret that we spoiled it by being late and could not have enjoyed a whole morning talking with you. I do not think I will be back in Lexington for a long time now. Our novice has been sent home, his health is not sufficiently good for this life. But in that case, I will expect you and Carolyn early in July, or even late in June. Whenever you like. Just let me know a little ahead of time. I am always able to be free about noon for an hour or so, as long as you let me know ahead of time. If you would like, rather than just sit around at the gatehouse we could go up to the lake or to some shady place. You can always have lunch at the guesthouse, but of course I know that really is no advantage as Carolyn would have to go to the Ladies' Guest House.

Yes, I do have quite a question forming itself in my mind. We can speak of it perhaps. Meanwhile, about the books: I may write to your friend to get some titles. I am interested in the ordinary titles that might be in the library too. But it will be a difficult job.

I look forward to seeing some more proofs in any case. How does Carolyn like the new version of the "Confession"? Perhaps the shorter one is better for a broadside. I like the broadside project very much.

God bless you. With all affection to both of you, in Christ
fr Louis

Does the library happen to have a book by I.G. Squire dealing with some Caribbean islands (The Corn Islands) off Nicaragua. Or anything else interesting on small Caribbean Islands like that?

June 18, 1959
Dear Victor.

I know this is the end of the Abbot-Milido story, but I do not know if this follows the page I sent you. It very probably does. Let me know if it does not. And if you want one hundred and one Desert Father stories that is fine. It all depends on you and your spouse. I look forward to seeing you in a couple of weeks. June 24th, 29th and July 2nd are *less good* days. The other days are fine.

   Blessings to you both—in Xt Jesus
   fr Louis

June 23, 1959
Dear Victor:

Here are the proofs again. I hope you got Abbot Milido all right— that "awful sight." I am glad we are progressing well with the book and that the end is in sight. I know it will be very fine, and I think your edition will have a very special character all its own which Mardersteig[61] will not measure up to. But I expect him to be very good too in a different way. I had to work to keep J. Laughlin from putting archaic decorations and woodcuts in the edition. It needs no decoration, the Desert Fathers are really not to be tied down in a "period." They transcend all epochs.

   A few more titles, if Carolyn can get them from the library. (I am sending some back today).

   Guenon, Rene: Crisis of the Modern World.
   Trevor-Roper, H.R. The Last Days of Hitler
   Kluckhohn and Leighton—The Navaho

Looking forward to seeing you sometime soon. With all blessings
Faithfully in Christ
fr Louis

❦

June 24, 1959
Dear Victor.

Here are the last of the proofs, with one correction. By the way do you
think you could give us some unbound sheets for three or four copies
and we could try binding them here? We can always use a few extras
outside the regular edition. If this is in any way inconvenient, then
let's forget it. If you want me to sign one or two of your copies please
bring them over when you come.
With all best wishes and blessings
in Xt
fr Louis

❦

Saturday June 25 '59
Dear Carolyn

I signed the sheet and sent them off yesterday. Thank you for the cards
and suggested titles—I am sending back 4 which you can bring with
you when you come—there is no hurry.
Here is also one I am very anxious to get—if you don't have it,
perhaps it is in the College of the Bible.

Butterfield—Christianity and History

I hope Victor is feeling better and I am sure he will be back on his
feet with a little rest. I keep him and you in my prayers. God bless
you.
Gratefully in Christ
fr Louis

1959
Dear Victor.

Here they are. I think everything is correct. So I am getting them back to you with the only corrections that I could spot. I am sure this will make an attractive cover. Eager to see you!

All the best to both of you.

In Christ our Lord

fr Louis

Friday [1959]
Dear Victor

I am terribly sorry to hear you are ill. I shall miss seeing you and Carolyn tomorrow, but that is not important, you can always come later. Any time will be fine. The important thing is not for you to rush over here but for you to get well. So take a good rest. And take your time. There is no hurry at all. If you want me to sign the sheets, just send them over. And if there is anything else I can do, just let me know. Meanwhile I will be praying for your recovery. So have a vacation, take things quietly. It will be the best thing for you.

Besides it is likely to be unpleasantly hot these next few days, this is the worst part of the summer. Don't be in too much of a hurry to bind all those books.

God bless you. Let me soon have the pleasure of hearing that you are resting and feel much better.

Faithfully in Christ

fr Louis

Tuesday, July 14 [1959]
Dear Victor

Thanks for your welcome note. I am glad the printing is finished and still more glad that the work was meaningful. I certainly derived profit from my share in it. I hope the Desert Fathers will all be praying for us in heaven and I am sure they will.

I will be expecting you both about noon on Saturday. If you have a moment to bring a couple of books besides the encyclopedia (!!) here are some possible titles.

Hearn, Lafcadio—Two Years in the French West Indies
Guenon, René—East and West.
Nicholson, R.A.—Mystics of Islam
Krivitzky—In Stalin's Secret Service.
Snellgrove—Buddhist Himalaya.

Bring the sheets and I will sign these and send them later—no need to do it while you are here, time is too precious.
Looking forward to Saturday—God bless you.
As ever, in Christ
fr Louis

❦

July 30, 1959
Dear Victor:

Here is a text beginning with "E."[62] I have cooked it up a bit, but I think it will do:

Erat in Scete quidam frater nihil habens in substantia sua nisi tantum Evangelium, et ipsum vendidit in pauperum nutrimento dicens: Ipsum etiam verbum vendidi quod jubet: vende omnia et da pauperibus![63]

This comes out a good length and has a good feeling about it, besides fortunately representing one of the sayings we have printed, more or less.

As to the text for the spine, I like better the one with the commas, and agree with you in not liking the brackets.

I think the cover will be very attractive and look forward to seeing

the proofs of it. But still more I anticipate your visit. Thank Carolyn
for the two books from the library which got in yesterday. I now have
to get down to some pressing work, so close in haste, but with all
blessings.

Faithfully in Christ Our Lord
fr Louis

❀

July 30
Dear Carolyn

How are you, and especially how is Victor? Can we look forward to
seeing you soon?

What I wanted to ask was: when you come, could you please bring
the best late book on William Blake—about him, his life and work?
And anything new on Mexico also.

Many thanks—and God bless you
fr Louis

❀

Aug. 12, 1959
Dear Victor:

Here are some off prints of the Pasternak article. Some are for you
and the rest for the library. The article was a small insert in a large
two page spread. I am having the editors send some copies of *Jubilee*
down to the library.

On looking over the Desert Fathers book at leisure, I am
confirmed in all my admiration of it. Certainly it is one of your very
finest works, and comes just about as close to perfection as one would
hope. It is a most beautiful book and everyone is in admiration of it.
I repeat that I am happy, and proud to have the occasion for such a
work and to have provided the material for it. It makes me very happy
and I think it is really something of lasting value. That is what a monk
should want, and it is not often that the desire is fulfilled. I do not feel

that I have done anything to deserve this, but anyway, the charity of Christ explains it. So, thank you.

No need to add that everyone is in admiration of the book. I haven't got Brother Giles' explicit reaction yet but he is very grateful. He will probably be writing me a note about it. I never see him, hardly see him more than I see you. He is always in another part of the monastery, the business end, from which I am extraordinarily and I hope permanently remote.

Are you sending a copy to Kurt and Helen Wolff?[64] If not, let me know, I can send them one of mine. I know they will greatly appreciate it.

Your visit the other day[65] was a pleasure. I hope that when the broadside gets under way you will be down again. Keep well, and God bless you both.

Faithfully yours in Christ
fr Louis

19. VIII. 59
Dear Father Louis: thank you for your kind letter—which was rewarding. However, let us not forget that things like that, books, simply ought to be that way and deserve no special admiration.—No, I am not sending a copy to the Kurt Wolff's in Zurich. If you send one, please remember me to them.—Harry Duncan[66] stayed here only overnight. He said he hoped to see you in St. John's, Minnesota, where you are going to deliver a paper—are you?—Here is the proof for the prospectus. Any change or improvement you want to make is agreeable to us.

Most thankful, in Christ
Yours C. + V.H.

Aug. 19 1959
Dear Carolyn:

J. Laughlin wants me to write to a certain Mina Loy about her poems.

As I gave you her book, with those others, when you were here,
I wonder if I could borrow it back for while, in order to write her
something intelligent. I forget the title.

How are you and Victor?

In haste—and with all best wishes,

fr Louis

❀

Aug. 24 [1959]
Dear Victor

The prospectus is perfectly all right—go ahead with it as you please.
I haven't heard from all those to whom I sent the Desert Fathers, but
those who have responded are literally swept off their feet by it. And
that is to be expected. I hope you are well—I will write more later.

With best regards to you both—God bless you.

fr Louis

❀

Sept. '59
Dear Carolyn—

If you and Victor come over on the 4th would you be able to bring
some of these books? I would be very grateful. I hope you will be
coming.

Faithfully in Christ

fr Louis

❀

Dear Carolyn

One or two more titles, if you have them in the library, please:

W. Barrett—Irrational Man.
Blackney—Meister Eckhart in a Modern Translation
Radhakrishnan—Mahatma Gandhi

E. E. Cummings—6 nonlectures Harvard 1953
H. Fast—The Naked God NY 1957
D.T. Suzuki Living by Zen.

Again, many thanks. I am sending back today the last of those
books you brought and have the small Russian readers etc. for which
many thanks. Is there any hurry for their return???
Faithfully
fr L

❧

Sept. 10, 1959
Dear Victor:

I wanted you and Carolyn to see this copy of a letter from Bob Lax[67] in
which he gives his characteristic impressions of the Desert Fathers book.
I hope you can read the photostat which is not very clear. The letter is in
Lax's own brand of English and I have had to insert a couple of words he
left out. I know you will enjoy it. Mark Van Doren also wrote praising
the beauty of the book. Other comments have not reached me.

Did you hear about Brother Giles going to Rome? This is amazing.
He is to work in the house of the Abbot General for five years. This
will keep him pretty busy and it will not be all beer and skittles I can
assure you. But I think he will have a chance to get around a bit and
see a few places, and that will be wonderful.

I have been sending back the library books gradually and think
I have most of them back by now. One arrived today however, the
Gellhorn, on War. Thank you, Carolyn.

Do you by any chance have:

Zernov—Three Russian Prophets
Zernov—Church of the Eastern Christians
Nicholson—Mystics of Islam

And did you ever get Jung's Secret of the Golden Flower?

The novitiate is a madhouse as they are tearing up a concrete floor in order to put in a drain for some new showers. So I think I will have to hide out in the woods for a while.

When are you and Carolyn coming over again? The weather in October ought to be quite nice—what we have had up until yesterday has hardly been decent.

Here is another off print you might like—it is from Cross Currents. Do they take that in the library? It is very worth while.

As ever, with all best wishes, and hoping you are both very well
Faithfully yours in Christ
fr Louis

❀

18.IX.59
Dear Father Louis:

Thank you so much for your letter of Sept 10; with the photostat of your friend Lax's letter. I still wonder why a thing made by one's hands for the praise of God speaks to people and speaks to them just for that reason. It doesn't speak to all of them, not to the masses however.—But when everyone will be a mass-man and the older generation dies out, and no Christians are left, and we travel to the moon, what effect will the handiwork of a man have on these people? And isn't that what Khrushchev wants and the Americans even more so? I am in a dark mood after having read your and Niebuhr's articles.

Yes Brother Giles was in Lexington to bid us good bye, the change will do him good, but it will not change him.

So far we have sold four books. Frank Dell'Isola[68] ordered one too, saying he is your bibliographer. We have sent him book and bill. I am going to send out three review copies: One to Publisher's weekly, one to the Literary Supplement in London and perhaps one to the Saturday review of Literature, or do you think that not necessary?

We plan to go to the east on October 4th. If we can manage to see you on our way to Louisville on that day we will certainly come and see you, and that would be possible only if we can drive to Bellarmine

College for the exhibition I shall have there, opening on 4th of October. Yet nothing is too certain yet.

I liked your article on Christianity and don't you see that this is exactly what the classic artist must do—not heading for beauty or anything else, only trying to open the eyes of those who might be able to see. But woe to him who tries to fake a work of classic art by trying to use the recipe for making one, he would fail as much as the Pharisees failed. Humility at least can prevent one from making a fool of oneself.

Yours in Christ
Carolyn and Victor.

❀

Sept 24, 1959
Dear Victor:

It was good to get your letter and Carolyn's books. I am happy to hear about the exhibit. What time will you have to be at Bellarmine? I wonder if I will be able to get in and see it. Would you be coming through here about noon, as usual? At any rate I shall keep an eye on the gatehouse that day. Let me know for sure if you will be out this way. Meanwhile, God bless you—

fr Louis

❀

Nov. 24, 1959
Dear Carolyn.

Here is the ms. of an article I wrote for a nun's magazine[69]—to enlighten the teaching sisters. It is for the collection in the university but I thought Victor might like to read it first. Also I thought you might like the photographs—I have been cleaning house, as you see. The photographs are for you and Victor, and were taken by Lax. I sent some others to be filed in the university. Care should be taken that they do not get printed as long as I am a living member of the Order.

I have no special news for you. J. Laughlin plans to come here about the middle of December and we might all meet then. If anything comes up before that, I'll let you know.

Always, best wishes and blessings to you both.

In Christ our Lord

fr Louis

8. XII. 59

Dear Father Louis: Thank you so much for your kind letter and the photos which we really cherish. Please let us know when James will be here, we would like to meet you both. Do you know the Book of Father Bruckberger:[70] Image of America? I think it is worth reading, and if you want it I can lend you my copy. Of course we all make mistakes and I cannot agree with everything he says, especially when he talks about Art—Picasso! The approach to the Visual is still mostly thorough literature, I am afraid, and this attitude will never change I am afraid too. Let us know then.

In Christ yours ever

Victor

Dec. 12, 1959

Dear Victor—

Thank you for your note of the other day. I have as yet no news when Laughlin will be here, and perhaps he may not come. Everything is uncertain except that we will not be able to come to Lexington this time—there is no possible reason for me to base a request on. I shall let you know when he gets here or is about to get here, so that we can perhaps arrange something. Would you want to come over? If the weather were nice I would hazard that perhaps we might all get together for a picnic lunch in the woods: but the way things are today, it would probably be wiser to build an ark.

I am sending you the *Christmas Sermons*[71] which we finally had printed in Louisville. I am ashamed to send you such a job—it really has nothing to it at all. Except that it is neat and tidy. Otherwise it strikes me more and more as silly, when I look at it. I tried a new type face . . . well, the less said about it the better.

I keep thinking that it would be so wonderful if you would make a tabernacle and candlesticks for us. Would you at least consent to look at the novitiate chapel? Here too, there is nothing that will offer much inspiration.

Apart from this I have no news whatever.

Thanks for offering me the Bruckberger book. I have heard about it, and perhaps I will get around to it some time. But at the moment I am rather swamped under other things that have to be read now.

With every best wish to both of you, and my blessing—a very holy and happy Christmas to you, (though I hope to see you before Christmas if J. shows up.)[72]

Faithfully in Christ

fr Louis

Christmas Day [1959]
Dear Victor.

We have put up the large crucifix in our novitiate chapel and the smaller one in the chapel of the infirmary.[73] I have not seen the latter in place, but the infirmarian is very pleased. The large one in our chapel is superb. It is very majestic and sacred and really one does not appreciate it fully until it is seen suspended at a certain height above an altar. It is so perfect for us that it seems to have been done especially for us and certainly we will have to buy it to make sure that it forms part of the finished chapel. Already the chapel seems transformed. Father Abbot agreed in principle to consider the paneling—but that will be at a rather distant future date since so many other things are to be done.

Thank you ever so much—yours was an inspired idea. I hope now we can go along with the tabernacle.

On the way home the other day, after my most pleasant visit, I stopped at Shakertown.[74] Could Carolyn get me a book or two about the Shakers, especially about their Kentucky colonies? I'd like to do a study of them.[75]

Best wishes and prayers for a happy New Year. I remembered you of course in my Masses today.

God bless you both—

In Christ our Lord

fr Louis

Jan 4th, 1960.

Dear Victor,

In this short note I want to make to you two large proposals. First of all, as a possibility for printing, I propose to you the accompanying text on solitude.[76] It would have perhaps a different and better title. I think though it has the character required for a small, simple tract—printed perhaps in the same type in which you set your notes on classic art, but in a larger size. Read it, please, and tell me what you think. The only thing is that it will eventually be printed in a book in New York, but not I think this year. I believe we have time for it, then.

The other proposal is to buy the crucifix—the large one. Now that we have it in the chapel, and see that it is indeed so perfect for the place and purpose, there is no alternative but to ask for it permanently. I know you once gave us a smaller price than you had been asking elsewhere, but forget exactly what it was. Was it a thousand dollars? I have received the approval of Father Abbot to buy it, if possible, for that sum.

And of course I hope this would be an added reason for going ahead with the tabernacle and candlesticks.[77] I believe that eventually we could panel the chapel also, as you suggested. But that would have to be rather a long while off, I fear.

At any rate, please tell me what you think of selling us the crucifix at that price, and if there is any other proposal you would like to make.

Please thank Carolyn for so promptly sending the books on the Shakers. I am very interested and will certainly do an article on them if I can. You know, I wish something could be done to make Shakertown a permanently protected place[78]—perhaps the university could take it over and use it as a study center of some kind. It could become a kind of summer writers' and students' colony, perhaps. Do you think that would ever be done? I would hate to see it fall into ruin, or just become a kind of state museum, though that would be better than nothing.

I spoke to Father Abbot about making paper, and he was very non-committal, as I expected he would be. I have no indication that he would be at all interested in such a project. One of the novices is very interested in it, though. And I really think it has possibilities. In itself it is wonderful, but in the concrete situation here there are too many obstacles. The mentality of the house is just not propitious to craftsmanship, and that is a great pity.

As usual, with very best wishes—God bless you both.

Faithfully in Christ

fr Louis

❀

January 7th 60

Dear Father Louis:

Thank you for your kind and good letter. I am—and of course Carolyn is too—very happy that the Crucifixus has found a permanent place at Gethsemani. After having been asked by the Austrian Government in 1948 to resume my post at the Academy of Fine Arts in Vienna my instinctive answer was: no, because I somehow knew my place was in this country; and now, after more than ten years I feel justified in my refusal, for this work of mine, the Crucifixus, is now in the place where it belongs—in your monastery. I accept the price of $1000.00 for it and am thanking Father Abbot and you.

I have pondered about the tabernacle and come to the conclusion that I best make it myself. We can talk this over when next we meet at Gethsemani and I might also take measurements of the chapel.

Though the paneling is certainly a far off job, I would have an eye on the cedar trees if I were you; the wood for that purpose should come from the grounds Gethsemani owns. As to the candlesticks, I would propose to have them made in France where the others have been made. I still have the drawings for those and after Father Abbot and you have seen them I can send them to my friend in Alsace and find out—if you want—about the price. The work done here would not be as satisfactory and certainly more expensive.

There are a few people here in Lexington, Louisville and elsewhere who are interested in preserving Shakertown. We will tell you about this when next we meet. There is a student at the university who writes his doctorate thesis on Shakertown and he too could be helpful.

As to your manuscript. First of all let me thank you sincerely. I have only read the first few phrases, realizing however that this is biographical matter at which you are always very good. So, please, let me read it before I say anything definite.—Yet I should say a few words on the type. If I am printing it for the Stamperia I would have to use the Uncial type as this is the only type connected with my Press. I know quite well how difficult it is for most persons— including you—to get used to it. You may even regret that the Desert Fathers have been set up in this unusual, and uncompromising type. It is the same with almost everything I am doing—conservative as I am, it takes people years and decades to see the reason why I am so severe, so uncommitting. And you will understand why I dedicate my work to God, not to men, and why I don't care for immediate reward.

Thank you dear Father Louis and please extend my thanks also to Reverend Father Abbot.

In Christ,
both of us,
Carolyn + Victor

8. I. 60. I have read the mspt. and I think that it would not matter if, for a while, it remains hidden behind my type. But I cannot do that without your consent. V.

Dear Carolyn

I am just sending back the last two books of yours that I had. Do you have these others:

Haskins, C.H., The Renaissance of the 12th Century
Krishnamurti—The First and Last Freedom
Davidson, B. The Lost Cities of Africa.
Obolensky, D. The Bogomils.

Also if you can dig up anything on the Ecuadorian poet Jorge Carrera Andrade I would be grateful, as I am doing some work on him.[79] He is a very fine and interesting person.

I am happy with Victor's ideas about the Solitary Life booklet and agree that it will be very fine as a companion to the other. Probably this will cross in the mail with something from him so I will add no more at the moment.

With best regards—hoping to see you soon[80]
Faithfully in Christ
fr Louis

P.S. I was wrong in saying these were the last books to return—I still have several on the Shakers. They will be a little while yet, if you will let me keep them. I hope no one else is looking for them.

30. I. 60

Dear Father Louis: enclosed find two copies of the first two pages— one for you one back for us—and I shall continue to send you 2 or 3 at a time. Should you want to make changes, it is easier for us to make them now, but perhaps not necessary for you.—I came across a short writing of Meister Eckhart: von Abgeschiedenheit. Obviously dealing with the same topic as do you. Yet there are centuries between you.—I have chosen to make this short treatise a companion, in appearance, of the Desert Fathers, to me the two seem so close. The title page has not found its form yet though I am working on it. The copyright note makes it always difficult, yet it must be there I realize.—I have done nothing, except a little thinking, on the tabernacle yet. We have to talk more about it because there are different approaches to the problem, yours and mine, and which one ought to prevail we will know only later.—I realize that I am a hermit in my art, not by way of the strength of conviction and character, but simply because I cannot help to be what I am. Sometimes I have tried to compromise, to adapt, but always with the same result—I have been found out immediately.

Yours ever in Christ—Victor

Carolyn sends her best and I do too.

Feb 5, 1960

Dear Victor:

Here are the first proofs with one correction. I am happy that this project is going ahead and that you like it. I thoroughly agree with you that it is a logical companion piece to the Desert Fathers book. The design will leave nothing to be desired, if the two are going to match one another. About the title page, remember that the copyright can be on the *back* of the title page. It does not have to be on the front, which is certainly disastrous for design. I look forward to further developments.

About the tabernacle: do not think that I am clinging madly to some idea of my own about how it ought to be. I leave entirely to you the external form and design of the tabernacle. The only thing that I *have* to be concerned about is that the tabernacle should conform to the canonical regulations. These are in brief:

1. That it should be in the middle of the altar (half way between ends)
2. That it be fixed to the altar or in some way un-movable.

3. It should be, interiorly, very solid and safe-like, so that it cannot be broken into, as far as possible. It cannot in other words be a plain wooden box. The outside casing can be wood. As for the inside "safe" you can go about that any way you like or even get someone else to make it. I do not know how to explain it in such a way that it will not deter you from the project. It just has to be very solid and secure. You can fill this prescription in any way you like as long as it is taken care of.

4. Inside, the dimensions should be such as to permit putting away a ciborium over 18 inches high. Or at least 19 inches. And there are some special ways of making the inside formal and lavish with silk or something, which I think is probably non essential, and if it isn't maybe some brother can take care of that here.

Really I don't think there has to be any special problem about this. What did you do for Kolbsheim? Surely theirs is regular.

I have been up and down with bouts of 'flu. This weather is miserable. I hope you are all right. From everywhere I get echoes of happiness from J. at the picnic we enjoyed together.

Thank Carolyn for the Nordoff book, which I have received. It is pretty definite that my photographer friend[81] and I will do a book on the Shakers, but I am not advancing very rapidly with study of the subject.

And now: when will you next come over? Let's give the weather a chance to clear a little. Perhaps early in March—the 2nd is Ash Wednesday and that would be bad, but the first, third, fourth or fifth would be all right. If you have some other choice, just let me know a little ahead so that I can confirm or change the arrangement. I hope to hear soon. God bless you both.

With every best wish
Cordially in Christ,
fr Louis

8. II. 60

Dear Father Louis: The red in the proofs are your underscored words. Of course the capital letters at the beginning of the 3 paragraphs will be in red too. As to the title pages—these are only trials and you can change them. The first page serves for the copyright. And I think you should find out from Washington what ought to be done in order that your publisher (New Directions?) is protected. Perhaps a copyright on this printing will not permit him to use it on the next printing. Or shall we say: privately printed, or: printed as a private edition. Would that jeopardize the publisher's rights? James L. should be able to find out about that definitely and authoritatively.—I rather liked your name at the end too and the place and date, as in the Desert Fathers. But this is entirely up to you.—I think I will try to cut the tails away on the *y* in that new type of mine. It will be more soignée anyhow, this is rather rough.—Hope you are well. Your paper (or book now) rather touches us, we read every word and it means so much. Your style is so clear and may I be permitted to say: classic, for that reason.

    In Christ,
    Yours ever
    Victor

9. II. 60

Thanks for your letter and the proofs. As to p. 7—I will see how the next paragraph comes out and then decide whether or not to put the 2 lines on the bottom of p. 7. Separating the 3 paragraphs this way is perhaps tearing them asunder, and there is that unity of the whole piece which might suffer.—About the tabernacle—I think we have to talk about that and I have to do some drawing. Of course I am concerned with the whole and the proportions of that small piece— the tabernacle—in relation to the cross, the height of the ceiling and all these things together.—Yes, let us wait a while for better weather, we might hit on another day like the one we had with J.—J. has sent the book of Miller on Rimbaud. These 2 windows in the front cover with the 2 pair of eyes looking out is a rum idea (I hope this is spelled right) otherwise the book is done very nicely.

Kindest greetings from both of us

Yours ever

V.

❦

Feb. 15 [1960]

Dear Victor

It took quite a long time for this to reach me—I only got it this morning.

I do not think we should put any but *Latin* words in red at least in the body of the text. So ignore please my other underlinings.

About the bottom of p 7. I think you are right not to break up the continuity by a strange arrangement. A simple new start would be better.

I took the liberty of making a couple of changes in the style—I hope you don't mind.

The title page is fine—the copyright should be on the reverse side, no? J. has only to reprint the same copyright line. No, this is not J. though, it will be Farrar Straus. I can find out. No emergency.

When will we see you? March 1st is out for me now. The other days are all right—and the next week except Saturday 12th.

As ever—with very best wishes

In Our Lord

fr Louis

❦

18.II.60

Dear Father Louis,

V. thinks that in your last letter to him—or next to last letter—you gave some titles which you would like to have sent from the library. Now we cannot find the letter and wonder if you will repeat your request? Can you?

At the moment we are all but snow-bound but happily warm and provisioned. It is really rather pleasant for these few days to be so quiet and undisturbed—and to have to walk. Victor is absorbed in setting your book and when you return the next proof I shall start printing it as there will be enough pages.

Sincerely,

Carolyn R. Hammer

☙

Feb 19, 1960

Dear Carolyn—

Yes, the snow is wonderful and I think it must really be especially wonderful in your warm little house. And with type-setting going on, and the smell of ink. What could be more monastic and contemplative?

But when it comes to remembering exactly what books I asked for, that is not so easy. Which shows that I can't be too set on getting them. Here however are the titles that I have had swimming about in my head for the past few days: I think they include what I asked for.

Krishnamurti The First and Last Freedom

Lytton Strachey—Eminent Victorians

Do you have Erasmus—Laus Stultitiae (Encomium Moriae) and
Enchiridion in Latin?

Schrodinger Nature and the Greeks

Oblensky, D. The Bogomils.

N. Lewis Volcanoes Above Us.

I know there must have been something else, but I cannot remember. If you can let me have any of these, fine. When are you thinking of coming again? Revising earlier statements, I can quote you March 9, 10, 11 as good dates, and also the 12th if you prefer a Saturday. In general, Mondays Wednesdays and Fridays are *less good for me* as in the late morning I have a conference.

I will break this off, with no more than a word to say that I am becoming very *classical minded* since reading F. M. Cornford. Have you anything by Jane Harrison? I understand she is good. Anything good on Aeschylus? I will talk more about my conversion to classicism later. Victor's good angel must have been working on me.

All best wishes and blessings—
In Christ the Lord
fr Louis

※

Dear Carolyn

One of the other titles I forgot has come back to me: perhaps you have it?

Haskins, C.H., The Twelfth Century Renaissance.
With best wishes—
in Christ
fr Louis

※

22. II. 60

Dear Father Louis: I have now added a dash after each paragraph since I did not want to indent them, and I think there can be no mistake about where a paragraph ends and the other one begins. And, as you see, I could manage p. 7 and have also done well with p. 12.

We will now begin to print the section from p. 5 on to p. 12. This will leave us time to decide about the title section, or front matter as it is called here, (very strange to me). As to the copyright page, which I prefer to set directly at the front, not ashamedly at the back of the title page, I believe you ought to write to Farrar and Straus and ask them what they think ought to be done with this edition of 50 copies, prior to theirs. It makes no difference to me, I would just as soon print it without the copyright passage, but I think you owe them an explanation beforehand and they should declare their stand too.

Whether the phrase: privately printed or private edition would protect your work and not impinge upon their right should now be clarified. But it is completely up to you for I have no interest in the decision reached.

You are entitled to any change in your text, without any charge, our time has no monetary value, we want the book to be written as good as you can do it and we will print it accordingly. I have made all your corrections and all three are a decided improvement.

The question is now: where shall your name appear in the title section and how would you like to have it. Is the mentioning in the copyright passage enough? It would be for me but this is not my book. Certainly this is 'the solitary life of Father Louis,' at least it is to me that, but this does not come into it. Again: you must make the decision, we only want to serve *you*. That is why I send the title section back.

The weather is awful, I haven't set foot outdoors since days. Yet we had longer and harder winters in Aurora.

As soon as we get the proofs back we will begin to print. I guess we will have 20 or 22 pages text and the book is certainly a companion to the Desert Fathers. How many copies for you, is twelve enough? We could extend this to fifteen, though not more.

Kindest greetings from both of us.

In Christ, yours ever

Victor

Feb 23 1960
Dear Victor

In this game of spiritual tennis I am returning the ball promptly. I have taken advantage of your kindness to make a few changes in the text which, I hope, will not be at all troublesome—and they will help I think. Would it not be better to have no names on the title page, just a solitary title. And if need be the author's name could go in a colophon. Bob Giroux[82] of Farrar Straus and Cudahy is here today and I will ask him about the copyright and let you know. The copyright line *must be* either on the title page or the reverse of the title page. Will you please ask Carolyn if the library has a book called *The Secret Country*—edited by John Peale Bishop, published by Macmillan in 1950? I would like it if possible.

Blessings as ever—hope it will warm up and that spring weather will bring you here!

Faithfully in Christ
fr Louis

❀

March 4, 1960
Dear Father Louis,

The following titles are on their way to you:

Erasmus: *Moriae Encomium*
(his *Enchiridion Militis* is in this library)—only on microfilm—
    sorry
Harrison, Jane Ellen : *Ancient art & ritual*
    "   "   "   : *Prolegomena to the study of Greek Religion*
    "   "   "   : *Aspects, Aorists & the Classical Tripos.*
Books on Aeschylus:
Aeschylus & Athens by Thomson
Aeschylus & Sophocles by Sheppard
Pindar & Aeschylus by Finley
(I can send others if wanted).

Of Krishnamurti, we have only the things noted on the attached slips; do you want? The rest of his work in print is being ordered including *The First & Last Freedom*.

Obolensky, *The Bogomils* is not here, nor *The Secret Country* edited by John Peale Bishop. Of the latter's work I find we have only his poems and essays.

The little car is only a fair weather car and we have given up the idea of trying to bring these over until Spring is more determined. Will you be able to see us on Saturday the 26th or any day of the week following?

Sincerely,
Carolyn R. Hammer

&

Mar. 8, 1960
Dear Carolyn:

Many thanks for your letter and for the books which I am expecting, and will receive gratefully. I am keeping the slips with the Krishnamurti references for a future date, as I don't want to be collecting too many of your books all at one time.

Saturday the 26th of March would be a very good day, and the next week is all right except that Monday is doubtful and Tuesday is not so good. Any one of the other days would be fine. Just drop me a line before you come, and I will be ready about noon. If you are coming before noon (which is all right too) then Thursday and Saturday are good, the other days not so good.

I have rewritten the solitary life piece to please censors for the book in which it is to appear.[83] It has been much changed, enlarged, and is almost entirely different. Hence the problem of copyright disappears. If in your limited edition which counts as manuscript Victor wants to omit the copyright altogether it would certainly make no difference now, legally. I leave it to him. But if he has the copyright all settled now, I mean if it is there to stay, Bob Giroux merely has to sign a document, or we do, but it is just a matter of signing something.

Last night we had a rather large fire—one of the industrial buildings, partly destroyed, with a few machines. There could have been some rather bad explosions, which thank heaven did not occur. I was milling around in the general confusion and still smell of smoke. Was lucky to be not one of those who were doused with freezing water from the hoses.

Looking forward to seeing you both when the weather is better—
God bless you and best wishes, in Christ.

fr Louis

The Secret Country was published by Macmillan about 1950 I believe.

☸

20. III. 60

Dear Father Louis:

If the weather isn't too bad next Saturday we plan to come and see
you. So we leave it to the weather since I don't want Carolyn to drive
if it snows and we are not too certain that it will not. Would you mind
having a picnic lunch with us? We will make it as lean and unpleasant
as we possibly can. Maybe we can even sit under the cedar trees. One
never knows in this climate.

It is not impossible that I can bring the rest of the proof sheets
with me. Carolyn has printed, that is she began the center section and
if she finishes it I have enough type for the rest of the book.

We still are not sure about the difference in the time you and
we have, but we start here at 9 in the morning and should be in
Gethsemani 2 hours later. Is that right? And I know you like the
coffee dark and hot. Carolyn wants me to make it perfectly clear that
we start here at *our* time, Lexington time. Is this too confusing?

Thank you, yours in Christ

Victor

☸

March 22, Tues [1960]

Dear Victor:

I just got your note. I will be expecting you Saturday unless it snows
cats and dogs. But let us expect nice weather for a change. You are an
hour ahead of us, so I expect you will be getting here ten or ten thirty
in the morning. I will remain in the novitiate and the brothers will
ring me up when you reach the gatehouse.

It seems a very long time since you were here last. I shall look forward to the visit very much, and I am sure we can accomplish much, in the way of work, and considering the chapel project etc. But more than that I shall be very glad to see and talk with you both again.

God bless you, then. With very best wishes

Faithfully yours in Christ

fr Louis

March 26, 1960

Dear Victor:

Your special delivery reached me this morning—is there such a thing as air mail from Lexington to Gethsemani? Anyway, everything is all right, I will be expecting you next Saturday[84] and hoping that the weather then turns out as beautifully as what we have today. It would be ideal for a sandwich "under the cedars." I am glad to see what I hope is the end of all this snow. May you have a very pleasant and fruitful visit with your friends, and I will look forward to seeing you, with proofs etc., next week.

Will you please pass the enclosed note about some books to Carolyn?

God bless you, then.

With every good wish—Cordially in Christ

fr Louis

April 7, 1960

Dear Victor.

At our last enjoyable meeting recently I forgot to mention that I had once again changed my mind in regard to the copyright line. It has occurred to me that if by any chance the book were pirated the consequences would be extremely unpleasant, as much attention would be drawn to those precise elements in it which should be more or less unnoticed.

Consequently, I think it is best to be on the safe side and have it copyrighted. The copyright line as you showed it to me, either on the reverse of the title page or the title page itself, would be quite satisfactory.

I cannot say how good it was to see you and Carolyn again on such a nice day.

Looking forward to hearing from you and seeing the book shortly and with best wishes for Holy Week and Easter—God bless you

Cordially in Christ

fr Louis

April 12, 1960

Dear Victor:

All I can say is that the meaning of the cross and the Resurrection is just that. Death is destroyed and sin is forgotten. There is a wonderful mysterious text in St. Paul somewhere, in which he says "even if my heart reproach me, yet God is greater than my heart." Meaning that (as he says in another place) we do not judge ourselves. And if we do, the answer of His mercy is more final than our self-condemnation. The reason why we talk of remembering sin is that it has to be remembered first before it can be forgotten. We are not birds or animals, living in thoughtlessness. What is done must be brought to mind and judged. But when it is judged the matter ends. It is forgotten. It is only in hell that sin is not forgotten. That is why it is hell. The cross is not a *reproach* for sin as so many people make it to be. (So many preachers simply threaten men with the cross, and belabor them with it.) The meaning of the cross is that the "writ" that is against us has been nailed to the wood and destroyed. It is that sin can now be forgotten, in so far as we are new men in Christ. If it come back, then it is again destroyed by His mercy and forgotten. All this is in St. Paul, but St. Paul is sometimes hard reading. And it is in the First Epistle of St. John, which would be a good one to read and meditate around this time, Easter.

Of course someone will say: there must be penance and reparation for sin. Well, the best reparation and penance is to have so much confidence in the mercy of God that one can forget it. But this implies a certain way of life which makes the forgetfulness real and not just a psychological suppression—it must be a new life in Christ. Which does not mean good bourgeois conformity by any means.

Here is a little card, not beautiful, which I got somewhere. The text is nice. I wonder if you would like to make something of it for us, sometime—not necessarily with a picture. I could ask Father Abbot if we could commission you to do a few hundred for us. It is a good word to give to many people.

And here is the proof. Many thanks.

God bless you and Carolyn, and all best Easter wishes.

Cordially in Christ Our Lord

fr Louis

☙

April 13, 1960

Dear Victor:

Just after I mailed my letter yesterday I received your note about the copyright. The copyright line you showed me before, for the Stamperia del Santuccio, is perfectly all right. You will have to get Form A from the copyright office at the Library of Congress, fill it in, have it notarized and send it in with four dollars. If you like, I could save you this bother by taking out the copyright in my name and doing all that here. But as to who has the copyright that is indifferent. You might as well.

I am no expert in the law. J. might be able to give you more information. As I understand it, once a thing is printed, no matter how it is printed, and once it is distributed, if it is not copyrighted, the author has no protection if someone else wants to print it. Printing a thing without copyright is tantamount to relinquishing one's right to exclusive publication of that text. Whether *pro manuscripto* makes any difference, I cannot say. There might be some legal angle. But then, I don't even know what would be the situation if a manuscript in circulation were taken and printed.

Strictly speaking, a non-copyrighted book that is printed by someone else is not pirated. Piracy in this matter would seem to involve a real violation of legal rights, the publication of a *copyrighted* book illegally (As happens when a book printed in another country is reprinted somewhere else, clandestinely, in such a way that it would be morally impossible, or too expensive, to prosecute.)

But, as I say, I am no expert.

Again, all blessings.

In Christ Our Lord

fr Louis

❀

May 4, 1960

Dear Victor:

Please forgive the red ribbon, I am trying to use it up. I am just writing to say that I imagine that you must be getting along with the book and will pretty soon be ready to come down with some of it, no doubt. And with this very fine weather there could be no better time. Apart from May 17 and 22–23 any day except a Sunday would be all right with me as far as I can see, though I am getting more and more involved in little things that seem to take time. How is Saturday the 14th for you—I just picked that because I think Carolyn likes Saturdays better, if I am not mistaken.

Rome has intensified the training schedule for novices and students in all the orders and that means I have more classes, but it does not affect our getting together since you usually arrive about 11 o'clock. By lunch time I am free.

I find I have been keeping a large number of library books for a long time, so I am sending some back, since I do not think I will be able to finish them now. With them Carolyn will find a book on the priesthood which is an extra we have here, so I am donating it to the library from the monastery. I don't know whether or not it is especially good, but it belongs to a reputable series.

A lady in Boston wrote me a most kind and enthusiastic letter about the Desert Fathers book, someone had just presented her with the last available copy. She is a friend of a friend of yours from Lexington who works in the Widener Library.

Last Sunday no fewer than fifty seven presbyterian men from Lexington showed up here and I gave them a talk which they seem to have enjoyed. They were from the Second Presbyterian Church. It seems I will be a little more occupied with work like this in the future, but mostly with rather special groups. I still prefer the "retreat movement" that includes spiritual conversations—and artistic ones— with you and Carolyn.

I have unearthed a man called Isaac of Niniveh, a Syrian hermit, of whom you might like to consider a few excerpts: again along the lines of the other two books. But I hesitate to suggest this because I really fear that you will be expending all your efforts on me alone and this would be really wrong.

In any case, I will be looking forward to hearing from you. Perhaps this letter may even cross with one of yours in the mail. God bless you both.

Very Cordially in Christ

fr Louis

May 11. 60

Dear Father Louis: thank you for your letter. The book will be finished today; and Isaac of Niniveh is most interesting we think.—I shall come on Saturday 14[85] at 11 o'clock or so. But this time a friend of mine, George Headley,[86] also a painter, will drive since Carolyn, most probably, will not be able to come. But we will have a picnic, either in the woods or in the car according to the season since we seem to have winter still. We start here at 9 it takes us 2 hours to Gethsemani.

Looking forward

In Christ yours as ever

Victor

Dear Father Louis, yes God and beauty do exist, but as soon as one tries to explain them they disappear as if they would not exist. Silence alone can express them.—I would like to be set right on the last judgment and on the river Lethe. Perhaps one day you could do that. In Christ

yours Victor

Monday May 16, 1960
Dear Victor:

Here is the poem. It is perhaps not long enough, but rather than add useless lines I think it would be better to divide some of the lines in two, if you so desire. I am marking several places where this is possible. I think it is a good idea for a cover. I think that short lines on the cover, with that remarkable initial, will be more effective than long ones. But I am perhaps no judge. I am very taken with that initial. I hope you can run off a few extra copies of the cover, say fifteen or twenty (is that too much?) I mean just the poem with the initial, in a folded page, or just a plain sheet, whatever is most convenient for you. I would like to send a few around. It would be nice to frame one and hang it on the wall. I can send it to some Carmelite nuns who would appreciate it, I am sure.[87]

The picnic of the other day was superb. It is wonderful to be blessed with such fine days. I am so happy with the book: it is in many ways more beautiful even than the other: being slightly thinner, for one thing. I have lent it to one of the Fathers who will understand it, but otherwise I would probably have spent the whole weekend just sitting and admiring it.

I forgot to speak about the little prayer card, where Christ says He forgetteth utterly. But I know you have been keeping it in mind and will do something with it at your own convenience. I am a little busy at the moment and Isaac of Nineveh, who has waited for over a thousand years, can wait a little more. And I enjoyed meeting George

Headley: the only regret was that Carolyn could not enjoy such a marvelous picnic.

Now here are those to whom the book may be sent. The others you can bring me some day when you come.

1. Mr Ernesto Cardenal—Monasterio de la Resurrection, Cuernavaca, Mor. Mexico.
2. Rev Pere Jean Danielou S.J., 15, Rue Monsieur, Paris vii, France.
3. Col. Laurens Van der Post, 13 Cadogan St. London S.W.3. England.
4. Mark Van Doren Falls Village, Connecticut
5. Mr Robert Lax, 3739 Warren Street, Jackson Heights, N.Y.
6. M. Czeslaw Milosz, 10 Ave. de la Grange, Montgeron, (S. et O.) France.
7. M. Louis Massignon, 21 Rue Monsieur, Paris VII, France.
8. Mrs S. Spender, 15, Loudoun Road, St. Johns Wood, London NW8 England.

And that will leave three others, then.

With all blessing and good wishes, until we meet again:
Cordially in Christ

May 17, 1960
Dear Victor

Do you mind if I make a change, in the list of those of whom my copies of *Solitary Life* are to be sent?

Will you please OMIT Czeslaw Milosz (who has a manuscript version already) and instead send a copy to Sister M. Therese, S.D.S.—St. Mary's hospital, Wausau—Wisconsin
Many thanks—and best regards—with all blessings
Cordially in Christ
fr Louis

✿

May 25, 1960
Dear Victor

Did you get the poem all right? I hope so, and hope that it is
satisfactory. I received from Geo Headley the things he said he would
send and am glad to have them—will you thank him for me if you see
him?

About the list of books to be sent, I think it would be better simply
to omit those on my list who are in France. This would simplify
matters a great deal in the long run and I think it would be advisable.

I hope both you and Carolyn are well. Here everything is as usual.
Tomorrow is the Feast of the Ascension, which I always enjoy.

God bless you both—
With very best wishes, in Xt
fr Louis

✿

26. V. 60

Dear Father Louis, Of course the poem is fine and we like it very
much. We even want your permission to print it for Christmas.
But the fact is that I haven't even tried to set it up, so I can't say
how it would do as a cover. The Seminarium Theologicum of the
Episcopalians has graduation ceremony on May 31 and I had to
print a number of diplomas. Only today I got back to my painting so
occupied was I the whole time with the printing. Ci vuole pazienza
as the Italians say who learned that in the course of their history.
They got rid of Mussolini, what comes next?—I shall keep the books
which are intended for France and wait for your decision. We won't
have them ready soon since they have to be bound first. Carolyn
was spending hours on a talk she had to give for her Monday
club. She spoke about the 2 months we spent at Kolbsheim while
I was painting the Crucifixus and it turned out to be a nice piece
of autobiographical—I won't say chat, just talk, and she had great

success. I wonder she should let you read it and judge it for it was suggested she send it to the New Yorker. For the 'solitude' we have quite a member of orders already, yet I am so happy we remain with our small editions: it is a labor of love and it seems God holds his hands over us and protects us. We are so moved by the poem that it is difficult to say something—you have said what words are not allowed to express. You will let us know how many copies you want of the printing and we shall do it for you in Christ, yours as ever C+V.

❀

Saturday, 1960
Dear Victor:

I have made two corrections and am keeping the second set of proofs—assuming that was your intention. Carolyn's letter came the other day after I had sent off the one to you. I look forward to getting the books she is sending. This is a hasty note, more later.

God bless you, and I wish you a happy feast of Pentecost.
Faithfully in Christ
fr Louis

❀

9. VI. 60

Dear Father Louis: here are the two proofs. I have to cut a new initial. Since this is a companion to the Desert Fathers the type must be the same on both the covers. In short, it took me longer than I expected, but it is now the right thing I believe. We are engaged in stitching and then binding the books, but hope to see you sometime soon before we finish. If you want to make any change, please don't hesitate, I can still reset the type. I prefer the arrangement on the yellow paper. We are well and think of you often.

In Christ yours as ever
Victor

June 10, 1960
Dear Victor:

What was my astonishment recently in Louisville to see on the front page of the newspaper a picture of a civilized man. It was you. I congratulate you on your honorary degree. I am glad the university knows enough to give you one. This is sufficient reason for a certain amount of rejoicing.

I am very glad that you liked the poem. I was not sure what your concept of the jacket was going to be, and if you want to change the length of the lines, making them longer, or anything like that, just let me know. Certainly if you want to use the poem for Christmas I am delighted. If you have some cards left over at that time I could probably, in fact certainly use them. As to the extra copies of what you print for the cover, I could use a couple of dozen. Is that going to be too much trouble? If so, fifteen would be all right.

I am glad Carolyn's talk was a success. And of course I would very much enjoy reading it. As to the New Yorker, it is always a good idea to try them. I no longer know the ropes around there. The man who used to handle stories in my day is dead.

About the copies I spoke of as going to France, I don't know what to do about them, but anyway, please hold them or bring them over when you come. When shall we plan on another meeting here? Toward the end of July perhaps. When you have had time to get the books bound. This month is going to be a busy one for me, and I will be pretty taken up in the first part of July.

I am enclosing one of the slips Carolyn made out for a book that is in the library, and which I would like to have if available.

With every best wish to both of you, as ever, and God bless you
Cordially in Christ
fr Louis

June 13, 1960
Dear Victor:

I agree with you that the way the poem is printed on the yellow paper is altogether better, and the idea of initials is rather undesirable I think. If I understand you correctly, the alternative is between the white paper version plus initials or the yellow paper one as it stands, without any additions. I think this latter is preferable.

You speak in your note of coming here sooner. That is very fine, and it can certainly be arranged. But it will mean finding a particular day, whereas later on almost any day will be good. But that does not mean that now is a bad time. Here are the possibilities.

The rest of this week is not good.

The beginning of next week would be all right: especially the 20th, 21st, or 22. The beginning of the following week would also be possible, for instance the 27th. The two best days for me would be the 20th and 22nd. I hope to see you on one of these. I will get this letter off at once so that you can reply and let me know when to expect you. If you arrive as usual about 11 our time, that would be excellent.

I am working on the offprints of Coomaraswamy you lent me.[88] They are very fine. I do want to study him well, so I hope you are not in a hurry for them.

All other business matters we can arrange with expert efficiency when you come. Always efficiency, production, and pep! Pardon my Irish wit.

With blessings to you both,
Very cordially in the Lord,
fr Louis

Could you please send a book to Col. Laurens Van der Post
13 Cadogan St.
London SW3.

June 27, 1960
Dear Victor:

I do not know what plans you may have about coming over: it is just possible that this may cross with a letter from you. But I want to say that this week and perhaps the beginning of next I may or will not be available. I am going in to the hospital for a check up. Nothing serious, just the necessary routine. So I will not be around these few days. But after that, yes.

How is the book coming?

I wonder about using the poem for a magazine or something, after you have sent out the bulk of your copies?

This is just a brief note, to prevent any confusion. I hope both you and Carolyn are well. I pray for you, and beg God to bless you.

Very cordially in Christ

fr Louis

Tuesday Jun 28 [1960]
Dear Victor.

As I expected, our letters crossed. The cover is very very fine, It just fits the book, but is a little tight. That is all right. I like the initial very much. And will like the other one, as a variation, on the Christmas Card.

I will be expecting you after the 19th. Have a good trip. Perhaps you will see J. We have been writing a lot with much interesting work going on.

God bless you all,

fr Louis

Will you please send one book to Prof. Jacques Maritain 26, Linden Lane Princeton, N.J.?

July 20, 1960
Dear Carolyn and Victor:

Your note said that you would be back Friday so I am answering it now to say I hope to see you soon. The last three days of next week, (28–30th) would be good for me and I suppose Saturday is best for you. Just drop me a line. If those days are not good, then perhaps early in the following week.

Bob Lax is the first to respond to the books you sent out and he is jubilant about everything, even the way it was wrapped. He wants to send you his Circus book. You do not have one, do you? I'll tell him, if you would like it.

It looks as though you are running into hot weather. But I hope you had a wonderful time in Vermont etc. Perhaps you saw J. in New York.

We can talk about it. Glad you are back.

With every blessing and good wish

Cordially in Christ

fr Louis

❀

July 27, 1960

Dear Victor:

Fine—I look forward to seeing you both Saturday at noon.[89]

Would it be possible for Carolyn to take a look in the library for any books on ancient Cretan and Minoan civilization? I do not know of exact references, but one title has come my way: "The House of the Double Axe."

And—do they have in the library a book by Fenollosa on Chinese ideograms and poetry? This too is vague. I hope it is enough to be of some value. But she should not waste time looking too hard.

God bless you both.

Very cordially in Christ

fr Louis

❀

7. August 1960

Dear Father Louis: I am returning your paper which I have carefully read twice.[90] I think it very good and since you speak of things which are so close to my mind and my heart I could not help finding it most interesting. I had, however, to realize how far I am in my own paper on classic art from rendering the pertinent facts in philosophical terms. My terminology seemed so simple, so earthy to me, yet it is not the one in common use and for this reason it is not easily understandable. But when I say: In order to understand modern art we must cast off all the strange notions of the artist as a genius, a prophet, a redeemer—I should have been readily understood. And are we not saying the same thing when I talk about the emptiness of all space-relations which constitute the core of classic art, or when I insist that all "art work" (what a word!) should be undertaken for the higher glory of God? And it was Fiedler who, more than 80 years ago in the last fragment said that the subject-object relation may be a necessary crutch for establishing scientific method, but that in all other human endeavors where truth is either created or revealed, it makes no sense nor has it any value, on the contrary—and Suzuki makes that very clear too. Not being a child of my age or society, I may bluntly add that I consider Picasso an able experimenter but in no ways an artist. And I also wish the terms beauty and creativity were banned from speech for at least a generation. Even in your paper, so clear and candid, that word beauty stands out as an opaque spot. It would be better not to use it at all. If we could make a clear and valid distinction between aesthetic and artistic worth, we would not need that word—it belongs to a much higher level and should not be used so carelessly.

Carolyn brought a book home which I asked her to order: L'esthetique contemporaine, une Enquete, by Guido Morpurgo-Tagliabue. When I opened it my eyes fell on that phrase:

La nature du beau n'est pas ontologique mais axiologique.[91]

This is out of the context I admit, but next time we are together I wish you could make me understand what that means.

I am sorry I cannot re-dedicate the book on Chinese characters[92] to you, it has already been dedicated to me by the printer. But you can keep it as long as you want, and I hope it will be of some use to you.

Enclosed is an aphorism by Fiedler. It seems to me it has some bearing on what you say in your paper. The translation is utterly pedestrian; I tried to change certain phrases as you can see, but more I could not do. This is a copy and you can keep it.

In Christ, yours as ever

Victor

9. VIII. 60

Dear Father Louis: thank you so much for sending the text of the broad side[93] and the letter from Rome—we enjoyed both. Carolyn will settle the question of your authorship when she has the proofs ready, which I hope will soon be the case. You can keep the book on the Chinese characters as long as you want—I also hope the chinamen will not change the roman letter, as did the Turks. Have you ever read Crankshaw's book on Khrushchev's Russia—if not I shall send it to you.

In Christ yours,

Victor

9⃝

Aug. 17, 1960

Dear Victor

Could you and Carolyn think about possibly coming over on Sept 3rd, or the 1st or 2nd? Or else perhaps on the 10th ? I think perhaps Ad Reinhardt will come down on the 1st, at any rate I have asked him to. But whether he comes or not, it would be nice to have you over on one of those days (always bearing in mind that the 2nd is a lean Friday and one would have to be careful of those great good sandwiches). I am glad you like the broadside. I am enjoying the Chinese ideograms. More later.

Every good wish and blessing

Cordially in Christ

fr Louis

✿

Sept 5, 1960
Dear Victor:

I would have written sooner but I have not found it easy to untangle
all the threads of the arrangements about those supposed to visit here.
At any rate Reinhardt is not coming right away, this month or next,
so he is out of the question. On the other hand a Benedictine and
another priest are here for a retreat next weekend so that knocks out
the 10th for our meeting.

Hence let us start over again. The following week is quite good
for me, almost any day at noon, but especially the 15th and the 17th.
I hope Clay Lancaster[94] will still be there. If the beginning of the
week is better for him, how about the 12th? I would rather have it at
the end of the week as far as I am concerned but I would like to meet
Clay.

Glad to hear the broadside is progressing. I read the little excerpt
from Fiedler and found it very illuminating. I wonder if people would
dare to say such things today, apart from wild persons like you and
me.

Hoping to see you next week sometime and waiting for a word
from you in confirmation.

Blessings—
Very Cordially in Christ
fr Louis

✿

Sept. 15, 1960
Dear Victor:

Thanks for your note. It was as I thought. And I have an added
complication, but I think it will prove an agreeable one. The 24th
is certainly all right, but a little after that there is a man from New
Directions coming down, Bob MacGregor, who is, I believe, J's chief
man there, he very much wants to meet you and I have told him I

would try to persuade you to come over while he is here. He is coming on the 4th, and perhaps you would like to come over on the 5th or 6th.[95] Can we plan on this? I know it will be in the middle of the week, but perhaps on this occasion we could make it. I am sorry Clay Lancaster has gone. Perhaps some other time.

Yes, do please bring over the Chinese book.

To Carolyn: many thanks for the Gandhi.[96] I am very interested in it and will try to make good use of it. I think it is very important.

If I think of some other book I might need between now and then I will send word. Meanwhile I am excited to hear about proofs. I have seen the page proofs of the Wisdom of the Desert from Mardersteig[97] and it is going to be very fine, very clear and chaste, and perfectly in keeping with the tone you have set, though different. Very classical. I am sending copies of Jubilee one of which has my article on Herakleitos.[98]

With very best wishes always, and God bless you,
Cordially in Christ
fr Louis

❀

Oct 17, 1960
Dear Victor:

Your letter with the proof arrived last week, about the 11th I think. It was postmarked on the 10th, from Lost Creek, Ky. I presume that Lost Creek is a post office that has no other purpose than to handle lost letters which are shipped up the creek by pixies. This is a curious facet of Kentucky life as yet unexplored. But in any case there is nothing wrong with the proof and I did not rush to say anything about receiving it as by now the broadside is probably finished, no?

I did not, need not, repeat how much I enjoyed the last visit, with Bob MacGregor here. Some time around the 19th of November would probably be good for the meeting with the anti-Catholic professor of political science who, I hope, will enjoy seeing Gethsemani. Does this seem like a good time to you? It is most convenient for me.

As the little house progresses,[99] through obstacles and misunderstanding, I must think of a few simple furnishings. Do you know of anywhere that they still make hand made furniture for instance back in the hills? If there were some person back there still doing things like that I would be happy to buy some chairs, a table, etc. I think of a very simple rug almost like sacking for the floor. Do you know of any possible source for such things?[100]

As ever, very good wishes and blessing to you both.

Cordially in Christ

fr Louis

I have had too long some library books, but I am working on the Gandhi carefully. Is there any rush for any of them to come back? I want to get through the Chinese art one if possible.

5.XI.60

Dear Father Louis:

Unexpectedly we have to go to Cincinnati on the 12th of this month, and since Carolyn cannot manage to go away for two consecutive weekends we will be unable to come to Gethsemani on the 19th, as planned. Which date after the 19th would suit you? Either the 26th of November or the next weekend of December third would be convenient for us. Any decision you make we will gladly accept. We have now your copies of the broadside ready and could take them with us.

I had a letter from Lexi Grunelius in which he enthusiastically expresses his gratitude for *The Solitary Life* which I have sent him. To him the poem is—als hoerte man einen Musikaccord mit himmlischem Nachhall.[101] He has shown the book to Père Cottier, a Swiss Dominican and friend of Mgr Journet.[102] Père Cottier thinks the piece should be translated into French and be published either in 'Nova et Vetera' or as an extra, little 'plaquette.' What a plaquette is I do not know, but you perhaps have heard that word and know what it means. Anyhow, Père Cottier is supposed to get in touch with you directly.

Lexi's letter contains sad news about Raïssa Maritain for whom, it seems there is no hope. The doctors artificially prolong her life—so she may still be on this earth. Maritain is beside himself; it seems Raïssa is not in the hospital but lies at home, in their old quarter in Paris, in the Rue de Varenne (I forget the number of the house). But I am not sure of this. I can say no more and cannot suggest any further move.

We wait for your letter and ask for your blessing.

In Christ, yours

Victor

❀

Nov. 9, 1960

Dear Victor:

Your letter arrived this morning. It is too bad you will not be coming this Saturday. But then perhaps the weather will be better on the 26th. Today is horrible, here. Cold and rainy. Let us hope that the other weekend will be better. In any case, the 26th is a fine date, as dates go. So I will be expecting you then, with the broadside.

I am glad the little book pleased Lexi and his friends. I shall take care of requests if and when they reach me. The fuller and more approved version[103] in the big book is what they should use. Have you got *Disputed Questions,* by the way? I must have given it to you last time your were here, that was my intention. But I have suddenly forgotten what I actually did about it.

Father Abbot approves your friend making some furniture for us provided the price is reasonable. Could he for example give us an estimate on how much it will cost us for him to copy your table? We can judge from that. There are splendid things in the pine furniture book. I shall be wanting some of the stools, and a desk. I thing a big chest would be good: both as a seat and as storage. My biggest difficulty is: what to have on the porch. The usual sort of thing they put on porches is hideous. Perhaps it would just be best to carry out chairs from inside. I will want to know more about those people who make chairs back in the hills.

I do hope it will not be too cold on the 26th.
Best wishes to you both, as ever, and blessings.
Cordially yours in Christ
fr Louis

🪷

Tuesday [1960]
Dear Victor

I saw Dr and Mrs Wygal[104] the other day and they expressed a wish to come down Saturday so as to see you and Carolyn again. I told them they would be very welcome. They will bring their own provisions. I hope we have nice weather. Looking forward to seeing you both.

Very cordially in Xt Jesus
fr Louis.

🪷

Dec. 1, 1960
Dear Victor:

It was certainly very pleasant to have you over here the other day and I enjoyed it immensely, but I think I would have enjoyed it more if there had not been so many people and if I could have talked quietly with you and Carolyn. Really I think the ideal group is you and Carolyn and myself with at times one other—so that you will not hesitate to bring over the Swedish girl who is seeking some kind of a center in life.

I am sending back the Pine Furniture book after having gone through it carefully.

Here are one or two things that I am very interested in having copied if your friend can see his way to do it. I do not want to start complications around here where people are not likely to be interested just in making something beautiful (some of course might be, but anything not immediately profitable is not encouraged)

1. The Shaker school desk, as in plate 118, (drawing 36) would be simple to make and very effective.

2. Perhaps as a seat to go with this desk there could be a stool, on the model of the one shown in drawing 16, plate 51, but proportionately larger. (Not a footstool, in other words).

3. It would be nice to have two of the so called "center braced forms" as illustrated in plate 63, (drawing 21).

4. The chest and desk combination in plate 110 is attractive. Also the stool illustrated in the same picture. There is no drawing but it should not be hard to make these things. Though it should have a *flat* top not a slanting one.

I wonder what would be the possibility and the expense of some of these, or all of them. Could we discuss this with your friend?

What size is the Christmas card going to be? I want to know in order to plan for the envelopes. Can you show me the size, or a sample of the envelope you plan to use, so that I can get some?

A book from the library: can Carolyn get for me Richard Rovere's Biography of the late lamented Senator McCarthy? Probably there are a lot of people reading it, and if there is difficulty I could try elsewhere.

I want to say again how beautifully the Mencius broadside[105] turned out. You said you would send one to replace the one I gave Jim [Wygal]. Perhaps the best would be to send this with my compliments to Senor Ernesto Cardenal, Monasterio de La Resurreccion, Cuernavaca, (Mor.) Mexico. He would be glad to have it. And, as ever, many thanks.

Very best wishes to you all again. When shall we plan to see each other again? After our retreat in January, I presume, or early in February?

God bless you,

fr Louis

There is also the problem of interesting light. There is no electricity in the house of course.

5. XII. 60

Dear Father Louis: Thank you for your nice, really sweet letter, we are so happy. I am answering immediately in order to settle certain things. To begin with: how blessed you are that you have no electricity in the place, you will find the right means of lighting it once you spend some time there. Your table will soon be ready and I persuaded the boy—David Rowland—to bring it to you himself. My further advice would be to wait for the chairs and in the meantime have two chests made on which you and your guests can sit and they also would provide plenty of storage space. [Editor's note: in the original letter, Hammer drew a picture of the type of bench that he wanted the furniture maker to build.]

The top board one can lift and all the space inside can be used. It is not the most sophisticated, thin metal sheet locker, produced according to a 'designer's' fancy, but one on each side of the table, or put against a wall if needed, is just what you will be satisfied with in the long run. The red wood soon gets a nice patina and is not too heavy. These things will not be dead right from the start but the toil that David put into it will make it alive as long as you live and after. Perhaps a few, quickly made and simple stools could be used on the terrace. The time may come when you want a grandfather's easy chair but you are still young and alert. These chests cannot cost too much.

Carolyn will take care of the book and replace the broadside by sending one to Senor Ernesto Cardenal. We shall come and see you as soon we can work it out and hope to be able to take the young Swedish girl with us. The Christmas card will be 9 x 5¾, I have it already in the press.

Carolyn sends her very best
in Christ,
Yours Victor.

Dec. 7, 1960
Dear Victor:

Your good letter just arrived. I think the chests are a good idea.
I shall certainly need two. But as the problem of chairs is solving
itself, I think we do not need the chests to go exactly with the table.
Hence we can make them less long, and deeper. I like your design
very much. But I think we need chests about three quarters the
length shown, at most, and wider and deeper. Two such chests. I am
thinking of places where they could be against the wall. Redwood,
of course. I definitely want these and hope David Rowland will be
able and willing to go ahead with them when he has finished the
table and he could bring them all over together, that would be fine.
We can check on measurements meanwhile. I will take whatever
suggestions you offer in the matter of measurements and will look at
the house and see how they fit the places I have in mind, then send
any modifications.

Does David want to try his hand or not at some of the things I
suggested in the Pine Furniture book? There he will find the stools
that seem to me to be ideal, I really want several like the stool I
mentioned in the letter. And the little Shaker desk would be simple
and nice.

One thing I will also need is a cupboard. I forget if I picked one
out of the book. But that will not be urgent.

Chairs: I have already managed to get one or two nice simple
chairs which obviously come from some farms back in the hills.
And there is a novice at Loretto[106] who is quite good at revamping
pieces of furniture and she has promised to fix up eight more chairs
for me. So I think I need not worry any longer about chairs. One of
those I picked up is a rocking chair so that my grandfatherly days of
retirement can begin at once. I do not feel there should be any further
delay.

Could I ask you to send just one more broadside to Frank
Dell'Isola?[107] His new address is 440 East 20th St., New York 9. I

think I ought really to send him this because I am going to have to write him a letter explaining why I cannot and did not send him the Sol. Life. The broadside ought to help satisfy him to some extent though really there is no reason why I should be satisfying his needs either. Though he has been a very careful bibliographer, but that does not mean that I am obligated to furnish him forever with an inexhaustible supply of rare books.

May I put down two or three more titles which I would be very happy to have from the library? They are on a separate sheet which you can give to Carolyn. That will be more convenient.

Let us soon think of a time when we can get together in January. Planning for that month means skirting around the annual retreat (18th to 25th) and a possible visit of the Abbot General who, however, may not come until February.

With every best wish and blessing to you both,
Cordially in Christ
fr Louis

12. XII. 60

Dear Father Louis, enclosed in a separate envelope perhaps, are your Christmas cards, 25 or so. I hope you can use them. Carolyn did a good job printing them. So you have to thank her.—David Rowland was here today, he intends to bring the table this weekend and promised to write to you.—I have to thank you for two letters, which I do herewith. However, I think it rather difficult for me to send a Ox Mountain parable to Frank Dell'Isola. He never paid for the copy of the Sayings which I have sent to him in good faith. Later on I wrote to him that I would send him an unnumbered copy free, if he would send the numbered one back. No answer. A woman from Brooklyn (where he lives) ordered a copy of the Solitary Life. We followed Bob McGregor's advice, sent her a pro forma invoice. No answer. Whether there is a connection between these two we do not know. My book will not do him any good I believe. He will always feel he wronged me who trusted in him. Even bibliographers have a conscience however subdued it may be. If you want to send him the broadside I can't help it. But you understand that I can not. I am independent because I am poor (not destitute however) that is, it enables me to print such books such as we do, a thing no rich man can afford.—We spoke about the lights in your hermitage. I have a whale oil lamp, but it would be too much trouble for you to fool with it, besides it will not even give as much light as a candle. A candle, that wonderful symbol of life that spends itself, would be the only answer for quite a time.—We think of you with gratitude and love.

In Christ yours as ever
Victor

Dear Father Louis,

The red initial is quite freshly printed and the paper still a bit dampish, so air them (the cards) for an hour or so; here also are two more parables, respectable enough for sending if you want. Victor can't bring himself to send one to Mr. Dell'Isola, so perhaps one of these will do?

Sincerely,
Carolyn

❀

Dec 23. [1960]
Dear Carolyn and Victor—

I expect a note from day to day saying when you will come, but any one of those days is all right, especially if you come as usual about 12. Meanwhile, there are a couple of books that perhaps might add to your cargo in the station wagon, if you can get them without inconvenience:

1. What is the best thing on *Maya Indian Culture* you have?

2. One of my artists wants to know if he can get Moholy Nagy's
   Anonymous Genius in Native Architecture (title?)
3. Jim tells me you have D.T. Suzuki's *Manual of Zen Buddhism.*

A very holy and happy Christmas—
   Faithfully in Christ
   fr L.

Dec. 27, 1960
Dear Victor:

By now Dave Rowland will have told you of his rather harrowing
afternoon here. The table is very fine, ideal for the place, and we got it
there all right. But then it started to rain, and on the way back David
got stuck in his car and had to leave it there for several hours while I
looked for someone to help him out of the mud. Eventually one of the
brothers pulled him out with a tractor.

I have no doubt he will have spoken to you of the three ideas we
agreed on, and you will have valuable suggestions to offer. I look
forward to further discussion about the plans, and I hope this will
bring you over here one of these days. If there is any need to talk over
the project soon, let me know. We could get together early in January.
Next week is not too good for me but after that, until the 18th,
everything will be all right. After the 18th is bad again and after the
25th is all right.

The other day in returning one of the books to the library, I also
made a package of three French books, or something of the sort.
Carolyn is probably wondering what they were: I was just getting rid
of them, as they are not needed here. I presume the library can use
them, and that is why I sent them.

I do not think I have officially thanked you and Carolyn for the
Christmas poem. It is superbly done and I am very happy to be able
to send it to a few people. So thank you both very much. I just sent
one to I. A. Richards[108] along with the Meng Tzu parable. As I said,

I am *not* sending Meng Tzu to our friend Dell'Isola. He had the crust to ask me again for the Sol. Life, when he has the copy you sent him. I told him to get his references from Lax's copy. Lax by the way may come down early in the year, this might be an occasion for you to meet him.

Do they have any of the following titles in the library, or can they be obtained anywhere in paperbacks, does Carolyn know?

Nicholson, R.N., Mystics of Islam
MacDonald, D.B., Religious Life and Attitude in Islam
Smith, Margaret, Al Ghazali the Mystic.

In any case I hope to see you in January.
All best wishes for the New Year,
Cordially yours in Christ,
fr Louis

Feb 2, 1961
Dear Victor:

Having been very busy, and on retreat, and also sick since I last saw you, I have not yet got around to writing the letter of recommendation.[109] And I am still wondering very much if I am sufficiently master of the mandarin formulas that will be required to make it effective. I would like to see a model of some such letter. Could someone obtain for me an approved form? Then I could follow it. I think that your own prospectus is itself here and there too simple and honest to be up to the required mandarin standard. I don't mean that you should be dishonest by any means, but I don't see that it will help you to say things like: "I can't tell you more than I have just said in these notes," and "maybe I ought to go and talk to Sir Herbert Read too."[110] I would be very definite on each point that it is quite essential for you to do these things or those things, and that you know precisely what you mean and what you want. I think many of the points you make are very well put and telling and I think you have made your classical standpoint seem quite strong. But why not stronger? In a thing like this one must not let modesty stand in one's way. No one asking for a Guggenheim should be diffident about his project or his powers in any way whatever. They should get the feeling that you are doing them a favor by letting them know about your work so that they can fulfill their purpose, their raison d'etre, by giving you money. I would even ask for more money. But perhaps in this I am too sanguine, as I say I am not in the mandarin class.

There has been some talk about getting someone in to talk to a group of the monks about right attitudes in regard to monastic work, especially in view of the building and remodeling we are doing around here now. Questions of taste, or orientation of proper outlook, of working like monks, putting up buildings as monks should, furnishing them as monks should. Bro Giles and I both suggested that you would be an ideal person to give one or two talks on this. Would you like to? Some Saturday afternoon. We could first have lunch together as usual, then the talk would be perhaps about one thirty or two, our time. There would be discussion afterward, and the purpose would be enlightenment of monks. I am sure something could be done, though I don't think all problems can be solved by panels and conferences.

Will you please let me know what you think of this, and what other information you would like. Of course, we would not expect you to do this without some remuneration.

I shall be waiting for some ideas about the way to write the letter you want. If you think it is really all right for me to go ahead by my own devices, then I will do so. But I think I ought to have a model to follow. Will they send me some kind of form?

I thought Bob Lax might be coming down but he didn't
As ever, all best wishes and blessings to both of you,
Very cordially in Christ
fr Louis

Feb 4. '61
Dear Carolyn,

I just came across a card of yours on Dec 12 in which you spoke of
sending the Richard Rovere book on McCarthy—did you ever send
it? For I never received it. I hope it has not been lost. I returned three
to you yesterday, including the big art book on Florence, Parody and
the one on the atom bomb. I will have a couple more.

    All best wishes—in Christ
    fr Louis

❀

Feb. 9, 1961
Dear Victor:

Here it is. I have done my best to promote useful knowledge. You
must now be loyal to the tradition of caves, and beware of the culture
of cities. While you are away I shall seek a small grant of about ten
dollars in order to spend a week doing some murals of my own in
some of the deeper recesses of our own Kentucky caves which have
so far lacked any form of artistic embellishment. My murals will be
completely abstract, without even the intrusion of an expressionist
element: it will be the emergence of a new cycle of so called "dead pan
cave art" and will be all the more effective because it must be
a) painted and b) viewed in *complete obscurity*. This will be my protest
against the fluorescent lighting which is currently characteristic of the
agora.

    I hope I have been literate and have not made so many spelling
mistakes as to prejudice your worthy cause. I got Carolyn's card and
am relieved that the Rovere book was not lost.

    When are you coming over again? When do you plan to sail if you
get the grant? If you come in the next couple of months would you
want to give a talk to the group of monks that I referred to? Any time
would be good except from February 15th to 28th. Perhaps the first
week in March? I hope we can arrange something.

I want to get this to you as quickly as possible, so I will not delay any longer. God bless you both:

With cordial good wishes in Christ

fr Louis

❦

February 20, 1961
Dear Victor

Would a week from Saturday, March 4th, be a good day for you to come over? The talk would be, in a general way, about the kind of attitude and outlook proper to monks when they build for themselves, or furnish their buildings, and it could spread out into the whole concept of monastic work. I think they would have very much to learn from an informal talk with discussion going along with it. The talk would have to be about 1.30 our time, (we could of course have lunch together at leisure first) and I doubt if you would get away much before 3 our time. Would that be too late for you? Is this date convenient? Really we can arrange almost any day, as far as we are concerned here. Hoping that all goes well. I wrote for you to the Bollingen people.[111]

Very cordially always in Christ

fr Louis

❦

March 8th, 1961
Dear Carolyn:

Many thanks for the copies of the broadside. The one you asked for has been signed and sent to the library. You do not need to replace it unless you have copies to spare. I really have enough for the time being anyway. Or rather enough, period.

A thought occurred to me as another "pretext" for printing, and I think it is a good one. A collection of "sayings" from Coomaraswamy, aphorisms reported by people who conversed with him, and texts taken here and there at random from some of his essays. I think it would be a very lively and salutary little book, and I could take the occasion to write a little essay on him as an introduction. Nothing long or elaborate. Don't you agree that this is a really attractive idea?

The only trouble is that his wife, Dona Luisa, might not completely agree. She has been very kind in writing to me and in lending me things, but I think she is perhaps rightly quite unwilling to let more of her husband's things appear all over the place at random while she is struggling to get his works in order in some sort of definitive text.[112] Anyway I will write to her and let you know her reaction.

If you or Victor want to leaf through the offprints that you have and pick out some possibilities, very fine. Perhaps if we get going on the project you could send me some of the material again. Did I ever ask you if there was anything much of this in the library there?

Now a problem of great magnitude: that Robert Graves book, which I am very glad to have: but when I was bringing the desk over I happened to leave the book around in the novitiate library and the novitiate librarian immediately picked it up and stamped it with the library stamp. I do not mean to suggest that it has become an acquisition, but if it belongs to the library of Kentucky it really poses a problem, doesn't it? If the book is Victor's personal property, that is bad enough, but I know Victor will accept an apology. But the library. . . . If there is a need be we will replace the volume for you, but it is not a book for our monastery, at least permanently, hence if it can be accepted back with our stamp on it, I shall be relieved. I am very sorry.

Do you have any of the following, and if so could I borrow one or more?

Sir Mohammed Iqbal—The Secrets of the Self.
S. Pacifici, Ed. The Promised Land and other poems, Anthol. (Italian Poets)
S. Pacifici Guide to Italian Lit. From Futurism to Neo-Realism.
Shirer The Rise and Fall of the Third Reich.
R. Trevelyan A Hermit Disclosed.

Again, many thanks for the broadsides, and best wishes to you both. Everyone who was there for Victor's talk really enjoyed it and I am sure he planted seeds that were waiting to be received. May they grow. Hope you will be back soon.

God bless you both,
Cordially in Christ
fr Louis

❧

March 27, 1961
Dear Father Louis,

This past week has been such a full one for me that I have had no time to gather together what we have by Coomaraswamy.[113] Victor and I are delighted with the idea you have and hope that Dona Luisa will also show enthusiasm. Shall we wait to hear from you before sending the off-prints?

Unfortunately we have none of the books you wanted except Shirer's *The Rise and Fall of the Third Reich;* this is much in demand, but a second copy is on order and I shall send it to you when it arrives. The only title we have by Sir Muhammad Iqbal is *The Tulips of Sinai*—interested?

I make notes of the books you request and from time to time can get them—so you may have a few yet to come. In the meantime, do let us know when you have any word of the possibility of our doing a collection of the "sayings" of Coomaraswamy. Victor has completed the INRI[114] for the top of the Crucifixus we have and will do the one for yours when he has again taken measurements. I will bring him over to do this when it is convenient with you. The last time he forgot to measure the depth of the panel.

Sincerely,
Carolyn R. Hammer

❧

March 28, 1961
Dear Carolyn:

I am glad that the novitiate stamp on the Graves book does not matter. It went back to you the other day and you have it by now. I did not have time to finish it, but I especially enjoyed the first story, I thought it was hilariously funny. Some of his lectures seemed to me to be a little empty and trite.

The book you sent recently is certainly instructive to say the least. It is a hair raiser, and the truths it points out are certainly very salutary. We have an awful lot to learn. The thirties are dead and gone, and so is the liberalism of that day. (I liked the old man's toast of "arms for Spain").

I have thought of another possibility for a printing project for Victor. If you have any Latin texts of Nicholas of Cusa in the library, or know where they could be unearthed, it might be a good idea to translate a short one.[115] I would be very interested in trying it. Do you have anything by or about him there in any other language?

What do we owe David Rowland for lumber to date? Perhaps it would be helpful to him if we paid our debt in this regard about Easter. Could you please find out from him and let us know? Also I didn't jot down his address so I have lost it.

And when are you thinking of coming over again? I hope we will soon be able to count on some nice spring weather.

Meanwhile, I will look forward to a reaction to the suggestion on N. of Cusa or Coomaraswamy. I haven't heard definitively from Mrs C. about this, and nothing from Victor, if he wrote it did not reach me.

Best Easter wishes, and God bless you both,
Very cordially in Christ
fr louis

March 29, 1961
Dear Carolyn:

Your letter arrived this morning after mine had gone out yesterday.
I still have no definite word from Dona Luisa but she is favorably
inclined at any rate and I think she will say yes. I think then this is
a better idea than Nicholas of Cusa but it won't hurt to look in the
library and see if there is anything there.

Why don't you and Victor come over on Saturday the 8th of
April, that is at the end of Easter week. It would be a fine time,
and the weather ought to be all right, I hope. Victor could take the
measurements then. We could also discuss any other business, and if
you would bring the Coomaraswamy off-prints just in case, as well as
anything you may have in the library, thought I might have seen some
of it before. The Tulips of Sinai by Iqbal does not ring any bells but
perhaps if you bring it, I could at least see what it is and I might be
able to use it.

If the 8th is not good, then perhaps the 22nd. I hope you can come
on the 8th. At the usual time. If you want to bring your Swedish girl
and cheer her up, I leave that up to you, I don't think one more would
make it too crowded unless we have to sit in the car again . . . I will
look forward to hearing from you about it. All the best until then and
God bless you both.

Cordially in Christ
fr Louis

❦

30.III.61
Dear Father Louis:

Thank you for sending the New Directions edition of the Sayings. I
was so touched by the kind words you said about my work and though
I feel it to be true I was so moved that you say you accept me as your
friend, and I am proud of it. Of course I must constantly try to live
up to this distinction.—As to the printing, I mean the very act of

it, the craft, I am still working, have recently printed 100 sheets of the Bachofen,[116] but Carolyn, now a partner in the Stamperia, takes over more and more the heavy work. The Ox Mountain Parable is completely her handiwork. We are happy about the possibility to print the Coomaraswamy, but still are very interested to see what you would choose from Cusanus. Carolyn will send you all she can find in the library. Once she gave me two of the Heidelberg translations. They are of course in German but the notes might still be of interest to you for they take almost half of the issues. I am not yet ready to tackle these books, rather wait and look for what your choice will be. I began to read in the "disputed questions" but am as yet not too far along; I will read again the Philosophy of Solitude which I have read only once. The sayings I find myself often returning to and reading them over and over again and thinking what a good thing it is that you gave them no special order.

How would you translate this passage of the preface to Job by St. Jerome: Habeant qui volunt veteres libros, vel in membranis purpureis auro argentoque descriptos, vel uncialibus, ut vulgo aiunt, litteris, onera magis exarata, quam codices, dummodo mihi meisque permittant pauperes habere schedulas, et non tam pulchros codices, quam emendatos. Migne, Patr. Lat. XXVIII, col. 1142 A. Your phrase in the preface to the sayings that St. Jerome lived and translated the scriptures in a cave at Bethlehem, made me aware of the possibility to get angry about big books when living in a small cave. How big was that cave and what facilities did he have there? Could it compare with your hermitage or not? We may, however, never underestimate the kind of luxury the ancients could afford. Did he know that he was a saint? His letters often show a quick temper, which in the face of sin may be excused. From which texts did he translate, was it Greek or Aramaic? I imagine that not a scrap from his hand came down to us.

We are very sorry but the weekend of the 8th is so crowded that we simply cannot fit a visit to Gethsemani in, much as we would like to do so. So we have to leave it for the 22nd. The Swedish girl is kind of big for our little car and we could accommodate you last time only because the seats were not there. So we must wait for a fine day to sit in the open.—David Rowland has, so far, spent $45.00 on the wood for the desk and the chest. His address is: 222½ Waller Avenue, Lexington, Ky.

Au revoir, dear Father Louis and please include us in your prayers.
C + V

❀

Easter Sunday
Dear Carolyn

If Victor and you are able to get over here next Saturday—here are some books that I would glad to see if they are available.

The Desert Fathers book looks wonderful. I am very happy with it. And I look forward very much to seeing you both. I remembered you and Victor in my Mass this morning.

God bless you both
Faithfully in Christ
fr Louis

❀

April 10, 1961
Dear Victor:

It was a pity you could not get over here Saturday, it was such a lovely afternoon, but I will be expecting you on the 22nd and I hope that will be even better. I have rather cooled towards Nicholas of Cusa because I find him rather wordy and cerebral. However there is much good in him, and there are possibilities to be investigated so I will be grateful for anything Carolyn can dig up.

As to the sentence from Jerome, I would render it: "Let those who like have ancient books, whether copied out in gold and silver on purple parchment or in what they commonly call uncial letters: such books are rather written baggage ("burdens") than books. Let such people only permit me and mine to have our poor copy sheets (?) and not beautiful books so much as correct ones."

Jerome is not my ideal of sanctity by any means, and what he says is very often likely to be hot air, or else something plainly uncharitable and even false. He was a headstrong and violent character and could not bear to be opposed in anything. Well, the Church thinks he is a saint, so I had better not quarrel with that judgment. As to his cave, it was probably a regular house cut into the rock, perhaps as big as my hermitage, but certainly nowhere near as nice.

I have sent David Rowland twenty five dollars, as someone made me a donation of that amount for the hermitage. The rest will follow.

Meanwhile I can be thinking of other possibilities for you between now and the 22nd. I still think the Coomaraswamy idea is the best, but his wife has said nothing definite about it.

All the best to you both, and cordial blessings in Christ
fr Louis

May 2, 1961
Dear Carolyn:

I just realized that the first Saturday in June would not be a good day for me to come over that way, as we have someone coming here to give some talks to the novices and I have to be here then. The end of May offers possibilities, but the Saturday is not so good. Would Thursday 25 May be at all possible? One thing I ought to do is visit Asbury Seminary when over there too. They would like me to come there very much. I don't know whether it would be better to go to Asbury in the morning and then come to Shakertown on the way back, or what. Tell me please what you think. And if that Thursday is possible at all. We may have to put it all off until later. The other day was just perfect, and I enjoyed it very much.

Ever cordially in Christ,
fr Louis

1961
Dear Victor:

The novice whom I deputed to take down the crucifix and make the measurements has done so. I do not know if they are what you want, but he assures me that they are quite exact and indeed that the paper was just as wide as the crucifix itself. I hope this is all right. If you want us to do some more, just let us know. I have a feeling that the side view is not complete. Yet the measurement is accurate I am sure.

I do not know if I am going to be able to get over to Shakertown soon, but I wrote to Carolyn about that the other day.

Will you please ask Carolyn if they have in the library this book:

McDonnell, E.W. The Beguines and Beghards in Medieval Culture, New Brunswick, 1954.

The weather continues beautiful. I have been writing a few poems. I will at this rate soon get to rewriting the letter about Sophia. The Neumann book does not really offer much inspiration, though. It is a cold compilation.

With all best wishes and blessings, as ever

fr Louis

❧

Monday, May 23, 1961
Dear Carolyn

Unfortunately a man is coming down from New York on publishing business[117] at the end of this week and I will not be able to plan anything with you for Thursday. In fact the end of this month is now out of the question. Could we put it off until later? Perhaps June— or if and when J. Laughlin comes down. I am sorry about this. I was looking forward to seeing you then. I have now rewritten the *Hagia Sophia* piece and it will be in the mail as soon as typed. All blessings to you and Victor.

fr. Louis

❧

May 24, 1961
Dear Victor

I have finally rewritten the bit on Sophia and here is the ms. It is a
little long for a broadside but I think it needs at least this much length
and I hope you will be able to make a small book out of it. It seems
to me that it is a more complete statement than I made, or could have
made, in the letter and I hope it is at least poetically clear.

It is a pity I am not able to meet you and Carolyn and your friends
this week. The card I sent to Carolyn should, I hope, have reached her
in good time. I am to be busy with some publishing business these
next few days. Perhaps towards the end of June we might be able to
get together as she planned. I will write more about this.

David Rowland came over with the cupboard which is very fine. I
am sending him the check which has been sitting here in this room
for some days.

Very cordial good wishes and blessings to you
In Christ the Lord
fr Louis

❀

26. V. 61

Dear Father Louis: Thank you for your letter and the poem. We can't
say more for the moment, because we are so overcome by the fact that
you were graced with the ability to say what moves your heart (and
ours) and say it so simply. Of course our thanks ought to go to Him
who has endowed us with his grace.—I shall do my very best as a
printer and am so happy that you have acknowledged the crowning of
the boy. More next time, in the meantime

Yours in Christ,
Carolyn + Victor
Carolyn was reminded of her first prayer she learned
Now I lay me down to sleep
And pray the Lord. . . .

We decided today to tell the Bollingen Foundation "to go jump into the lake." The letter is written.

❦

June 9th, 1961
Dear Victor,

I was very happy with your good note and glad you liked *Hagia Sophia* as I thought you probably would. I am of course very interested in your plans and eager to see how they are progressing. On the other hand it does not look as if I am going to be able to get over to Asbury or Shakertown for some time, as J. is not coming this month. Perhaps in September.

Would you and Carolyn like to come over some Saturday? The best days for me are July 14th and failing that June 17th, next week—which has the advantage of being sooner, but perhaps you have by now other plans.

Glad to hear about Bollingen—I feel you are very wise to turn them down.

Very cordially as ever in Xt
fr Louis

❦

18. VI. 61

Dear Father Louis, This was a crowded week and I missed completely to tell you that we could not come yesterday. We are however determined to come on July 15 Saturday. It is of course always the same. Carolyn has to make up the time beforehand or afterwards when we drive to Gethsemani. This is why the Saturday is the most convenient as she is only busy in the mornings of that day. I feel she takes too great a burden upon herself and she should not accept social duties too easily but she finds it hard to say 'no.'—We have read again the poem on Hagia Sophia, Carolyn read it aloud, it is very fine indeed. She wants me to make a criblé of the center panel and print it as the title page. It's an idea that appeals to me very much, but when to do it is the great question! Goethe in his old age said that old people—and I am one of them—should eliminate projects they had in mind to execute, in order to complete some and not take on new ones. And there are two Irishmen printers in Dublin who want me to cut an Irish type face. They now use the very first one I made and which I do not like too much. Too many new projects! Well we shall see. As it is we are very much looking forward to the 15th of July.—I almost forgot to tell you that there is a young man at the new medical center who lived 3 years in China and reads Chinese. He is a good linguist and every week one evening we draw together and work on a translation of Fiedler's aphorisms. His English seems very good, at least he has a liking for it and he understands *what* he translates, so he does not only translate the words.

Au revoir—then

In Christ, yours C+V

I have finished the first draft of my paper on classic art and am now polishing it a little. Then Carolyn will take over to iron out the language. My young friend, Wayne Williams,[118] will then read it for the contents and I would be very happy if you would read the Mspt. in its more or less final version and talk it over with us. There are always things I take for granted though they are not known to the reader. In fact there is a passage which contains the gist of what we discussed one day as to the dangers of fascism we face in our own country. I was stuck with the dialog but this carried me over the hump.

Carolyn would like to know whether you have a book of, or about, Nikolaus Cusanus from the library. She does not know where it is.

June 21, 1961

Dear Victor:

Thanks for your good note: the 15th of July will be fine. I wondered if you had gone on a trip somewhere, or if my letter had got lost. There is just one slight possible hitch. A Jesuit from Europe[119] is supposed to come down here some weekend in July. He is a very fine scholar and no doubt he would enjoy joining us if he were here. Or perhaps it would be better to change the date if he happens to be here that weekend, as I might not have any other time in which to talk with him. I don't think this is likely though. Provisionally I will assume that even if he comes we could all get together on the 15th anyway.

I do not have any book on Nicholas of Cusa or about his work. Carolyn never brought or sent any. Perhaps though something was sent and got lost in the office here before being given to me. I can inquire. Is Carolyn sure she gave it to me, or any such books? I have only the Shirer on Nazis from the library at Present.

It is good that you like the poem. I am not sure I understand what you intend to do about the title page. We can talk of that when you come, and I will understand. I do think you are right not to take on too many projects but I am glad you have someone who can work with you on the Fiedler, which is more than just a project for you. The same can be said of the classic art. We have to distinguish "projects" from things that are as essential to us as breathing. Breathing can never be a project.

All the best, and every blessing,
in Christ
fr louis

July 11th 1961
Dear Victor:

By all means, I am expecting you Saturday. Bring your friend along. There will be no one else involved here. I look forward to seeing some proofs of Hagia Sophia. There is a power mower operating outside the window and I cannot hear myself think, so I will not try to write any more. See you Saturday. God bless you.

Very cordially in Christ
fr louis

24. VII. 61

Dear Father Louis: Here are the proofs and there is only one
question on my part and you would have to decide: the four periods
at the end of the poem. I have made two different proofs and you
can decide which one you prefer. For a long time I thought that the
four periods have a sweetish taste and only one would be stronger.
But I am not so sure now whether or not I am right—so I shall wait
for your decision. The four periods may carry a meaning in spite of
its sweetness.—We enjoyed the hour with you and Wayne Williams
has written a poem about the meeting, perhaps we will show it to
you on occasion. His translation of Fiedler promises to be really
adequate and—readable. We are going away for a weekend and hope
to be back on August 2nd.

In the meantime
In Christ yours
Victor

July 27, 1961
Dear Victor

This looks wonderful. I am very definitely against the dots at the end,
and think one period is what we need. I had forgotten I had done
this, indeed I did it without thought. What was not noticeable in the
typescript became starkly evident in your type. Again I owe much to
your uncial. Certainly when men wrote out their works in this hand
it had a tremendous influence in shaping their thought. I should have
written this so, but unfortunately I cannot.

The visit with Wayne was, as usual, very enjoyable. Maybe you can
get back some time in September.

Can Carolyn please send me whatever is best, that is available on
Mao Tse Tung and Chinese Communism? And a volume of the Latin
Eckhart if any. There is a remarkable new book out on Eckhart in
French by Lossky.[120]

All blessings, always.
Cordially in Christ Our Lord
fr Louis

❀

Aug. 10, 1961
Dear Carolyn,

Were you able to find anything in the library on Mao Tse Tung? Have you anything especially good on contemporary China?

Here are a couple of titles I am looking for—

S. Voros American Commissar
Edgar Snow Journey to the Beginning
Kraemer The Christian Marriage in a Non-Christian World
K. Marx The Holy Family.

That last is an unusual sounding title for Marx, isn't it? It is one of his significant lesser works. I would like very much to have one or another of these if possible.

How is *Hagia Sophia* coming? Are you and Victor about ready to come over again soon? How about the 2nd or 9th of September?

I hope you weren't all too depressed by the poem about Auschwitz.[121] Its reception has been very "various."

Best wishes to you both and to Wayne. All blessings
In Our Lord
fr Louis

❀

19. VIII. 61

Dear Father Louis: I am now working on the drawing for the print of Hagia Sophia which will be on the first page. When the drawing is done I shall begin the plate itself for the print. Nothing of "industrial enterprise" in the whole book, I shall keep it clean—sacred, and alive. I have certain suggestions for the title page and perhaps also for the colophon, but will wait until we can talk about, writing is too complicated for me. We will come Sept 9 (the second is too close to Labor Day) if this suits you and very much look forward to it.

In Christ yours

C + V

⁂

Aug. 22 1961
Dear Victor,

Many thanks for your letter. I am happy to hear about the drawing and "no industrial enterprise." And also that you will come on the 9th, which is fine for me. I will expect you at the usual time. All blessings

Cordially in Xt

fr Louis

⁂

Friday
September 1, 1961
Dear Carolyn—

I am sorry the 9th is not too good for you. However I have so far no obstacle on any of the other Saturdays. Perhaps the 16th? If I don't hear more from you I shall expect you then—your letter did not reach me until today.

All best wishes

In Christ

fr Louis

⁂

Monday—Sept. 18, 1961

Dear Carolyn
Your card reached me this morning . . .

Do you have in the library a thorough and recent history of one or both of the following:

The Taiping Rebellion (China—19th cent)
The Opium War (China—19th cent)

And do you have available—Proceedings of Pugwash Conference of International Scientists on Biological and Chemical warfare—1959?

It was good to see you and Victor the other day—Such a nice day too. I was only sorry that the visit was shorter than usual because of your time change. I had a good session with the Protestants afterward.

Best wishes and blessings always
In Christ our Lord
fr Louis

Sep 28, 1961
Dear Carolyn—

I am sending over to the library some books and magazines which have got here somehow and which are, generally speaking "inappropriate" for us. You will know whether or not they are of any use to your library.

Thanks for the two books sent recently. All the best to you and Victor—

Cordially in Xt
fr Louis

Oct 16, 1961
Dear Carolyn:

Today I am sending off a couple of packages to the library: one of books that I am finally returning with thanks, (I hope I have not kept them too long), and one of oddments that I am presenting, if they are of any use to you. I don't remember whether I sent the Dutch version of Seeds of Contemplation before. It doesn't matter. That is one thing I have plenty of, Dutch versions of Seeds of Contemplation. It is good to have plenty of *something*. I have plenty of other things too, French versions of Thoughts in Solitude, for example.

How is Victor coming along with the print? No rush. I am just wondering whether November or December would be a good time for him to spend a few days over here as he planned. We will have to do a little planning ahead, as I would not want him to be here when I am engaged in talking to a large numbers of retreatants. Weekends are not absolutely the best time for me but they may be for you. Saturday is all right though. Could you let me know when you would like to come and then I can plan from there. The first weekend in November is not good, nor is the first one in December. Personally I would be inclined to suggest some time around December 11th, or that week. It is not necessarily a very gay time of year, though.

Did I send to your library a book of poetry called *Overland to the Islands* by Denise Levertov? I think I did. Could I borrow it back, please?

Do you have any of the following books, that I could borrow?

P. Leigh Fermor, Mani
Randolph Bourne, War and the Intellectuals
Anything by Jean Giono
E. Mackay, The Indus Civilization
Tillich, The Protestant Era.

I would be very grateful for any of these, if available.
    With best wishes and blessings to you and Victor
    Cordially in Christ
    fr Louis

Nov. 2, 1961
Dear Victor,

The best times for me would be November 17–18 but failing that the 10th and 11th. If those do not serve we will have to wait until

December. Mr McCallister wrote that he would be over here on Monday 6th with E.D. Andrews who is quite a student of the Shakers and has written several books about them.[122] They invited me to Shakertown this Saturday but it was impossible for me to get there. I am glad you are taking time with the drawing in order to get everything just right. And I look forward to seeing the new classic art. I have been busy with polemical articles about peace,[123] which I feel are necessary.

    With all blessings to you and Carolyn,
    Cordially in Christ
    fr Louis

Nov. 9th 1961
Dear Victor:

Fine, I will expect you at lunch time Friday 17th about 11:30?[124] Will I be able to read while you work? It doesn't matter—whatever is best. Looking forward to next week! All blessings—

    Very cordially in Xt
    fr Louis

Nov. 22, 1961
Dear Victor.

I have come across a most suitable quotation that might go under the woodcut, except that it is a bit long:

    Wisdom will honor you if you embrace her
    She will place on your head a fair garland,
    She will bestow on you a crown of glory. (Proverbs 4:8–9)

But we might omit the second or third line. I leave that to your discretion. In any case this seems to me to be a thoroughly suitable verse for the book.

146

Your two day visit was most enjoyable and I am so happy that it was fruitful for us all in every way.

I forget whether I gave you the mimeograph (very poor and hard to read) of Clement of Alexandria. There are in Clement many excellent "pretexts" for printing. He led me also to the above quotation, as he is a great friend of Sophia.

All blessings and best wishes to you and Carolyn

Cordially in Christ

fr Louis

Dec. 19, 1961

Dear Victor.

I was very sorry to hear Carolyn had to go to the hospital but on the other hand it was good news to hear that everything turned out well. Of this I am glad. I hope you will both have a good rest over Christmas, if such a thing is possible.

About the woodcut—I am sorry you have had to make a second try at it. I suppose really it would not be easy to make one that exactly fitted in with the typography. Perhaps the best thing is simply to do what works out most favorably, and if the book will look better without the woodcut then that is the way it ought to be. And I suppose the only way to judge that is to try it and see.

So perhaps in January we can consult on this. It is possible that J. may come down for a quick visit as we are working together at a book of articles on peace.[125] I will let you know.

Best Christmas wishes to both you and Carolyn and all blessings. Perhaps I might translate a page or two of Jean Giono for you to print some day. We can speak of this.

In Christ our Lord

fr Louis

20. XII. 61

Dear Father Louis, I suppose you never got the letter I wrote to you about 10 days ago where Carolyn came back from the Hospital. So I repeat with a much lighter heart that all went well, no malignancy, and though slowly, she is on her way back to normal. Let us thank God and rejoice for a while.

Enclosed find a proof and I would like to know about the copyright. So far I haven't assumed this nor that, whether or not. It is up to you. We shall print no more than 50 copies, if not less. How many for you then? The illustration faces the first page of your text. You will get more proofs of these first 4 pages (one empty), according to your decision. You will understand silence and delay, so please excuse.

In Christ
affectionately yours
Victor
Carolyn joins in greetings

Dec. 23 1961
Dear Victor

Many thanks for the proof. I think it will do very well in the book. It is very simple and austere. Are the lines in the hand holding the crown too heavy? This strikes one a bit. But the woodcut is I think very fitting and good, and I am glad it turned out well, after your misgivings about it.

How many copies can you spare me? I forget how many I asked for last time, and do not know what measure to place upon my greed. Will six be too many? I now forget whether I have promised that many to people already. I half promised to give one to St. Mary's College Notre Dame and then drew back and said no they had better buy one. I don't think I am a good salesman. But we'll see. If it worked with them I may do it to all those to whom I first promised one, and then enter 1962 with an air of executive abandon.

I wish you again all the best of the season's graces. Good health and joy to you in the New Year, and blessings especially to Carolyn. I will let you know if I hear that J. is coming.

Very cordially as ever, in Christ

fr Louis

Jan 5, 1962
Dear Victor:

It was good to get your letter and I am happy to hear of the painting in progress. It is a good subject and I liked your previous treatment of it. What will it be now? I am very interested.

The dust has settled a little after the Christmas festivities which even here are more of an upheaval than necessary. January is still going to be rather taken up with things which exclude a visit, however, as we have the annual retreat from the 18th on, and I have a couple of ministers to see at the end of the month.

Let us plan on one of the Saturdays in February: I give you the choice of the 9th, 16th or 23rd. Let me know which one you think will be best for you, tentatively. It is a pity we cannot tell this far in advance what the weather is likely to be, but in any event if I have a choice I would rather you came sooner, and thus we might hope that the 9th would be a fairly sunny day? I hope so, but you may have other things determining your choice.

I continue to have small motives for twinges of conscience for having spoken out in favor of Congdon's (abstract expressionist) "paintings."[126] It is true that I appreciate his motives, but after all it is silly to praise a man just because he means well and because he has a taste for this or that color. Perhaps after all I have no need to be modern at all, I have just continued to be so out of habit. But why do anything just out of habit?

The monk who translated the Cassiodorus is Father Augustine

Wulff. My bits from the Desert Fathers were practically all translations, with a little editing here and there to make the story shorter and more succinct, but they can be called translations and are not re-tellings.

All the best New Year wishes to you. Did I ever send the Chartres letters? Here is a copy.

All blessings, as ever,
Cordially in Christ,
fr Louis

Jan 18, 1962
Dear Victor

I was so sorry to hear that both you and Carolyn had been ill. It was a pity you and I and J. could not get together. It would be nice to see you, and I wish we could have got over to Lexington but there was no time and I hesitated to ask permission. Perhaps later on in the spring when the weather gets better we can see you here and we can bask in the spring sun, speaking of the good things with which God continues to bless us.

J. and I were working on a book about peace which I think will be quite effective. Meanwhile tomorrow I go into retreat for a week.

I was down near Lexington, at Asbury, but it was just not possible to get over there, as I had to be back early. I stopped at Shakertown and took some photographs which came out quite well and now I am musing on a project of a little simple book, of perhaps only a dozen pages, with pictures and a kind of prose poem along the lines of Hagia Sophia. This would probably do for some magazine, but I think it would be my contribution to the "cause." I will keep thinking about it.

I still have one or two books from the library, and have been very slow to get them back. But I will get busy and return them. They are a couple of Gionos and one other.

How is Hagia Sophia? J. said you were still having trouble with the woodcut. And the portrait?

Well, I must close now. I think under separate cover the novices are sending you a couple of recently mimeographed articles on peace.

With best wishes and blessings always,

in Christ

fr Louis

Dear Carolyn:

Do you by any chance have one or other of the following—

R. Niebuhr—The Irony of American History

L. Barzini—Americans are alone

Something on America by Denis Brogan

C. Wright Mills—The Power Elite

J. Larteguy—The Centurions (in English or French)

M. Spark—The Prime of Miss Jean Brodie

Blessings to you and Victor. Get well quickly again. Do I still have any of the library books? I seem to see more around here.

Ever Cordially in Christ

Father Louis

21. I. 62

Dear Father Louis: Thank you for sending us your notes on the nuclear bomb.[127]—About a year after the first one was released on Hiroshima I listened to a lecture by R. Oppenheimer in Cornell. He said that the only way to escape destruction was not to use the bomb. He had no more to say.—there is a clipping from Time Mag. What do you think of brain washing? What is it and how to escape that with all the newspapers and means of mass communication around? So I am going to print only 50 copies of your essay.—Is the cut now right, does it go with the type? The one proof shows the first section with the title and the pro manuscripto 1962. Do you want

the copyright and if so what have I to say? Why do you not write
to Washington and find out what the "pro manuscripto" means and
legally does? This would at least be an official answer, and settle this
affair once and for all. The second proof is only to show the cut and
the text together. I think I better fit the third line of the proverb in as
well, this would lead to the text in an unmistakable way—only for the
eye of course, and I am concerned with the eye, my poor eye! Yet the
one I have left serves me well enough and I am grateful.—We were
sorry to miss the opportunity of seeing you and J. as well, but Carolyn
is not yet ready to drive that far and back in one stretch. We will have
to wait for better weather anyhow. Hope you feel well. All our good
wishes and best greetings

    In Christ yours

    Victor

Continued on Jan. 24. If one works for the higher glory of God one
cannot say: this is good enough, one must give one's own best and
even if it is no more than the farthing of the widow. So this is now the
best I can do: I scraped the cut once more and made another one. And
this is it. Can I go ahead or not?

Jan 28, 1962
Dear Victor:

As we came out of our retreat I found in the pile of mail your proof
and letter. First of all the proof is fine, I am very sorry you felt you
had to do the cut over again, as it was quite good before, but now
it is much better it seems to me. So therefore I am both sorry and
glad. The new cut is lighter and more free. Or so it seems to me. So
by all means go ahead, everything is right and ready as far as I am
concerned.

    The copyright problem as I understand it is not one that can
be changed by dickering with Washington about the phrase "pro
manuscripto." That may work with the censors but it does not work
with the copyright office. I will make some kind of an effort to

work this out for sure sometime when I am more in the clear, but for the moment I think we just have to put copyright by the Abbey of Gethsemani, or Victor Hammer, one or the other. Let me know which and I will apply to Washington for the copyright and at the same time will ask about pro manuscripto, without hope of finding out anything relevant. The copyright line should read:

Copyright 1962 by, . . . (whoever it is to be.)

It must be on the title page or on the reverse of the title page. That is, probably on the one where you have pro manuscripto. If you think the whole thing is foolish, then let it go, but it will make it difficult for J. or whoever publishes the piece later in a book commercially.

Frankly I think it would ruin the pro manuscripto and look senseless, so if you feel you want to just let it go, then please do so. I think the way the page looks is more important than anything else, and hang the copyright. At least that is what I think, really.

So now you have a full range of opinions to choose from. If you just forget about the copyright you have my full approval, there is no point in ruining the book for that.

As for brainwashing, the term is used very loosely about almost anything. Strict technical brainwashing is an artificially induced "conversion," brought about by completely isolating a person emotionally and spiritually, undermining his whole sense of identity, and then "rescuing" him from this state of near collapse by drawing him over into a new sense of community with his persecutors, now his rescuers, who "restore" his identity by admitting him into their midst as an approved and docile instrument. Henceforth he does what they want him to do and likes it, indeed finds a certain satisfaction in this, and even regards his old life as shameful and inferior.

In the loose sense, any mass man is a "brainwashed" man. He has lost his identity or never had one in the first place, and he seeks security, hope, a sense of identity in his immersion in the pressures and prejudices of a majority, speaking through TV, newspapers, etc. Having no real power or meaning in himself he seeks all in identification with a presumably all powerful and all wise collectivity.

Whatever the collectivity does is right, infallible, perfect. Anything, approved by it, becomes legitimate and even noble. The worst crimes are virtues when backed up by the all powerful collectivity. All that matters is to be part of the great, loud mass.

It seems to me that the great effort of conscience that remains for modern man is to resist this kind of annihilating pressure, this defection, in every possible way. The temptation comes unfortunately from very many angles, even seemingly good sources. The Cold War is the deadly influence that is leading western man to brainwash himself.

When the process is completed there will be nothing left but the hot war or the decline into totalitarian blindness and inertia, which also spells hot war in the end. The prospects are very dark, aren't they? Yet I think that perhaps some providential accident may happen that will wake everyone up. Some kind of plague of radiation, perhaps, something unexpected and unforeseen that will force people to their senses. But can we say we have done anything to serve this? I hardly think so. Fortunately, if we only got what we deserved, we would never have very much of anything good. God is not simply just, He is also and above all merciful. I wish that this had not been so thoroughly forgotten.

The clipping was interesting, and I had already started a note to Carolyn which had that book included in a short list of other items. The French situation is very disturbing indeed. Much evil can come of this. Everyone expects De Gaulle to get it this year some time, and I wonder how long he can survive. He has been a good man in many ways, yet perhaps mistakenly messianic too. But what could any reasonable human being have done with Algeria? If he goes, then France goes too. And this may be the spark that will finally ignite everything. The next few months will tell us a thing or two. And the next three years, or four: well, to call them fateful is putting it so mildly as to be ridiculous.

I wonder if there is going to be much left of the Western World by 1984, to fulfill George Orwell's prophecies?

Meanwhile, we have only to be what we are and to retain the spirit and civilization which we were blessed with, and to keep as human as we can. I hope you and Carolyn are well, and that Carolyn is gradually getting better. I look forward to seeing you then, perhaps in March?

God bless you always.

With all friendship and affection to you both in Christ

fr Louis

❧

[February 1962]
Dear Victor:

Bro Bernardine assures me that they do not have the book you want and for some reason it will be some time before they get it.[128] His solution is to return your check, so I am doing that, together with his note, which may make more sense to you than it does to me.

Today, Sunday, the weather is so nice that I hope it is inspiring you and Carolyn to plan to come over soon.

In haste, but always with the most cordial good wishes and blessings, in Christ

fr Louis

❧

Feb. 13, 1962
Dear Victor.

March 3 will be fine as far as I am concerned, and I hope the weather will be nice. If it is not we can always remain in the car.

As for the eyes, well, I think probably greenish blue or greenish grey—there seem to be a lot of funny colors in there, I did not know an eye was so complicated.

Here is one of the Brogan books I could probably use—and I am grateful to Carolyn for the information.

Yes, the bomb is a great invention of benevolence: it ends wars, saves lives, makes everybody happy and even ends worlds.

God bless you, cordially always in Xt

fr Louis

9. V. 1962

Dear Father Louis: enclosed find a proof of an unfinished metal-cut which I attempted to make for the poem because I was not satisfied with the wood-cut.[129] I have spent about a month on that thing, but now have decided to give it up completely. I still think it holds a promise, the faces I believe not bad at all and the composition too I could defend. But to finish it is beyond my power, that is, beyond the power of my eye-sight. I have probably pulled about 300 or more proofs while working and more than 100 I kept while the rest went into the waste basket. I worked with a binocular loupe, two pairs of glasses and 2 magnifying lenses alternatively. But now, when I began to stipple the dresses I could no longer continue. The punch with which to stipple, the hammer with which to drive the punch and the binocular lupe with which to look were in each others way, I could see no more than a quarter of an inch of the area to be stippled, while looking through the lupe. When I wanted to check with the proof I had to put one pair of glasses on my nose, then lay it aside and look again through the loupe, picking up punch and hammer. This year, God willing, I shall be eighty, it is time to resign myself to the things I still can do and leave my hands off from those that demand younger organs for execution. I can still paint with that one eye which is left. Indeed I have finished now a portrait which shows no sign of decay. On the contrary, it is one of the best things I was allowed by God's grace, to do. So I shall stick to painting.

The text of the poem is printed and the proofs of the title pages and the colophon are enclosed for your approval or correction. I think I can still print: for in doing this kind of work I need only one pair of glasses, my ordinary ones, and a magnifying glass alternatively. It takes a little more time, but the tools do not interfere.

We often speak of you and in our thoughts you are always with us. When will it be possible to see you again? We plan to go to New York during the fourth week in May (20–26) partly on business, partly for seeing friends. We shall try to see James Laughlin.

We also thank you for that masterpiece of understatement: Original Child Bomb [the published version]. "Zart Gedicht, wie Regenbogen, wird nur auf dunklen Grund gezogen";[130] light on this earth seems to need darkness, for it would not shine otherwise, so God seems to need the devil. Sad, but true.

Your blessing we need and we thank you for it.

In Christ yours devoted,

C+V

The colophon will be the same as in the Solitude [*The Solitary Life*].

May 10, 1962
Dear Victor:

I was glad to get your letter, and Carolyn's card about Jonathan Greene[131] came at the same time. Thanks to you both.

You have certainly had a time with that engraving. I might have guessed that you were still fighting it. The struggle and its issue show that you are not satisfied with the possibility of finishing the print to your satisfaction. The steel engraving looked promising, yet you are right. I think it is better for the book to be without any illustration, and that in its simplicity it will say more than the picture which cannot satisfy you, and which has never the less cost so much. I am grateful to you for so much trouble. Whatever fruit it would have had in the finished engraving will find its way in some hidden way into the book itself. I am returning the proofs, of course without any correction.

I was thinking of writing you a note to find out what the news was and whether you were coming down again soon. It is too late to get you here this Saturday I suppose. And on the 19th you will not want to come as that is just before your trip to the east. What about June 2nd? Or the following Saturday?

J. will tell you about the book of essays on peace which seems to be coming along: we have a good group of authors. I am just going to get down to the proofs of my own contribution. But this business of writing about the war and peace issue is not much fun. Nor should one expect it to be. Every once in a while you stop to think what you have just said. It is unbelievable to be calmly talking about such issues as the destruction of continents. Yet it is still more unbelievable not to be talking about them when they so obviously threaten us.

More and more I see that it is not the moral principles which are at stake, but more radically, the whole outlook of modern man, at least in America, and the basic assumptions which tend to guide his thought, if it can be called thought. We are living in an absurd dream, and a very bad one. And it is the fruit of all sorts of things we ought not to have done. But the whole world is in turmoil, spiritually, morally, socially. We are sitting on a thin crust above an immense lake of molten lava that is stirring and getting ready to erupt. Nothing will stop this eruption. But at least we can refrain from setting off bombs that will start it in some far worse way than it normally would.

In addition my higher superiors have suddenly decreed that a monk does not know there is danger of war and consequently should not make any observations on the fact. I am hoping nevertheless to get a little book on the subject published,[132] and observation that has already been written, and comes before their hieratic utterance.

Here is a prayer which was read in Congress by a good man who was military governor of the prefecture of Hiroshima and helped them rebuild the city.[133] J. will probably tell you more about him. I am also interested in the steps being taken by Leo Szilard for peaceful policies in Washington.[134] This seems to me to be about the sanest thing that has come up so far. All the rest is either way out, like the CNVA[135] (the nonviolent movement, which is largely amoral and beat) or ineffectual like the more solemn movements that do nothing.

Do let me know when I can expect to see you. I hope you have a good trip to New York. J. will be happy to see you.

With all blessings and best wishes, in Christ
fr Louis

May 29, 1962
Dear Victor

I look forward very much to seeing you and Carolyn this Saturday, June 2, at the regular time.[136] I hope we will have some nice weather.

God bless you always

fr Louis

June 26, 1962
Dear Victor:

I am glad to hear that the printing is finished and that you are ready to bring the opus over. Since there is a question of measuring the titulus for the crucifix, Sunday would not be a good day as there is always a crowd around in the novitiate. But let us make it Saturday the 7th.[137] I look forward to seeing you then.

Now I have a little idea for something to print. It is a beautiful prayer of Cassiodorus at the end of his *De Anima*.[138] Perhaps by the 7th I will have a rough translation finished for you to see. And of course I would write a little introduction. In all, it would probably be almost the same length as Hagia Sophia.

In fact I am thinking of doing more work on Cassiodorus. I have been reading a lot of his work. I wonder if Carolyn has in the library the critical edition of Cassiodorus's "Instituta" (done by R.A.B. Mynors, Oxford, 1937). Or if she has anything else on him. All I have is Migne and a couple of Catholic journals that have some articles on him.

Also perhaps Carolyn might find for me a good history of the late Roman Empire, especially covering the Barbarian invasions and the state of affairs in the 6th century. This would be useful for background to Cassiodorus.

I look forward very much to seeing you both. Meanwhile, God bless you. And all best wishes. I am still happy about the painting.

Ever cordially yours in Christ,

fr Louis

July 18 1962
Dear Carolyn:

Today I remembered finally about the text for the cover. It had been gone from my mind for days. So I have got some material on paper. With interlinear English this ought certainly to be long enough. And of course you may even want to cut some of it. I hope it will be satisfactory.

Do you think it would be possible for me to borrow a volume of *Speculum* (the magazine) out of season, if I promise to get it back in a big hurry?

There is an article by Rand "The New Cassiodorus" in Speculum XIII (1938) p. 433 f.

There are also apparently three Columbia dissertations on him. Then there is a book I meant to refer to you, published by Columbia in 1946.

L.W. Jones, *An Introduction to Divine and Human Readings* by Cassiodorus Senator, trans with an introduction.

I am sending back the large volume of Notker and will keep the small one until I have read some more of the poems.[139]

Are we agreed on August 23rd? Or do you prefer the 30th? The 23rd is slightly better for me, but there is not that much difference.

Is Maritain at Kolbsheim now? I might write to him if he is. In any case please give my warm regards to Alexis, for whom I prayed yesterday, the Feast of St. Alexis. And I wish I were coming with you.

With all best wishes as ever

Most cordially in Christ,

Tom[140]

I might as well keep the record straight and be consistently Tom with *all* my friends outside the monastery.

P.S. many thanks for the [?] *Reporter* our librarian deeply appreciates. Also of course Nicholas of Cusa.

July 23, 1962
Dear Victor.

This looks really fine. I have hastily inserted translations for the two added verses.

Please thank Carolyn for the Buddhist book which came last week.

I will look forward to hearing when you intend to come. The sooner the better.

With all good wishes in Xt

Tom

July 26, 1962
Dear Victor:

Here are the final proofs. I tried to carefully spot every little slip, and I find one must look closely to correct your uncial, as "a" and "o" are liable to look much alike. I think I got everything, including my own mistakes.

Could you please ask Carolyn to have them send me the following titles by MLW Laistner:

Beda Venerabilis
The Intellectual Heritage of the Early Middle Ages.

I may be going to the hospital for a checkup early in September or late August so if you come sometime around the 23rd it would be best for me, or even earlier. There is nothing wrong with me, I just have to get an ex ray once in a while.

This is just a hurried note. Bless you both.

Cordially in Christ,

Tom

I just have not been able to write that piece about the Shakers. My mind has been on other things.

Aug 11, 1962
Dear Carolyn:

You have already sent me the book from Columbia. It is the edition
of Cassiodorus's "Divine and Human Readings" by Jones. In fact you
sent two copies, of which I returned one. I am glad to know of the
two dissertations however, but there is no immediate need for them. I
will keep them in mind. Many thanks.

Victor had mentioned the 23rd as a possible day, and I thought I
would put in a Thursday for a change, but if you want to come on the
25th that is even better. Whatever you like. Drop me a line and tell
me whether to expect you on the 23rd or the 25th. I will be equally
ready, in fact the 25th is the Feast of St. Louis.

Could you have someone *list* for me the works of Erasmus you
have there in Latin? I can't get to this right now, but will want to
eventually. Also, what do you have of Cusanus now in Latin?

And finally could you let me know what you have *about* Lucretius,
just the more recent and important studies if any. If it is not too much
trouble.

This poem was written about a child's drawing of a house.[141] I
thought you and Victor might like to see it.

All best wishes and blessings always,
Cordially in Christ,
Tom

Aug 12 [1962]
Dear Carolyn

Another possible reference—supposed to have good material on
Cassiodorus.

Courcelle, Pierre, "Les lettres Grecques en Occident" Bibliothèque
des Ecoles Françaises d'Athènes et de Rome, Fasc. 159 Paris, 1947

Do you by any chance have it?
Many thanks—as ever
Tom

❦

20. August 1962

If Saturday the 25th is still convenient, we shall come then (not the
23rd). You will hear this week from the library abt. the titles you need.
    Sincerely
    C.R. Hammer

❦

Aug 22, 1962
Dear Victor

Now there is *no* difference in time. We are on the same time as
you—I will expect you Saturday 25th at about 11.15 both your time
and ours.[142] Looking forward to seeing you all, Carolyn and Wayne—
and yourself.
    All blessings in Xt—Tom

❦

Aug 22, 1962
Dear Victor,

In my card yesterday I was confused. You should come at 12.15 your
time and ours, otherwise you will come when I am going to give my
class. Everything is an hour later now. Temporarily.
    In Xt—Tom

❦

24. IX. 62 [Monreale, Italy]

Dear Tom: As I have your image with me we have not lost touch with
you. Carolyn recovered completely during the 10 days on board. She
is stunned by the things she saw in Monreale. These churches are not
propaganda they are religion and one can feel it still today,
    yours Victor
Victor too is 'stunned' once again—CRH

27 Oct [1962] [Dordogne, France]

Dear Tom: Just out of the caves we are happy to be in God's light again. But it was necessary for me to see the paintings with my own eyes. Photographs distort, are only good for recollection. It is rather chilly at the end of October. We are looking forward to seeing you again.

In Christ our Savior
yours C+V.

27

Nov. 21, 1962
Dear Victor.

Thanks for all your cards from Europe, especially the guards from Venice which I have on the wall behind me. When will I see you and Carolyn again? Any Saturday in December will be good—I wonder if we will ever have decent weather again it has been rainy and foggy for days. Let me know which Saturday is suitable for you and I will expect you 11.15 *Eastern Standard* time—All blessings as ever—

In Xt
Tom

27

Nov. 24, 1962
Dear Victor:

I was glad to get your card this morning and to learn that you are back. It is perhaps late to plan anything for next week, but if you want to consider Thursday the 29th or Saturday the 1st of December, that would be fine. Monday the 3rd and Wednesday the 5th would be fine. The 8th is no good.

On any of those days, if you can come about 11:15 eastern standard time, great. Or a little later. Perhaps the best would be to plan on the

29th, unless I hear otherwise. In any case, perhaps the simplest way to let me know would be to call Bro. Bernardine or whoever is at the gate and give them a message just before you are starting out. Make sure that they get it to me, though.

I will be looking for you on the 29th, then. If that date is out, and you think one of the others better as of now, perhaps you could send me a note.

Have been rather busy. I will have a copy of the new *Reader* for you, and other small things.

By the way, do you know what happened? I lost the two transparencies of the picture. This was very foolish of me and I don't know how it happened, but I have not been able to find them anywhere. You don't suppose I slipped them into a book which you took back with you, by any chance? It is so long ago now that there is no hope of finding it, I suppose.

It is so good that you are back. Very best wishes always, and blessings:

Cordially in Christ

Tom

❀

Dec. 11, 1962
Dear Carolyn

Now that it snows and is cold, I think with pleasure our meeting last week and the little fire in the grate. It was most enjoyable.

Here are a few books I have seen well reviewed—esp. in the Saturday Review. If you have, or get, them, I would enjoy reading them.

Randall Jarrell—The Sad Heart at the Supermarket
R. Rovere—The American Establishment
Benjamin De Mott—Hells and Benefits
Dwight Macdonald—Against the American Grain.
Alfred Kazin—Contemporaries

Mary McCarthy—On the Contrary.
Ottiero Ottieri—The Men at the Gate.
John Strachey—The Strangled Cry.
Heydecker and Leeb—The Nuremberg Trial
C. Wighton—Heydrich.
E.B. White—The Points of my Compass.

That is quite a list—of course I don't expect to see them all—but in case you get some, please remember me.

Best regards and blessings always in Christ

Tom

✿

Dec 25 [1962]
Dear Victor and Carolyn.

I think of you on this Christmas morning and will remember you both as I go down to Mass. May God bless you both, and bring you closer to Him always.

Looking forward into the next year, January for various reasons is pretty occupied, with a long retreat period when everything is closed up, and I think February would be best. Pick your own day and let me know. So far all is free. The 5th would be good.

All blessings,

Tom

Carolyn—May I keep Mason, Rilke, Europe etc. beyond Dec. 31? Only past New Year?

✿

Saturday [February 9, 1963]
Dear Victor—

Sorry I am not seeing you today but doubtless it is best for the wind is cold, the clouds are dark and it looks like snow. Next Saturday, the 16th will be best. I hope it is nice. The Saturday after that will be no good for me, alas. I hope we don't have to put it off.

All best wishes and blessing to you both, in Xt
Tom
P.S. I found the transparencies.

March 3, 1963
Dear Victor:

It was a good thing you did not come down in February, it would have been much too cold. But today looks more hopeful. I know one cannot bank too much on appearances, but shall we assume that March is going to be a little better than February was? There are three especially good Saturdays, as far as I am concerned: the 16th, the 23rd and the 30th. Can you make it one of those days? I am looking forward to seeing you. It has been quite a long time.

I doubt if this will be in the library, but perhaps I might as well suggest it, in case Carolyn might want to get it:

Masunga, R. "The Soto approach to Zen" Tokyo, 1958.

Are any of these available:

N.O. Brown, Life Against Death, the psychoanalytic meaning of history, Wesleyan U, 1959.
R. May, Existence New York 1958
G. Kepes, The New Landscape, Chicago, 1956
L.L. Whyte, The Next Development in Man New York, 1948
E. Erikson, Young Man Luther, New York, 1958.
H. Marcuse, Eros and Civilization, Boston, 1955.

I forgot what exactly was on my previous enormously long list, but wonder if any of it came in. I do not know if I kept a copy.

I hope you are both well and working hard at good things.

All blessings, in Christ,
Tom

March 4. [1963]
Dear Victor.

I too have been thinking about seeing you and Carolyn again
though today the weather is hardly lovely. However these next few
weeks are not the best, with Easter coming up. One possibility
would be Saturday the 21st, though. We could keep that in mind.
Better however would be the 4th or 11th of April. Still nothing on
Leopardi.[143] I am in censor trouble again, it seems worse than ever.
I wonder if I should even think of Leopardi at this time? Of course
it might not raise any problem as a limited edition would not need
censorship. In any case I would like to see the translations to which J.
refers in his admirable letter.

Let me know what would be the best date and I will expect you.
I will try to remember to confirm it this time, but if I don't all is still
well. One advantage of coming on March 21st would be that the time
would be as usual. After Easter we do everything one hour later, while
remaining on Eastern Standard time.

All best wishes to you both.
Cordially in Christ
Tom

Tuesday 19th [March 1963]
Dear Victor

I am so glad you are coming Saturday—and hope it will be nice.[144]

Does Carolyn have in the library any other works of Fenelon or
of Madame Guyon? I could use anything they may have in French or
English.

Hoping to have a good visit with you both—
All blessings in Xt
Tom

Carolyn—Can I have the address of the people who published N. de Cusa?

❦

April 7, 1963
Dear Victor and Carolyn:

You probably realize the quandary I am in. I just got a letter from the President of the U. of Kentucky, with about a normal delay (dated April 2), and I observe that I am to be Queen of the May. This is a new role for me.

Precisely, in case you don't know the full news, and you may not, I have been awarded an honorary LL.D.[145] Which suggests that someone there is under the delusion that I can read and write. Perhaps so. But also, and of this they are aware, I am not able to appear at the foot of the maypole and receive my degree.

They have asked me to get someone else to do it for me. Obviously the first person I think of is Victor, but at the same time I am sure he is even less disposed to be Queen of May than I am. I do not know exactly what it involves. I am not sure whether a speech is required, and whether I am supposed to write one and have my noble proxy, whoever he may be, read it. I certainly do not want to inflict this on Victor. But if it is just a matter of sitting there in a top hat, and then receiving the sheepskin and making a bow of some sort, then perhaps he would not mind. But as I say, I would not inflict this on him for worlds, if he does not want it, or if it is too much bother. I can see that it probably is.

Anyway, Victor is my first choice. After that, I could probably embarrass a professor at the College of the Bible into doing it. Or else I would have to look around in Louisville, or perhaps I could get Dan Walsh here to do it. That might be a solution except that *he* has got to be Queen of the May at Bellarmine, and I don't know if it is on the same day.

I am really very pleased to receive an honorary LL.D. I will wear my cap and gown all around the monastery for a full week, including in choir, and make myself entirely odious to everyone. But really, I think it is very kind of them, and when I find out who is to be my proxy, I will write a letter of thanks. Can you tell me if I have to send a speech or statement?

In haste, and looking forward to seeing you early in May,
With all blessings and good wishes,
in Christ,
Tom

꙳

Dear Victor

I am so glad you will be able to "represent" me to "make me present" at commencement and receive the degree for me. There is no one by whom I would rather be represented. Thank you very much for consenting to do this.

Meanwhile, I look forward to seeing you before that—on the first Saturday of May—Derby Day! I hope this still stands and that it will be nice weather.

Have you heard from J? I am hoping he will come down, bringing a Hindu writer with him. We'll see. It would be nice if we could all get together.

All best wishes to you and Carolyn
In Xt
Tom

P.S. I sent a statement to Pres. Dickey but it was *short*.[146] Does he want something longer?

꙳

June 7, 1963
Dear Victor and Carolyn:

Thanks for your note, and I am especially grateful for Victor's Trappistic exploit as my secret agent. I shall look forward to seeing you next Saturday, the 16th or rather the 15th, and am happy that because of the august doctoral hood, you will be coming sooner than you otherwise would. I hope it will be a nice day. I have just had five superb days of retreat up at the hermitage, and they have been invaluable for me. I hope the joy and peace have not worn off by next Saturday. Thanks again, and I will be expecting you Saturday. But then it will be about 12.15 as I have a class that day. *If you come Friday, you can come earlier,* say about 11. On that day I have no class. Thursday of this week, the 13th, is a Feast Day and I would not be free. Tell me at once if you are coming Friday and remember that this affects my diet.

    All the best, always.

    Every yours in Christ, with all blessings,

    Tom

July 16, 1963

Dear Victor and Carolyn:

Not having heard anything from J., I presume he is not going to come down in July, and I am going to be too busy in August (several visiting firemen, so to speak, which will use up the best of my time). In that case, I won't be able to see you until September, unless you want to come over July 27th, whether or not J. comes down. If this reaches you in time and you prefer to come the 20th, even better. I thought I would let you know. If you can come the 20th or 27th, fine: otherwise we will have to put our next visit off until some time in September.

    Hoping you are both well. By the way I forgot to say how much I liked the little books, Carolyn's history of the press, and Victor's digression.[147] I thought Carolyn's was particularly good reading, a very good little book. The dialogue on the Roman letter is very well done too. I appreciated the remark about men not proceeding gently, and "even the gentle teachings of Christ have not met with success." That is unfortunately quite true.

    Best wishes to you both. Hope to see you soon.

    Yours in Christ,

    Tom

Aug 16, 1963
Dear Victor:

I was sorry that Carolyn's mother was ill and that you could not come last month. I hope everything is going better now. I have been very busy with visitors the past week or two, mostly semi official things, French Benedictines for whom I had to interpret etc.[148] Now things are calming down again a little, and I can look forward, I hope, to seeing you both again. Two dates occur to me: August 31, and Sept. 14. Sept 7 is also a possibility if it is better for you, but the 14th is much better for me, and on that day I think you will be able to come earlier if you like. But in any case I can meet you about 12.15 on any of those days. Let me know if they are good. I am just sending back to J. the proofs of a book of verse he is bringing out this fall.

Best wishes to you both. Hoping you are well.

All blessings, in Christ,

Tom

🪷

September 4, 1963
Dear Victor—

I was sure I had written today Saturday 7th would be fine, but in any case I sent a telegram today to make sure.

Hope to see you this Saturday at noon.[149]

All the best to both of you

Tom

🪷

September 15, 1963
Dear Victor—

I am in the hospital in Louisville with a cervical disk, besides bursitis and arthritis.[150] Things are coming along well, however.

About your book, I wanted to say how excellent it is.[151] I like its informality and its *reality*. There is no nonsense in it, and it is very simple and perfectly right. It is a unique book. I want to quote your lines on Dalí in my own book, if I may—my book is very silly in comparison.[152]

One correction—on page 14 the later quote should read Eritis Sicut Dei—the word 'gods' has to be plural, not singular (in Genesis).

About the preface to your catalogue—my hesitations are due to a whole new situation in regard to such things. I have resolved to put all this in the hands of a friend in New York who was my agent once and who will help me to keep straight and out of difficulties. I get so many requests and I have been assuming too many. There is no question about my wanting to do this for you, but I really think I should not because I have simply got into a rut of writing irresponsible short statements of every kind, and it has to stop. So I am afraid I must refuse this one, because I would not do it intelligently enough.

I am enjoying the Leopardi[153] book in the hospital and will look forward to doing the translations.

All best wishes and blessings to you and Carolyn

Yours in Christ always,

Tom

❀

Sep. 29, 1963

Dear Tom: Thank you for your kind letter of Sept. 15th. We were very sorry to hear about your sufferings but were relieved to know you were in good hands at the hospital. I hope this letter reaches you as a convalescent in the monastery. All good wishes for your recovery.

The news about your agent in New York who endeavors to keep you out of difficulties by cutting down on the demands which are constantly made upon you, such as blurbs and similar things is very good news indeed. I am glad to hear this happened. You need not apologize to me for I made similar demands. I realize now that the

text of my book—which you so kindly and seriously reviewed—
will be the appropriate text to accompany a supposed book of
reproductions from my pictures.

I admit that my proposal was rather naive, thoughtless perhaps. I
fancied a layman faced by these pictures, definitely out of fashion now,
and telling what they mean to him. But the layman is not what he
once was and how I wish him to be. In bygone days the layman was
after the artist because he needed his work. The priests of the religious
orders defined exactly what they wanted and needed as painted stories
on the walls of their churches, in order to teach the believers who
could not read but were able to see. Though the wishes of the clerics
(laymen too regarding the arts) were set down exactly in writing and
contracts with the artists made, no patron, as the Church was, would
have expected the artists to "express themselves." Yet the artists were
free to strive after artistic truth as they saw fit.

This kind of layman no longer exists, and church art became as
poor as it is. The churchmen do not know what they want and actually
they don't want anything specific; they wait for what the artist offers
and meekly accept it, or after a while reject it for the wrong reasons.
As the Abbot of Scheyern, when I asked him when the frescoes on
the barrel vault of their Romanesque church were painted, said: Oh,
that was when we had too much money.

You will understand that in this sense you are not, and cannot be
a layman, for you are a child of our age just as I am myself. Therefore
it was thoughtless of me to ask you. It has become a sort of excuse
to admit one is a layman. But the laymen who built the cathedrals
thought of themselves as patrons who hired the craftsmen and took
the credit for their work. The Sistine chapel is the creation of Pope
Giulio II and he knew why he hired Michelangelo to execute it.

Colpa mia to ask a man who knows how to write (a craftsman of
the pen or of the words) to add his to the reproduction of paintings.
Sad world in which we live and involuntarily take part of the spirit
that reigns in it.

Dear Tom, you are of course free—as it honors me—to quote

Victor Hammer, *Thomas Merton* (1962); drawing for the tempera-on-panel portrait, 33 x 28 cm. This drawing was purchased from Victor Hammer by Rudolf Serkin. After his death Mrs. Serkin gave the drawing to the Abbey of Gethsemani.

Victor Hammer, *Self-Portrait* (1925); mezzotint, 9.7 x 7.7 cm.

Victor Hammer, *Miss Carolyn Reading* (1953); silverpoint, 23 x 16.5 cm. Carolyn Reading married Victor Hammer in 1955. This portrait is now in the collection of her nephew W. Gay Reading Jr.

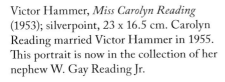

Victor Hammer, *Christ and the Adulteress* (1962–1963); tempera on panel, 53.5 x 84 cm. This is the fifth and last version of Victor Hammer's effort to tell a story by purely visual means. The images are a circle amid uprights, as he writes in *Fragments for C.R.H.:* "He gave no answer to the Pharisees but instead enacted a visual parable. With His body He had formed a circle—a circle that meant: do not accuse by remaining proudly separate, forgive by recognizing that you too are sinners as this woman is one, forgive and from your upright position bend down as I do, kneel down. But none of them understood His silent gesture and they continued to bait Him with the spoken word. Then He lifted up again and spoke the words that finally silenced them. And again He stooped down and wrote on the ground." The painting is in the collection of W. Gay Reading Jr. Photograph courtesy of the Library of Congress.

Victor Hammer, *Crucifixus* (1957–1958); tempera on gold-ground panel, 127 x 99 cm. This is the second of two replicas and is now in the Chapel of Our Lady at the Newman Center at the University of Kentucky, the gift of John R. Gaines. The first replica was intended to hang in the chapel in Alsace, which Victor Hammer was commissioned to create by his patrons Alexandre and Antoinette de Grunelius. The chapel at Kolbsheim was completed in 1935, with the exception of this rood. In 1957 the Hammers went to Kolbsheim to put the completed rood in place, but finding it too small for the space, Victor Hammer repainted it in a larger size, which now hangs in the chapel. The intended rood, the "first replica," was bought by the Abbey of Gethsemani for the novitiate chapel at Thomas Merton's request. It now hangs in the infirmary chapel. Photograph courtesy of the Library of Congress.

Victor Hammer, *Hagia Sophia Crowning the Young Christ* (1953–1956); pedestal triptych, tempera on gold-ground panel, 68.5 x 72 cm. Originally commissioned as a Madonna and Child by Carolyn Reading, it reached its final composition over the course of three years, considerably transformed from the initial plan. Victor Hammer writes (in *Some Fragments for C.R.H.*) "One day, Father Louis (Thomas Merton), our friend, came from his monastery in Trappist, Kentucky, to bring an ill novice to the hospital in Lexington. . . . We had prepared a simple luncheon and I welcomed him to sit with us at table. From where he sat he had a good view of the triptych on the chest and he often looked at it. After a while he asked quite abruptly, 'And who is the woman behind Christ?' I said, 'I do not know yet.' Without further question he gave his own answer. 'She is Hagia Sophia, Holy Wisdom, who crowns Christ.' And this she was—and is." It is now in the collection of W. Gay Reading Jr. Photograph courtesy of the Library of Congress.

Victor Hammer, *Resurrection* (1964–1967); unfinished pedestal triptych, tempera on gold-ground panel, 94 x 61 cm. This triptych was never finished because of Victor Hammer's cataracts, which increasingly compromised his vision. It is part of the Hammer Collection in the Art Museum at the University of Kentucky. Photograph courtesy of the Library of Congress.

The Kolbsheim Chapel (1933–1936), entrance, with figures sculpted by Victor Hammer above the door: *Adam and Eve* on the left, and *The Saints* on the right. This is a private chapel built behind the village church of Kolbsheim, Alsace, on the grounds of the château of Alexandre and Antoinette de Grunelius. It was consecrated as La Chapelle du Préciéux Sang de Kolbsheim. Victor Hammer accepted their commission to build a chapel to house the Blessed Sacrament between Masses, as the church was used by both Protestants and Catholics. Victor Hammer was responsible for all sculptural ornamentation and interior decoration, including the *Crucifixus*, which was not completed until 1957. Photograph courtesy of W. Gay Reading Jr..

The Kolbsheim Chapel, interior: crucifix, altar, tabernacle, candelabra. Photograph courtesy of W. Gay Reading Jr..

Victor Hammer and Thomas Merton at a picnic on the grounds of the Abbey of Gethsemani. Carolyn Hammer's Morris Minor is in the background, with picnic hampers in view. Photograph by Carolyn Hammer, courtesy of Paul Evans Holbrook Jr.

The Hammers with Thomas Merton, picnicking in a tobacco barn on the grounds of the Abbey of Gethsemani. Photograph by Robert MacGregor.

Thomas Merton in the living room at the Hammers' residence, 220 Market Street, on Gratz Park in Lexington. Photograph by Carolyn Hammer.

anything from my book, and thank you for the good words you had
for it.

In Christ yours,

Victor

For more than forty years I felt a gentle, but constant urge to give
definite visual form to a conceptual idea that is behind the story of
the woman taken in adultery, so succinctly told by St. John in his
gospel.[154] In the course of these years I have painted two complete
versions of this story, besides a great number of trial paintings,
unfinished and abandoned attempts to reach the final form. I have
now finished a third panel and with it I went as far as I was able to go
with my brush. Yet I have not uttered one word, I only used my brush
for making a drawing, a design, a graph, a gramma.—things which
ought to be seen and cannot be heard.

Beyond its decorative value the painting contains a message, just
as Christ's gesture of silently stooping down meant a message to
be understood by the Pharisees. The painting only perpetuates this
message. Christ reacts to the tempting questions of the Pharisees first
by a gesture that is not understood, then, lifting himself up, He raises
His voice and speaks in words. He does not dismiss the Pharisees, He
asks them an indirect question which they could answer only in one
mood—by turning away.

I read St. John's report in the gospel and painted the attitude of
the woman, the Pharisees and Christ's gesture. Christ speaks first
with a gesture, silently; then He writes and then He raises His voice
and after that repeats His gesture. But the message is never delivered
directly, the message which says in words: do not accuse—forgive. St.
John reported what he saw and heard.

Is it so difficult to see what Christ meant with His gesture, are we
blind, must we take recourse to words, to hear what He wanted us to
see? Addressing the eye again with the diagram which underlies the
painting, those who can see are seeing five separate vertical lines and
one undivided round line: the circle. Christ gestures first by stooping

down, then with His finger He writes on the ground, and finally He lifts Himself up and raises His voice. And again He stoops down and writes on the ground, and with all of that He communicates.

Whether intentionally or not, Ortega y Gasset does not mention this story in the note to the "Commentary on the Symposium of Plato," postumously published under the title of: The Difficulty of Reading. (Diogenes magazine . . .).

[Editors' note: Victor Hammer attached a short essay he wrote in 1950.]

"One day, back in the 1920's, as I started off on a short trip I slipped a copy of St. John's Gospel into my pocket. On the train I began to read. I read until I reached in Chapter VIII the familiar story of the woman whom Jesus refused to indict for the crime of adultery. When the story came to the point where 'Jesus stooped down and with his finger wrote on the ground,' all of a sudden I beheld a mankind divided against itself, each individual accusing the other, groups against groups, fighting each other with the help of law and prescribed punishment. There they stood, each one rigidly upright and alone, blind to the presence of God in their midst. The countenance of Christ, indicative only of his human appearance, tempted the scribes and Pharisees to set for him a trap after their own legal fashion. But Christ answers not. Rather he assumes a non-accusing attitude, stoops down and from an upright position moves into the circle, pointing with his finger toward the earth. The Pharisees do not understand his attitude; they do not see what it expresses, and continue to question him. Then Christ lifts himself up and gives the famous answer which silences them. Again he resumes his attitude, waiting until they are gone. Later he talks kindly to the woman.

"I was struck by the visual content of the tale: incredible is the congruity between the visible attitude of all the actors in that scene and their behavior. I realized the constituent elements of a picture, a clear geometrical pattern, a circle as against so many uprights. What could be more expressive, what more easily understood? Then I remembered Titian's painting which I had so often admired in the

176

museum at Vienna. And I began to wonder whether this painter had been blind when he read the story, or whether he had read it at all.

"I did not read much further on the day, for I had already begun to give the stirring message visible form. Thereafter I was haunted by the subject; and yet I kept silent about the meaning of my story, for I was curious to see whether other people had recognized or would recognize, what I had seen, would recognize it without the aid of verbal explanation.

"A number of sketches convinced me that it was necessary to provide the right setting for the figures. At that time I was much more dependent on direct stimulus from nature than I am now. Hence I started on a trip down the Italian peninsula, sketching in many places, until I found the cathedral of Siena to be the right background and the right setting to be the front steps. Following this experience I decided to move to Italy for a while. We settled in Florence, where I began to paint the panel. I showed it in a biennial exhibition in Venice. However, it was not really finished, and I did not like it. But after a few years I began a new version, this time it turned out to be much better balanced. The circle and the uprights were more determined; all the accusation was focused upon the movements of the hands of the actors. Christ became a young man with blonde hair, though I don't really know why. This version was exhibited at an international Carnegie exhibition in Pittsburgh. It remained in that town.

"I was interested to see how other painters had treated the subject. Though I made no extensive study, I did find from brief investigation that only a few painters had chosen this particular scene. Poussin and Michael Pacher painted it. Both were anxious to show Christ's face. Both made him point to where he supposedly wrote, while the bystanders watched him or listened to what he had to say. And again I wondered whether these painters had not got the content of the story only from what they had been told from the pulpit.

"My work at Pittsburgh was received coolly; yet no one asked the question I was so eager to hear. I remained silent but was ready to quote St. John's tale when asked. Was I seeing things? Or were the others blind?

"While still in Florence, I made a sketch of a coronation of the Virgin. I intended to treat it as a separate picture, but once I had made another sketch with the coronation above the scene of the woman taken in adultery, there was no question that it somehow belonged there. At that time I had a pupil who owned a life-size mannequin; he draped it as a model for me in the position of Christ holding the crown. Several times, on the way to his studio with me, this student tried to dig out my ideas about the meaning of the combination. I grew cautious, and said that I attached no special meaning to it, which was not untrue, since the coronation just happened to fit the panel. Whatever story I might have painted there would have done the job, that is, repeating above the oblong square the figures on the bottom. Therefore I refused to attach a meaning to the new picture, after all it existed only in my head and in a few rough sketches; I authorized the boy to refute any interpretation as willful and arbitrary.

"Years passed, painful years. I emigrated to the United States, for I could not stand the idea of being claimed by the Nazis as a Teutonic painter. Before I left Vienna, I had tried to paint the version of the two themes together; yet I never finished that either. Still I was not through with the haunting story, and several versions which I have painted in the United States are extant. Some of them are sketches, and some were at one time finished paintings which I destroyed afterwards; only remnants of them have survived. In all of them the combination with the Virgin is discarded, and only the upright and one circle are stressed.

"At the end of the year 1949, a part of my belongings arrived in Lexington from Austria, among them portfolios containing my old sketches and drawings. Friends wanted to see them; and when I moved into the old John Hunt Morgan house and had plenty of space at my disposal, I complied willingly. One evening I showed drawing after drawing, together with those I had done in Lexington. When I looked at all these sketches, among them the first drawings for the adulteress, I resolved to try the subject once more, this time with the coronation. But I kept silent until I found time to begin the new panel. It is now finished, and now I believe I have been granted success. I feel that I cannot go further, that the visual part of the theme is definitely stated, and that only now I understand my own work.

"Through the thirty years stretching from the inception of the picture to its completion, apparently not one of those who saw it was ever awakened to the visual power of St. John's story. And to my knowledge no one else has commented to that end upon the story in the Gospel. In fact, that aspect of it which I have treated in my picture seems not to have been touched upon. Only careful readers of the Bible may be aware of it. People who, in front of my picture, were articulate enough to ask such questions as: Is that kneeling figure Christ? And what is He doing? Does He write? And what is it He writes? seemed as intent upon knowing about Christ's activity as a writer as they seemed blind to everything else. The eye served them only as an organ of reading. It is only too true that language, though an isolated and unique form of reality, distinct from all others, represents for the great majority of mankind almost the only existent reality.

"Since my painting is now finished and the visual part of the theme definitely stated, I might as well venture to try, in terms of conceptual thinking, to open the eyes of a few.

"In the story, as told in the Gospel, Christ realizes that he is facing a trap which the Pharisees are trying to spring on him. He knows also that there is no legal, that is to say, no verbal answer; so he remains silent, stoops down and points to the earth on which all of them stand. It is a gesture, a language directed to the eye, and as such perfectly understandable, especially to Mediterraneans, who even today are not infected by Anglo-Saxon restraint.

"The Greek text reads: 'He stooped down and with his finger wrote on the earth.' Of course this is a translation and the words *GE* and *earth* have a different background; so have *graphein* and *to write*. Many years ago I heard the famous Adolf von Harnack lecture on that very subject. The title was something like: 'Christ's writing as recorded

in the Gospels,' and among the *writings* was that from St. John. I
do not remember anything, except the trite statement with which he
concluded his lecture: 'We do not know what he wrote.'

"But did Christ write at all? Did he write in the sense that we use
the word nowadays? That is to say, did he write words on the ground?
The Latin text uses the verb *scribere;* but the Greek text, which I
have incorporated in my panel, says: *to daktylo egraphen eis ten gen.*
The word *graphein* originally did not mean writing words. It meant
scratching, scratching signs into something. The Greek of the Gospels
is very different from the Greek of Homer and Hesiod, because many
words changed their meanings during the centuries. Yet the original
meaning of *graphein* was still in use, along with other meanings, and
could be here intended.

"In the light of my experience this story has mainly a visual
significance. Christ gives no verbal answer, but uses an unexpected
language a gesture: he makes himself round, indistinguishable,
undivided. He stoops down, points to the earth, which knows no
sin, and scratches it. St. John, the messenger, reports what either he
or his informant had witnessed. The dialogue is rendered verbatim.
In addition to that, Christ's gesture is recorded, and also the
important fact that he repeated it. The word *egraphen,* having still
several meanings, does not necessarily imply that Christ wrote words
on the ground, as we would write words into the sand with the
finger. The recorder of the instance interprets Christ's gesture in his
own way, not as an artist but as a reporter. This is natural enough.
Yet, while seemingly disregarding its meaning as I understand it,
which is to demonstrate to the Pharisees that they should not go
on accusing others but should turn their eyes inwardly towards
themselves, he has, on the other hand, recorded like a photographic
lens what actually happened and what only Christ could have done.
There is still the possibility of assuming that the reporter understood
Christ's gesture rightly, and purposely refrained from explaining it,
knowing perhaps too well that it is not for mortals to make the blind
see.

"The plastic arts have a medium of expression peculiar to themselves. So has poetry, for poetry does not use language in the ordinary sense. There is, however, an experience common to both arts which the following quotation from Norbert von Hellingrath's foreword to his edition of Hoelderlin's poems effectively reveals. He says: 'Hesitatingly, and only as I became aware that it could be useful even to those well versed in Hoelderlin, I decided to add explanatory notes [to the content of the poems]; for, it is always a resignation to discourse about the meaning of something unsurpassedly said, and almost dangerous in this case, because we are only too readily inclined to mistake a poem for what it conveys in words.'"

V.H. 1950

Oct. 3 1963
Dear Victor

Thanks for your good letter. I am back in the monastery and getting along fairly well. It will be slow.

Yesterday I finished *Art and Anarchy* and am returning it.—really an exceptionally good book. All the essays were solid and full of new insights (or old ones perhaps that had been forgotten). I particularly liked the one on "Art and Mechanization," a topic that is too seldom regarded as presenting problems. I know how much you are concerned with this. It is very good about the dangerous implications of things that everyone takes for granted (Skira books on painting!) precisely because they are "good" (technically). These things need to be said. Yet he never gets into a mere dirge or Jeremiad, and this is good too. Thank you for the book.

When can you come again? October 26th might still offer nice weather. November 2nd is possible but not good. November 9th and 16th are also possibilities. I think I will not at that time be mourning over my shoulder—at least I hope not. It is doing well enough.

The people at Bellarmine are starting some sort of collection of things by me and want to exhibit something—they might want to *borrow* the painting. Fr John Loftus may get in touch with you about it.[155]

With best wishes always to you and Carolyn.

All blessings, in Christ,

Tom

☙

October 31, 1963

Dear Victor

This is just a reminder that our monastery timetable is changed and I will expect you at 11.15 Eastern Standard Time, Saturday [November 2, 1963]. I suppose you would be coming at that time anyway. Looking forward to seeing you and Carolyn—

Blessings—in Christ

Tom

☙

1963

Dear Victor and Carolyn:

Here is Victor's text, and my own piece on Shakertown,[156] as I promised yesterday at our very pleasant encounter. I still don't know what Jubilee will do with the Shakertown piece but I see no reason why it should not be printed privately, and I could do some editing on it. As a matter of fact, if this is to be printed in connection with the restoration of Shakertown I could go a little more fully into the history.

Bless you always, in Christ,

Tom

☙

Nov 9, 1963

Dear Victor:

I shudder at the thought of attempting a long didactic poem on art. Yet who knows, someday it may happen. I generally end up doing what I never expected to do, and I suppose that is a very good thing. However, I am firmly resolved to do anything but this at the moment.

Of course one could approach the subject of art as a way of "knowing" and seeing. You sometimes cannot see a thing at all unless you take pains to make something like it. And yet not like it. Nothing gets to be known without being changed in the process.

As to saying "what is art," well, I don't think there is much chance of making any sense out of the question if one is looking for a pure essence. On the other hand the question is not without *meaning*. It is a matter of communication, not of discovery: not of defining the thing and getting command over it, but of clarifying one's own concepts and conveying what one means, or does not mean.

After all, one has to be able to say that abstract expression is *not* art, and I think that clarifies most of what needs to be said about it, both for and against. That is precisely what is "for" it: that it is not art, though it seems to be. I know this statement is scandalous, and I think the ambiguities are bad ones in the long run (it should not pretend to be art, which in fact it does). I do not think that throwing paint on canvas and saying "this is not art" merits twenty thousand dollars. It is too obvious. However, even the obvious has its place.

If I write a long didactic poem on art it will certainly not be about this.

Best wishes to you both, always,

With all blessings,

Tom

I keep thinking about the Shaker project, and wonder what Carolyn thinks of the article.

30 November 1963
Dear Father Louis,

We are so sorry to have kept this for such a long time; but, three people on the Shakertown committees read and kept it to talk about and it had just recently been returned to me.

First, they want to know if they would be permitted to have two copies of this made in order that all board members could read it? (They—the three—were very 'moved' by it and feel that nothing yet has been written to so bring out the ideal and spiritual qualities of the Shakers.)

Secondly,—if Jubilee publishes it, could off-prints be obtained, and under what circumstances as to copyright, etc.?

I, for the time being, can serve as a go-between.

Victor and I so happily recall our last beautiful day at Gethsemani—the country is so lovely. I am ready now to bind the copy of Victor's book and he will send it to you soon; he is stitching away as all of our other binders are too occupied until after Christmas. Stanley Morison[157] was with us the other night (by courtesy of IBM). He has asked Victor to paint a Resurrection.

Sincerely yours,

Carolyn R. Hammer

Dec. 4, 1963
Dear Carolyn:

Jubilee has run off offprints in the past, on occasion, but they have not done so recently. They might provide extra copies, but on the other hand if the Shakertown committee is sufficiently interested to share in the expense, he might do it on this occasion. I would be glad if he did, as I could use a few myself. Why not have someone write to him from there, and I will also mention it in my letter to him. The article is to appear in the January issue so there is not much time. Some of my photographs of Pleasant Hill will be with the article.

Write to:

Edward Rice, Jubilee, 168 East 91st St., New York 28.

Certainly I have no objection to copies being made of this. I can return the text you sent me if they want to copy it there. Too bad I did not mimeograph it here, but now we are in the Christmas cheese rush and I can't detach anyone from the crew to do this job at the moment.

If they want to mimeograph it they are perfectly welcome to. That might be a solution if Rice does not want to make offprints, though that would be better as pictures would be included.

Yes, your last visit was so pleasant and the conditions were so fine. When will you come again? When can we plan on so nice a day? January is variable, but we might risk it. The only time so far that would be excluded would be from the 18th to the 25th when we are "on retreat." Do let me know. And let me know if you want the Shakertown mss back for someone to copy in Lexington. I have still another copy here, so I will not be inconvenienced in any way.

The Resurrection painting sounds exciting. A great idea and I am very happy about it. May it prosper. All my best wishes to you and Victor.

Cordially yours in Christ,
Tom

❀

10 Dec 63

Dear Father Louis, we have written to Mr. Rice of Jubilee asking him about the offprints (and just a few minutes ago the dialogue, your 'remarks' or statement, & the Shakertown piece arrived in the mail). Thank you on our behalf and on behalf of the library and on behalf of Shakertown! I am having the latter (Shakertown) copied today and will return the original to you. We will also check the titles which may be of interest to you and send those if available. I am glad that you work on Cusanus. Victor asks me to say that January often has very propitious days for journeys (though our oracle with meteorological instruments is never dependable). Rather, we would sniff the air ourselves and then write for permission to come.

Sincerely,
Carolyn Hammer

❀

Dec 10, 1963
Dear Carolyn:

Here is the Shakertown piece for xeroxing. And I have added a couple
of other things.

Do you by any chance have any of the following books available,
and if so could I borrow them, please?

Jules Henry—Culture against Man
E. Rice—Renaissance idea of Wisdom
K. Jaspers—Way to Wisdom
Kristeller—Studies in Renaissance Thought and Letters.

All would be useful for Cusanus. You will see I have made a small
translation of one of his works, and as next year is his centenary I
might try to do a study on him.
    Best wishes to you and Victor,
    Most cordially in Christ,
    Tom
Extra copies of the mimeos are for the library.

❧

13. XII. 63

Dear Tom, Carolyn wrote about Stanley Morison and his suggestion
to paint a Resurrection. I am already making sketches and will soon
start on the drawings. The only thing which bothers me is the white,
red crossed flag which appears in all the paintings; Christ arises with
the flag out of his tomb!
    Grünewald combined Resurrection and ascension and left out the
flag. So did Michelangelo in his drawing. Is the flag really necessary
and what does it mean? Indeed it seems to me puny, if not outright
silly, Christ carrying that flag. It seems a very late invention, and not
of the best kind. Please let me know your attitude toward this.—We
would like to come in January. Carolyn is overburdened, takes things

seriously that others simply shrug off but she is that way and it can't be helped. It would certainly be good for her to take a day off for the trip to the monastery but it takes one more day off her duties.— So let's wait and see. I am reading Pascal, wonderful prose, but he wants everybody to be a saint, and that simply will not do—and certainly would be dull. I often think of you and what you mean and are for us.

God bless you and you bless us
In Christ
yours Victor

☙

Dec. 18, 1963
Dear Victor:

Thanks for your good letter: I find you much more scrupulous about the treatment of religious subjects than most artists would be. In fact the use of the "vexillum" or cross-flag in the iconography of the Resurrection is not common these days. I suppose it is a late medieval motif, suggested by the Crusades. In any event there is no reason on earth why you should even give it a second thought. The flag is simply a sign of victory, and I suppose it means that the artist wants you to recognize the resurrection, in case the tomb does not look sufficiently like a tomb. There are certainly other ways of doing this.

Today is a bright snowy morning, and it helps make one ready for Christmas. I hope that January will bring us some nice days. The middle of the month is out of the question for me, (from the 18th to the 26th) because then we are on retreat and incommunicado. But in any case, things will work out and we will be able to get together in due time. Just let me know when things seem convenient for you, and we can plan something.

I like Pascal, and of course he was a fervent devotee of Port Royal where they took the spiritual life seriously. I wonder if I sent you the meditation on Julien Green?[158] I enclose one, it may have something in it of a sardonic comment on that background, but on the other hand I have no notion of saints being dull. It is only the pseudo saints that are oppressive. The real ones, from what I have read, are exceedingly lively. Of course canonization manages to wash all the liveliness out of them and reduce them to safe limits, so that the bien pensants will not be disturbed.

I wish you all the best of everything for Christmas. May the joy of the season be fully yours. My blessing to you both, and I promise special prayers on that day.

Most cordially in Christ,

Tom

❀

I. I. 64

Dear Tom—I have read your paper on Green's book again. Since I don't know the book your remarks about it relate—with me—to a kind of void, and though your criticism may be consistent, it is—for one who does not know the book—not solid, and the meaning of Saint Sulpice escapes me entirely.

But when you talk about Mercy and that Grace is "inconsistent," it is, at least it is to me, as if a light would shine, as if truth would appear in all her glory. She speaks through you, and there is no question that you say the truth.

The funny thing about your paper is to me that in my writing Carolyn always wants me to be consistent, especially about (at, or with or in) the tenses, which I rarely am. I accept her criticisms for I can hardly prove that 'inconsistency' is a virtue—for it is not consistent.

As to Pascal I hope I did not say that Saints are dull, for most of them, if not all, were sinners before they became Saints. I meant to say that a community of Saints *on this earth* would be almost unbearably dull. Is Pascal humorous when he so aptly describes human follies? May be that this is his way of being comic.

There is only one Saturday left for us to come before the 18th (the

11th). The next is Feb. 1, and with all that snow we are hesitating, though we badly want to see you again.

Pazienza, e ci vedremo

In Christ yours

Victor

❀

Fri. 3rd [January 1964]

Dear Victor—

It is warmer today and it may be warm next week. Why not gamble on Saturday the 11th as a good possibility. If it gets very bad you could call it off. I will expect you and Carolyn on the 11th unless I hear otherwise—good?[159]

In Christ

Tom

❀

10. III. 64

Dear Tom: the 21st would be fine but in case of bad weather, either snow or rain, we would not come and you will be able to judge this event at the morning. Rain meaning that kind of weather we have now.—Would it be all right to bring a friend of ours, a man who regularly comes to Gethsemani for a retreat: Dr. Edmund Pellegrino[160] from the Medical center. He is a competent Latinist I am told and I believe it. You may talk Latin with him. But I am not sure he will be able to come, but in case may we bring him?

thank you

In Christ yours

Victor

❀

March 13 [1964]
Dear Victor

I will look forward to seeing you and Carolyn on the 21st, a week from tomorrow. If you bring Dr Pellegrino that will be fine. I hope the weather will be all right. If you are not coming perhaps it would be simpler to call and leave a message with Bro Bernardine.

All the best to you both, in Christ
Tom

❧

Friday [March 28, 1964]
Dear Victor

I look forward to seeing you and Carolyn on the 4th of April at the same time and hope the weather will be as it is now!!

Happy Easter.
Tom

❧

April 11. [1964]
Dear Victor.

I was not sure if you and Carolyn would come today, it would have been a fine day. Can I expect you on the 18th? The 25th might still also be a possibility but the 18th is better. And it is long since you have been here. Hope to see you soon!

Blessings in Christ
Tom

Did you get the note I wrote about 10 days ago?

❧

Monday [April 14, 1964]
Dear Victor—

Your note came today and I will expect you soon on the 18th—next

Saturday.[161] I hope the weather will be good. I am glad the angel lifted the stone and since he has done it you do not have to. So you can rest. See you Saturday.

    Best wishes, in Xt

    Tom

You sent your note to Bardstown and it was delayed.

June [1964]

Dear Carolyn:

As I am today sending you some books on Yoga for the library I will also put in this note a word about the next possible visit, in reply to Victor's welcome card of Le Douanier Rousseau (whom I certainly think classical and very fascinating in every respect. One of my favorites).[162] Victor spoke of coming down soon: at the moment things are bad as this is a crowded time of year for me. I hope things will be better toward the end of June. How would June 27th be? I don't suppose you would want to drive on July 4th which is the next Saturday. Is June 27th all right, or is July 11th altogether too far away? I think it is, myself. I hope you can make it on the 27th. Please let me know. All the best to you both.

    Blessings in Christ

    Tom

16. VI. 64

Dear Tom, Carolyn gave me your letter you wrote to the library. Though the 27th would be possible, we must refrain from coming since I shall be operated on Monday 29th or Tuesday 30th, removing the Cataract. Dr Tounes in Louisville will do it and it will take at least 10 days at the hospital. Perhaps you have a chance to come to Louisville too, library or doctor's checking up? We will see what happens. I am looking forward to that operation, and the slow diminution of my eyesight being stopped. Pray for your friend.

    Victor

✿

June 20, 1964
Dear Victor:

I am sorry to hear you are having an operation and that on this
account we will not be able to get together next Saturday. I do not
know if I am going to be in Louisville at the time while you are
hospitalized, but if I am I will try to see you. What hospital will you
be in?

I shall pray that everything goes well. I hope all will be most
successful and that your vision will be greatly improved. Best wishes
to you and Carolyn, and let me know when you will be well enough to
travel down here. I think almost any Saturday in August will be good
for me.

God bless you always.
in Christ,
Tom

✿

3. VIII. 64

Dear Tom: now, with the help of a magnifying glass I am able
to write. The operation went according to expectations. Today
we take it as a matter of course but still, I can't help seeing the
healing power as something of a miracle and, let's term it—the
hands of God. A grace, not a merit. Next week I go again to the
hospital for a hernia operation and then, I hope I have a few years
ahead for praising God by the works of my hands.—This occupies
at least the first half of the month and I think we cannot plan
to come before the 22nd or the 29 of August. I so badly want to
see you and talk to you, as I have a Latin project in mind—all
my projects due to the hoped for new eyesight (expect my new
spectacles in 2 weeks time)—which I want to discuss with you.—
Fortunately I have your portrait just opposite my bed on the shelf,
next to the picture of Christ and the woman taken in adultery,

then my daughter's portrait. We did not see you since we came back from N. York.

Schluss und grüss gott[163]

yours Victor

❦

Aug. 5, 1964

Dear Victor:

It is good to see your handwriting again. This is a sign that things are going well and that you are recovering after your operation. But I am sorry to hear there is another one on the way. However, if it will be of some help, then that is good. I hope it, too, will be successful.

Will you be ready to come over on the 22nd? If so, that would be a fine date for me. The 29th is all right too, but less good. There is the 5th of September also, though that is Labor Day weekend. I do hope you can make it on the 22nd, and will be planning accordingly. We are now on our summer schedule which means that though still on Eastern Standard Time, we do everything an hour later. Thus while I can easily meet you at 11.15 in the winter, it will have to be about 12.15 in this season. In any case, unless I hear otherwise from you or Carolyn, I will look forward to seeing you at 12.15 on the 22nd.

Please thank Carolyn (this time I have spelled it properly) for sending the two reprints. I think I could use half a dozen more, if they can be spared. I believe the Shaker Foundation at Pittsfield wants to get reprints too.[164] If anyone corresponds with them, they can be advised to apply to Jubilee. It is perfectly all right, as far as I am concerned, if any number of reprints are made.

Your Latin project sounds interesting and mysterious. For my part I am working on Celtic monks.[165] They have some wonderful poetry, not of course that I can translate Gaelic but I read it in English when I can get it.

I am enclosing a note for Carolyn, in case she can find some books in the library for me.

With best wishes and blessings to you both,
Most Cordially in Christ,
Tom

❁

Aug. 5, 1964
Dear Carolyn:

Many thanks for the reprints. As I mentioned in Victor's letter, I could use half a dozen more, but it is not urgent.

I thought I had better add this on a separate sheet to you: these are some titles of books I have noted down and wonder if by any chance they are in the Library and if I might be able to get them: In many cases I do not have the complete reference:

Trenholme The Story of Iona, Edinburgh 1909
J. Chagnolleau Les Iles de l'Armor, Paris 1951
H.G. Leask Irish Churches and Monastic Buildings, Dundalk
    1955
WF Skene, Celtic Scotland, ii vols.
Von Derkheim The Japanese Cult of Tranquility
Renan La Poesie des Races Celtiques, Paris 1913
J.M Synge The Aran Islands
Waters EGR The Anglo Norman Voyage of St. Brendan, Oxford,
    1928

I realize that these may all draw a blank and will not be surprised if they do. But anyway there is no harm in trying.
Best wishes and blessings to you both
Cordially in Christ,
Tom
Hoping to see you on the 22nd.

❁

8th of August. 1964

Dear Tom—enclosed find a letter of Lexi Grunelius that might
interest you. We wonder who that martyr was and whether or not he
had the edition of the Stamperia. Tomorrow I am going again to the
hospital and I hope it will not last more than a week. Fortunately St.
Joseph's is in Lexington this time, not in Louisville, it makes things
so much easier. Again dear Tom, please enclose me in your prayers.

    yours ever
    Victor
Letter, please, return.

Aug. 12 1964
Dear Victor:

Perhaps your hernia operation is all over by now. I hope so, and hope
that it has been successful. May you have a good rest and rebound
in happy strength. After that I will look forward to seeing you and
Carolyn here some time soon. I will be eager to hear when it may be
possible.

Your letter and the letter from Lexi reached me. Actually, the book
that I sent to Clyde Kennard[166] was a copy of your Hagia Sophia, and
I know he was very glad to have it. He was then dying in a hospital in
Chicago, of cancer. He had been "framed" by the Mississippi police
for trying to register at Miss. State University, and had been put on
a chain gang and very badly treated though he already had cancer.
The story as I heard it was simply that he had been very pleased with
the book and that it had given him some joy in his last days. It seems
the story is becoming a bit amplified now. But still, it is good that
we are both able to think we have helped such a person and brought
something meaningful into a tragic life, which however was full of
meaning because of his own dedication.

I hear that Jacques Maritain continues in good health, and I am
glad of it. I have not heard from him for some time.

Please let me know when you will be well enough to come over. I think you must have received the letter in which I suggested a few possible dates. All best wishes to you and Carolyn and many blessings.

With all friendship, in Christ,

Tom

17 August 1964

Dear Father Louis,

Of all your request, only Waters, The Anglo-Norman Voyage of St. Brendan by Benedeit is available; this is on its way to you. We have an Engl. ed. of Renan, *La Poesie* . . .—shall we send?

Victor is still in the hospital and very weak. However, these last two days he seems better. Actually the operation was more serious than we'd thought, and there was at the same time a foreboding happening to one of his eyes. It has not been too easy for him and now he may have to wait several weeks for glasses, if all goes well from now on. Therefore, all plans to bring him to see you are 'waiting.' He appreciated your letter. He will be at the St. Joseph's here until we know more—I hope within the week. I am back in the library for the first time today.

We hope all is well with you and the Celts; worthy subjects of interest.

Sincerely,

Carolyn R. Hammer

October 14, 1964

Dear Carolyn:

I have not heard from you or Victor for some time, and am writing to find out how Victor is getting along. I suppose that he is slowly recovering and that, inevitably, one cannot expect him to be able to get around so easily. But I do miss you both and it is a long time since we have been able to get together. Is there any chance? I admit, November is not going to be too good for me, as it is rather crowded, and from December on there is not much good weather. I wish there were some way of my getting over there. However, since I cannot come in person I send a photograph. It is by no means such a "presence" as Victor's painting and is considerably less spiritual.

All summer long I have had trouble with the skin of my hands, beginning with what seemed to be poison ivy and going on with some kind of dermatitis for which there seems to be no satisfactory cure. It is a little better at the moment, however.

Do you know that Marco Pallis[167] is coming with a small group of musicians to this part of the country? He is stopping off here on the way from Louisville to Berea, on October 24th.[168] They give concerts of ancient music, as you probably know. You might be interested in hearing them. I hope they may play something for us here, but am not yet quite sure how it is to be arranged.

Please let me know how Victor is and if there is any chance of our getting together. It has been so long since we have had a chat, and I hope one way or the other we can meet.

Very best regards to both of you, and all blessings.

Most cordially in Christ,

Tom

❀

October 28, 1964
Dear Carolyn:

The other day I finally mailed back Leopardi, and perhaps you have him again now. It was with great regret. But I am afraid I just see no way of getting around to those translations, so I might as well face the fact. Perhaps some time in the future.

Fortunately I have some good news: the book on peace, much changed, but perhaps improved, will finally appear in the new volume (with other articles) that is coming out soon.[169] So it worked out after all.

Do you by any chance have in the library, either in French or in

English, a book called "Logique et contradiction" by S. Lupasco?
And would it be possible to borrow anything by Ionesco that you have
available.[170] I am interested in some of his plays but also in essays he
may have written. Preferably in French. I know there might be a run
on this stuff, since it is mad, and all that is mad is popular. I would
promise to get it back in short order.

I do hope Victor is getting along, and hope to hear some good
news of his progress.

Cordial good wishes to you both and all blessings in Christ,
Tom

30. X. 64

Dear Tom: Today is the first day that I don't feel so weak as I did until
now. That is why I couldn't face even writing a letter. My phlebitis is
also much better. Nothing new in my life except waiting for recovery.
I have given up—at least for the moment—my project for Latin
proverbs or sentences to print them with exact accents and English
translations, but who knows I might come back to it. I am already
working to gild the base for the picture of the Resurrection. This is
not exerting my physical abilities. Getting back some strength is now
the aim. I miss so much our visits to Gethsemani, and, to say the
truth, your company. Whether we will be able to come before the end
of the year is still a question—and no chance of seeing you here for
an hour or two. At the back of the picture of the Resurrection I will
write—in gold letters—a giving of thanks to God for the returning
of light to my eyes (my father died blind and I had already accepted
this sad fact for myself). In the Greek Anthology are several epigrams
of scribes who donated their tools to the gods at the temple because
a 'veil fell over their eyes' and they were unable to continue to write.
Anyhow my inscription would give thanks to God that He had
restored my sight. I thought of asking Robert Graves to write such
an inscription for me in Greek. But I wonder if you could compose
one for me in Latin. It could be quite long—or short, perhaps a Latin

poem. Think it over.—We were quite sorry to hear of your plight, you were too sure of yourself, regarding yourself immune to poison ivy and oak. But you seem to have recovered somewhat. So, dear Tom, forgive my long silence and please pray for my recovery as we will pray for yours.

In Christ yours ever

Victor

❧

Nov. 3, 1964

Dear Victor:

I was so pleased to hear from you and to know that you are at least fairly well, that though I am no Latin poet I immediately attempted a poem. Here it is. I do not know if it scans. All I can say is that I think it does. The lines are supposed to be hexameters. If you hear a strange noise it is the whole choir of Latin poets turning in their graves.

It is certainly good to know that your eyes are serving you well again and that you are working along as usual, or more or less so. I can well understand that things might be tiring to you and I hope you will not attempt a trip over here until you are sure that it will not be a burden. Meanwhile, perhaps something else might offer itself. We shall see. But we can be patient and look forward to our next meeting whenever and wherever God wills it to be.

My hands are still afflicted with skin trouble though I can use them all right. But it is a nuisance. I suppose I will finally have to take some tests and find out precisely what the trouble is and what is to be done. My assumption is still that poison ivy started it all, but I never heard of it going on as long as this.

If you should hear news of my exhibiting strange blobs of ink in Louisville,[171] ignore the information: it is not worthy of your notice. As always, my feelings about it are very mixed, but it was something that presented itself in such a way that I thought I could do it without harm to anyone. I think I have made plain to all concerned that I do not regard it as "art" and that they are not supposed to either. If that will help.

Today I did not vote for Goldwater, but I heard he had come out in favor of Mammoth Cave. Or perhaps for enlarging it?

With very best wishes always to you and Carolyn,

Most cordially in Christ,

Tom

A prayer of thanksgiving written for Victor Hammer.[172]

O Tu Pater splendoris Dator luminis
Ad Te gaudens precor restituto lumine
Da quaeso mihi servulo tecum perpetuam
Nox ubi non contristet corda vel umbra diem.

O Thou Father of splendor, Giver of light
To Thee I pray in joy, with light restored
Grant I beg to me Thy servant everlasting
Day in which no night makes sad the heart, and no shadow.

November 3, 1964
Dear Father Louis,

For once, we have the titles you wanted. If you don't have enough of Ionesco, let me know—we also have most of his plays in English translation.

We are most interested in the book on peace—when will it be available and from which publisher?

Victor is so-so. By now you have his note?

Sincerely,

(Mrs.) Carolyn R. Hammer

Head, Acquisitions Dept.

Nov 11. 1964
Dear Carolyn:

Many thanks for all the Ionesco. I am sending back Renan today. There are very interesting things in it but I do not want to keep it too long.

Do you by any chance have a book called "Strategy and Conscience" by Anatol Rapoport? It sounds very interesting and I would like to borrow it if it is available.

Best wishes always to you and Victor,

Cordially in Christ,

Tom

17. XI. 64

Dear Tom, we were so touched by the poem, it moved us to tears. Thank you, that is all, and the only thing we can say as we truly mean it. I have made a tentative drawing of the lines and would be very pleased if you could scan them as you feel it or know it. I have to learn it by heart. The copy is actual size as it would appear on the back of the panel. You can imagine what the whole thing, the picture and the inscription mean to me. Also your letter, for which I thank you very much. I realize the importance of subject matter, the material without which artists are lost, and nowadays are thrown back on 'self-expression,' a meaningless, empty substitute. But it obviously means going back to chaos from which a new order can spring—as I tried to say in the last paragraph of my 'Concern.' Thank you once more and I hope to see you, perhaps even this year.

in Christ yours

Victor

Dec. 4, 1964
Dear Victor:

Yesterday I asked Father Abbot if I could perhaps have an exceptional permission to get over to Lexington to see you. He said that someone is driving over to the doctor on Dec. 16th and that he would let me go with them and have lunch with you, if this were possible. So I am writing to ask if that would be a good day for me to come over for lunch? It is Wednesday. I think that if that day is impossible for you, if you can suggest another thereabouts I might be able to get a ride. But in any case I hope I can see you and Carolyn and have lunch in your fine studio, as monastic as any monastery, and in fact more.

For my part things are going quite well. There is every likelihood now that I will be able to live at the hermitage continuously. In fact I am already sleeping there and coming down for some of the offices and for my work in the novitiate, which still takes up quite a bit of time, but anyway in the night hours and in the afternoon at least I am in the woods and it certainly agrees with me. It seems to me that this is really what I came here for, at last, and that the community life has been somehow provisional and preparatory. However, we shall see what develops. Part of the agreement may end up by being a cutting off of contacts with visitors, perhaps almost completely. But as I say, we shall see. I will do my part and leave the rest up to superiors with their concept of how things ought to be.

Meanwhile I look forward to the joy of seeing you. I hope that everything will work out. If that day is no good, please just let me know any other day (except Sunday) and I will try to arrange something, but can't promise. Otherwise I hope to see you a week from next Wednesday, and will try to get there about noon.

Very best wishes to both you and Carolyn. Yesterday I sent a copy of the new book, which is not like the others in many respects. God bless you. Is it really five years since I was last in Lexington?

Cordial and warm good wishes in the Lord,
Tom

✺

Dec 5 [1964]
Dear Carolyn

Do you have this in the library and if so could I please borrow it.

> R.F. Goheen—The Imagery of Sophocles' Antigone—Princeton
> 1951
> Also perhaps R. Latimore—The Poetry of Greek Tragedy,
> Baltimore 1950

I wrote Victor yesterday about possibly coming to Lexington on
the 16th . . . Hope it will work.
All the best, in our Lord
Tom

✺

[December 9, 1964]
Dear Victor:

Fine: I shall plan to see you on the 16th, a week from today. I hope
that everything will work out all right. I hope to get there about 11.30
or 12. And will probably have to leave about 2, hoping to get a ride
to the doctor's office where the other Trappist will be, and then we
can take off at once for the monastery. It will be marvelous to see the
picture and the poem. I liked very much the lettering you sent.
All the best and all blessings in Christ,
Tom

✺

Dec 28, 1964
Dear Carolyn:

My friends at Stanbrook Abbey say they are sending an exhibit of
their printing to this country and that it will travel about.[173] I wonder

if they could get it to the library there at the U of K. Have they written to anyone there about it I wonder? I should be very interested in knowing about the possibility of its coming there.

I look back with great pleasure to my visit with you and Victor,[174] it already seems a long time ago. The trip by car is not pleasant, but it is worth the sacrifice to be there with you in that wonderful little house. Do please give Victor my best wishes for the New Year. I greatly enjoyed seeing the beginnings of the "Resurrection."

Do you by an chance have Edith Sitwell's "English Eccentrics"? I would very much like to have it if possible. And also a book by one Gunther Schwab, on technology or something of the sort, perhaps in French. You may not have this, but Victor may have heard of it in German. I would not want to try reading it in German, it would take too long.

Tomorrow I will mail back the three books of yours that I still have, or rather I will keep one more, Panofsky, and send the other three. Ionesco and Rapoport.

Best wishes to you and Victor and I hope the New Year will be happy and peaceful.

Cordially always in Christ,

Tom

❧

7.I.65

Dear Tom: I have read the 3 papers you left with us when we had you here, and I have read "From Pilgrimage to Crusade"[175] now for the second time. It is important, a gripping thought, for you imply—so it seems to me—that to attain peace and keep it is not in man's nature. That you see 'scientific research' and its natural fruits in the light of redeeming our 'sins,' and that we try to do penance by wandering not only on earth but beyond its limits is a sign that we realize that 'more sitting at home, meditating on the divine presence' is not enough for our time—this is what strikes as true and even new in your thought. If I weren't so weak and so engaged upon my picture of the

'Resurrection,' I would like to print this piece of yours.—In these days
Carolyn and I discussed another idea: of publishing reproductions
of my religious paintings: the crucifix, Hagia Sophia, Sta Notburga,
the woman taken in adultery, certain portraits with the cross in the
foreground. I thought you could write something that may open the
eye of the layman, for the subject matter is important in all these
things, indeed it is the prime mover in them. I am so glad that we had
the chance of seeing you here and I am very thankful to the Father
Abbot that he allowed you to come.

In Christ our Saviour,

yours Victor

I wonder about the title of your paper, it seems plainly historical—
which in a way it is—but there is so much presence, actuality in it
which one realizes only at the end. In fact, when I read it the first
time I almost laid it aside before reading it to the end. Should the title
not keep us on the suspense? In expectance.

Jan. 9, 196[5]

Dear Victor:

Thanks for your letter. I am glad that you liked the "Pilgrimage" piece
and I think you are right about the title. I will have to give it some
thought. A more complete text with footnotes etc. was published
by a magazine called "Cithara" at St. Bonaventure University, New
York. I had not thought about the title problem at that time however.
Marco Pallis also asked me to let him submit it to some magazine
in England, for which he himself writes.[176] Incidentally, I have been
trying to get the Columbia Record people interested in recording some
of the work of Marco Pallis' Group, called "The English Consort
of Viols." They must play a lot of things I would like to hear,
especially settings of sixteenth and seventeenth century songs. Does
the university library have a record collection from which one can
borrow? Perhaps not. I would be interested in some of the original
settings of songs by Edmund Waller[177] etc., if they exist and are

there. But I suppose this is rather a complex and difficult request. You can suggest it to Carolyn, but probably nothing can be done.

Certainly I would be delighted to write some notes on your religious paintings for a booklet of reproductions. I think it is an excellent idea. I would have to look more at the paintings to get my thought in order. We shall see what comes of the project. But I am certainly willing to get into it, though of course I cannot right at this instant. I still have a couple of prefaces and reviews hanging over my head.

Here are the best of the pictures I took, or rather two of them Carolyn took. They are not as bad as all that, in fact in every case I was disobeying the advice of the camera. So that just shows that one must not always bow to technology. In fact I am sure that if I did what the camera wanted and took the pictures with a flash, they would have been very stupid and insipid. As it is they seem to me to have a little character.

It was very good to see you, and it is good to hear from you. Your writing is as firm and regular as ever, and I am sure that working on the "Resurrection" will keep your hand in trim. It is a pity you can't print "Pilgrimage" it is something I would love to have in a booklet from the Stamperia.

Best wishes and blessings. Keep well. May God give you peace health and joy.

Blessings to both of you.
In Christ Our Lord,
Tom

❦

20. I. 65

Dear Tom: It is now certain that in April there will be an exhibition of my work at the North Carolina Museum of Art. Dr Bier,[178] the director, suggested that a short foreword by you to the catalogue would be a most valuable ornament attached to it.[179] Since, except for the portraits, most of my work has a religious character, even the pagan themes, you could avoid being taken as an art critic. The Crucifixus I have here, photographs of the chapel, Christ and the Moneychangers, Sta Notburga, Hagia Sophia, all these things would exclude the emphasis on the artist and the eulogy lavished on the man. The importance of the subject matter, the role of the artist as a servant, yet a master in his craft, would be things the public of today should be told. The priest, God's servant too, could, perhaps, resume again his neglected role as a mediator. Tempi passati [past tense]. I know I am an anachronism and my work too is of another time—perhaps one to come and I know my time may be not yet. I am silenced by my time and I was silent for the 25 years I am now in this country. I may be allowed to speak once more, tentatively perhaps, for, as Carolyn said, I cannot expect much, or anything of that exhibition. Yet I shall try and if you raise your voice too that public* which exists, but has no voice yet, may listen and be comforted. I enclose a few thoughts I have jotted down on the subject a few days ago, you may be interested to read them. I am working steadily on the 'Resurrection,' may be I can finish the painting for the show. Thank you.

In Christ

yours ever Victor

*pp. 13–14 of the *Concern*,[180] i.e. the chapter: On the cross roads

The anonymous Craftsman of the Middle ages existed in his work.[181] He was admitted to a guild only when he proved to be able to do good work and more or less consciously he worked for the higher glory of God. He was a member of a society that took care of him for what he contributed to it was in a sense religious and God did not care for profits so much as he cared for good or quality work. The mediaeval craftsman did not need publicity while today an artist who is not known does not exist, he too is anonymous for nobody cares for him.

The modern tax payer has no need for religion nor has he need for works of art. He is unable to commission one for he would not know what to commission. But as public conscience is still uneasy when it feels it neglects cultural demands it trusts the care of them to officials appointed especially for taking care of these demands. How futile. No temples then, no cathedrals and even bank houses need no longer the trappings of columns and gables. Architecture is turned over to the building engineer. So the artist is freer than ever he was before. Those who were patrons before turned into the completely anonymous, impersonal millionaire who foots the bills, but must be careful to make it clear that the acquired 'treasures' are paid for the cultural benefit of the 'public' (Mellon's case at court for evading income taxes). The public then is induced to see the works of art in the museum and is bent on learning about the artist, his unconscious life and its appearance on the canvas. Professors, university chairs on art, on its history, on individual artists, students, art books, philosophy of art, but almost no works of art, willed by the lay people and simply enjoyed by them at home. Reproductions, almost as good as the originals which are kept in the museums, the precious cemeteries of works of arts, to which the public is enticed to flock. There the visitors are counted and the attendance is taken as a sign of interest or of growing 'knowledge' about art. That good, cheap meals and ice cream are served is taken for granted. Thousands of paintings, of sculptures, of graphics, done by professionals, doodlers, amateurs, and plain lunatics—all 'art' and collected as historically interesting objects.—An artist transplanted from Europe 25 years ago goes to an art dealer. The dealer sees that his work has 'value,' but is not too sure whether he can rely on his own judgment, he must also consider his wife's opinion and her reaction to these 'works of art' which the artist refers to. The dealer kindly corrects him saying: Let us not talk about 'art,' this is merchandise for me and I will treat it as such. Well, these twenty or so panels, partly on gold ground and pain stakingly executed over years, partly commissioned but not accepted (fortunately) are perhaps not 'merchandise,' having no mercantile value, at least not for the moment. And the academicians of today will see to it that they remain unnoticed.

Victor Hammer (20. 1. 65)

20 Jan. 1965
Dear Father Louis,

I also write to you regarding the short foreword which I hope you can find time to do by mid-February if possible. The exhibition is scheduled for some time in April. Although the plans for the catalogue are just being made now, I gather that your foreword may serve as a key-note. Edgar Kaufmann[182] (unknown to us) has offered to finance the publication, so that there will be a number of reproductions in black and white and at least one in color. Dr. Bier thought also that someone would write about the portraits, someone else about the books, etc. In your foreword, the mention of Victor's gold-ground religious and mythological paintings would have emphasis. No one picture need be mentioned unless you want. Victor's letter and the notes he appends may suggest something to you. The paintings in the category above would, for your information, be: The Hagia Sophia triptych, John VIII (Christ and the Adulteress), the Crucifixus; the progressing Resurrection (with its 20th century soldiers guarding the tomb!), Saint Notburga, Mnemosyne and her Daughters, the Muses triptych, Aesop and Rhodopis; Mrs. Joseph Graves owns Christ Driving the Money Changers from the Temple—I don't believe you ever saw a photograph of this? She will probably lend it for the exhibit. I list these just for purposes of recollection. When V. wrote to you a few weeks ago about writing something concerning each picture for an eventual publication, he did not of course know what was planned for the exhibition. The two will not overlap; the other publication is the one we hope to do one day in color. I am happy indeed that there will be a catalog—a survey of all V.'s varied interests. I am writing to Lexi Grunelius about the chapel (there will be photographs of it)—perhaps either Lexi or Jacques Maritain would write something on the chapel as a 'place.'

Sincerely yours,
Carolyn Hammer

Jan 22. 1965
Dear Carolyn

Just a brief note to ask if you have any of these and if I might borrow them—

E. Wood—Zen Dictionary
T. Hasumi—Zen in Japanese Art
Baudelaire—Journal Intime (English or French)

I hope you and Victor are both well—Best wishes and blessings to both of you—
Cordially In Christ
Tom

PS After I wrote the above your letter and Victor's reached me. I will write the note, in fact I already have it on paper. It ought to reach you some time next week after it has been typed. So glad about the exhibition and all that goes with it.
T.

1 Feb [1965]
Dear Father Louis—

We received your notes 'on' Victor. Thank you so sincerely. V. is writing, but I wanted to say something too.
Carolyn Hammer

3. II. 65

Dear Tom: with your words you have silently embraced me, I feel the touch of your hand on my shoulder, so kind. We are tools in the hands of God, we have to remain sharp and true. It is a fine duty and is the only rewarding turn for what we do. You have sensed this and said it. However much or little we can give or rend, we ought to be content with the fact that we did not cheat and this too is no merit but grace.—Shall I thank you for what you said—or just be glad that you could say it—for this too is only grace.

In Christ our Saviour

yours ever Victor

6 March 1965

Dear Tom, V. is back in the hospital with another heart attack as of Tues. morning; however, this one not so severe but he will be in an oxygen tent for a week and then around in his room a few days before coming home. In the meantime, we have somehow managed to get the pictures, mezzotints, etc. listed and off with the help of two friends to do the typing. Now I am answering letters and getting other 'notes' to read. Yours of course was sent quite some time ago, but in re-reading the copy I had made for myself I came across this sentence which on first reading seemed clear—on second, not so clear. Would you check on page 2, lines 12–15:

> "One must first accept the tools and materials with which to become oneself quite real in choosing to do an authentic, etc., etc."

The phrase, *with which to become oneself quite real . . .* * is not clear to me. Do I need a little punctuation perhaps to help me out?

I am so grateful to you for having written this bit on Victor. It looks as though he will not be able to go to the exhibition—nor I—but I still plan if at all feasible to go down, just for a quick look.

And thank you so much on Victor's behalf.

Sincerely,

Carolyn Hammer

*If there is a change, please let me know and I'll send it to Mr. Williams in N.C.

March 10, 1965
Dear Carolyn:

I am sorry that phrase is not clear. Commas around "oneself" might help. One might change it to "attain to self-realization" except that this is pretentious and it is not really what I mean. But if you think it is more effective, by all means do that. I think the commas will probably make it less unclear.

In any event it was a pleasure to write these notes and I am glad to hear that everything is going along well, in preparation for the show. But I am not glad to hear that Victor had another attack. Still, as these things are to be expected, and as it is not too bad, one can be thankful for that. I hope he will have a good rest in the hospital. I am sending you some translations that might interest both him and you, and give him something to divert him in the hospital.

Talking about diversion, I never said how much I liked Hebel's stories. They have a completely wonderful tone and atmosphere, and one never gets tired of them. Thank you for the book.

Please give my best regards to Victor, and tell him he is as always in my prayers, as are you also. Best wishes to you both and God bless you.

Cordially in Christ,
Tom
By the way, do you have the following by W. H. Auden in the library?

—Letter from Iceland
—Journey to a War
—The Dog Beneath the Skin

Are they much needed, or could they be borrowed? I will soon send back the others. Many thanks for them.

21. III. 65

Dear Tom: I am sorry to bother you again with all urgent reply—here
is Maritain's letter, or rather his contribution to the catalogue, and
also Lexi's letter which accompanied it. There is also a translation of
Maritain's text and we are puzzled about the meaning (translation) of
the two words—romans—romane. Whether 'dépouillement'[183] and
'recueillement'[184] is translated well, as we tried to do, is also bothering
us. I have urged Lexi to give me his English translation but his reply
will come only in about 5–6 days. Lexi made also an error, for it is:
redimisti nos in sanguine tuo. Should you find the time to produce
your own translation of Maritain's text we would of course be very
happy, but we do not ask you directly to do it, as we know it takes
your time. So . . . I think I am improving, at least I feel well today
and maybe it was to my advantage that I had to face, and do, things
I usually leave Carolyn to do—washing dishes, cook meals—for she
had a terrific headache (she is already much better now). Tom—we
think of you, we are grateful to you, hope you are well.

Thank you
In Christ
Yours Victor

(our tentative translation into English)[185]

THE KOLBSHEIM CHAPEL

The Kolbsheim Chapel is filled for me with so many blessed
recollections and it is so closely connected with everything dearest to
my heart, that it is difficult for me to speak of it solely from the point
of view of art. Nevertheless, I shall say that Victor Hammer, with his
varied gifts and his honesty, has created here a work which achieves
an altogether special place because of its architectural dignity, its
simplicity and its humility. One thinks of the austere graveness of
Romanesque structures, but the restraint here is greater, and the quiet
proportion of the age of classicism is joined to the graveness of the

Romanesque. Everything in this chapel built of grey native stone promotes a spirit of meditation (and what a relief it is to be delivered from reinforced concrete, the hideous ruins of which, in centuries to come, will be a desecration on the earth). And the total effect corresponds to the three notes which, according to Saint Thomas, constitute beauty and which are so typical of the house and garden at Kolbsheim: Integritas, Consonantia, Claritas. I especially like those moving groups, carved in rose-colored sandstone, which form the tympanum above the chapel door. It is a perfect sculptural melody.

Jacques Maritain

(La sculpture expresses perfectly the theme given to the artist: the redemption by the sacrifice of the Lamb (redemisti nos in sanguine tuo); to the left, Adam and Eve ejected from Paradise, Adam consoling Eve by showing her the Lamb to which he points with his right arm extended—the Promise; to the right, the Fulfillment, the saints in Paradise singing the praise of the Redeeming Lamb—the canticle of All Saints.—*Note on the sculptured group,* A. de Grunelius)

March 24, 1965
Dear Victor:

Thanks for your letter. I was glad to get it because I had been thinking about you and wondering how you were. I am happy to hear that things are going better.

The note of Maritain is splendid and I am delighted that he sent it. Your translation, as far as I can see, leaves nothing to be desired. You are correct in your rendering of "roman" and you need have no misgivings about it. I am returning Lexi's letter and the copy of the Maritain note.

I have been pretty busy, and have had the usual series of slight mishaps, trouble with an eye which was accidentally injured and so on. There is a fair amount of 'flu about in the monastery and I seem to be getting a bit of it. But that is all quite usual at this time of year. Later, after Easter, I am hoping that J. will be down.

Did I send you the notes on the eremitical life I put out recently?[186] I think you might be interested. In any case, I enclose a copy, as I have plenty of them. Naturally this is the kind of thing I am most interested in at present.

Carolyn sent the books and they arrived safely this morning: I am grateful to her. And as for you, keep well and I hope you will progress quietly with your work. I keep you both in my prayers.

With my most cordial good wishes as always, in Christ,

Tom

April 18, 1965
Dear Victor

It is Easter morning and your Rood cross which has been veiled during Lent (according to our rule) is once again unveiled, and is once again a splendid and substantial presence. So naturally I think of you, especially as the fine catalogue of your "retrospective" reached me, with extra copies, the other day. Really your whole and unified work is a most satisfying achievement—much more than most men can claim. You have certainly no need for regrets!

As to solitude: I have had a quite "solitary" Holy Week, only coming to the monastery for the most important offices and never has Easter meant so much or been so clear. One *must* be solitary in order to recover contact with the same and ancient traditions. All my woes and regrets are to be traced to efforts to be "in contact" with the world and its movements (and I include "movements" within the Church!). So be thankful for your extraordinary solitude, for it is a most precious gift.

All blessings to you and Carolyn, in the Lord.

Tom

May 13, 1965
Dear Carolyn,

See we are very American Uncial on our stationery. I was sorry to hear Victor was laid up again and hope he is resting well. I got another attack of intestinal flu the day after the visit,[187] but it did not last, and did not spoil the effect of that wonderful day. I enjoyed if fully too.

Here is Chuang Tzu[188] whom I delayed sending—you can use any part of it you like.

Best wishes to you and Victor, and don't let him overdo things. But age is age and no one can change it—and it has its irreplaceable values too. I liked the Mumford[189] article on Gideon.

Cordially in Christ,
fr Louis

May 30. [1965]
Dear Carolyn

This Friday, June 4, I have to come to Lexington for some Ex. rays and tests. If I am lucky I ought to be finished by about 12.30, and might be free to see you and Victor and have a lunch[190]—on a simple scale as my stomach is upset. (Rice never upsets me however.) I cannot say definitely, but I will in any case call from the Doctor's and if you are not free or not there,—it does not matter, so do not make elaborate plans. But I would not want to miss another chance to have a few words with you and Victor. If you drop me a note as to where would be the best place to call, that would be good. I do not definitely know when I will finish at the Doctor's or when and in what condition he will let me go!

Best wishes to you both and blessings
Tom

June 23, 1965
Dear Victor and Carolyn:

Here is an uncorrected carbon copy of the complete Chuang Tzu ms.
I will need it back before too long, so what I suggest is this: that you
look through it and pick out the pieces you want, which you can copy,
and if you like I will proof read the copy to make sure it is all right. I
do not mean to rush you, and certainly you can take a reasonable time,
but I would like to have the ms. back say about the middle of August.
Would that be all right? I hope you find it fairly legible.

Things were quite unpleasant in the hospital but they found out
that the trouble was, as I thought, an infection. They gave me some
antibiotics which have cleared it up quite efficiently. So I am grateful
for that. I was kept very busy the morning I was there, and called you
before leaving, but you were not at home by that time so I assumed it
was too late to catch you and that you had probably gone to see your
new graduate.

I have very much enjoyed the Tao of Painting,[191] which I will send
back soon. Duveen is priceless. But I am afraid it has almost fallen
apart. Could I borrow your copy of Eric Gill on *Clothes*?[192]

Carolyn, I have here a copy of Giles "Confucianism and its rivals"
which you sent me. I have never been clear if this was a loan or an
extra that you wanted to get rid of. Could you please let me know?

Best wishes to you both, and God bless you. Any likelihood of
your coming over this summer?

All the best always, in Christ,
Tom

❀

July 65
Dear Victor:

I would not call these few the best. But as I do not have the complete
ms., I cannot make a selection. Perhaps when I get a copy back from
the censors. I think the butcher should certainly be in it. Why don't

we make a selection of all those that have to do with "art" in the broad sense, including the wheelwright, the fighting cock even, the woodcarver, the symphony for a seabird perhaps??? I could pick them if I had the ms. Thanks for the designer's name. We will be carefully considering the question.

Best wishes to you both and all blessings in the Lord
Tom

I am sending this collection of Irish poems,[193] which has beautiful possibilities for printing.

July 3, 1965
Dear Victor:

Here is something that might interest you and Carolyn: not to print necessarily (though you are welcome to if you like) but just to read. It is not proofread but I think it is fairly legible.

Can you tell me this: we need someone to help us design and get printed a book of photographs about the monastery.[194] Routine job. Is there someone in this area, Lexington, Louisville or Cincinnati, who would be good at this, and would also help us to get a good printer and especially a good engraver? He would have to be willing to come down here and talk over with us the material we have, which is good, and also help us with the printer and engraver and the business end of it. We are in a word publishing the book ourselves. We could also if necessary come to wherever he is and get together with him if required and if it would save him trouble. Any suggestions would be appreciated.

How are you? J. is pleased with the longer Chuang Tzu and since it is so big he has changed his plans a little. I am glad of this.

Best wishes to you both. Hope to hear from you soon. Keep well. And God bless you.

Cordially in Christ,
Tom

Aug. 28, 1965
Dear Victor:

Thanks for your very good letter about the Symbolism notes.[195] I
knew you would like them. I agree with your remarks on ornatus.
In the Vulgate text of Genesis on creation, God is spoken of as
finishing the heavens and earth *and* all their ornatus. I think that a
lot of the austerity so called of the moderns is just a pose in part at
least. But of course there is a justifiable, though perhaps not always
reasonable, reaction against false ornamentation. Well, in this as in
everything else, we are in turmoil today, and no one really knows the
full explanation, except that we can say it is a manifestation of sin: the
primal sin of hubris and of making ourselves the beginning and the
end of everything, collectively, as a race, and as individuals.

Well, one reason why I have not written is that it took time to
get all my affairs in the novitiate settled and move completely to the
hermitage.[196] I have been here in practically complete solitude for
a week now, going down to the monastery once a day only to say
Mass and get one cooked meal. I hardly see anybody, even in the
community. I can see that this kind of life is not altogether easy, but
it is what has been appointed for me by God and it is what I will try
to do to the best of my ability. I do not claim to understand all the ins
and outs of it, but I can see that it is a real and uncompromising task,
and therefore must be done, whereas for me what was going on in
the monastery was not, apparently, that much to the point, though I
cannot criticize anyone or anything.

I don't know whether this means the end of your visits over here, I
have not gone into all the details of that. I hope the door is still open
and I think it is, but I do not think we should plan anything right
away. I am sure there will be more opportunities. We'll see.

The writing, of course, continues.

One thing I miss, having had to change from the novitiate chapel
to another place for my Mass, I no longer say Mass before your
crucifix. I miss it very much, it had come to be a very important

element in my worship. Now I am in another quite different sort
of place, modern, in both good and bad senses, with one of those
twisted metal Christs they do these days (some brother made it) and
I am afraid the effect is not at all the same. I may have some taste
for some modern art but so far none of the so called modern "sacred"
art has made the slightest appeal to me. I think it is grotesque and
pretentious, for the most part, and a pose. I have no particular choice
in this, as this is the best place for my Mass according to the time at
which I say it.

I think often of you and Carolyn and wish I could see you, but
we must wait. My health is pretty good, and being in this hermitage
certainly seems to have improved it, at any rate. I will refrain from
eating too much of my own cooking, and thus be safe. Being pulled
this way and that in community was not much of a help and it is good
to get to a completely unified and primitive life. It is strange to think
that one is one of the few people in our society actually living such
a life today. Rather an awesome responsibility. Or not. I don't know.
God bless you. Keep well and rested. And work, and write when you
can.

All the best always, in the Lord,
Tom

26. IX. 65

Dear Tom: it seems to me strange that even you have missed the
meaning of the passage in the Vulgate; you quote—God finished the
heavens and earth *and* all their ornatus. It should read—God finished
the heavens and earth by all their ornatus—I have emphasized that
in my four dialogs. First on p. 3: architecture is 'mimetic' because it
tries to follow God's activity to 'build' a world pleasing to the sense
of the eye, to vision, by saying that it is now 'finished' ornatus, that
the time for being content with what has been done, that time for
rest, has come: sunday. "Beauty" cannot be defined as a noun, nobody
has ever been able to do that not even St. Thomas; 'beautiful' is an

adjective, integritas, claritas, consonantia, are not of the same quality, of equal quality. Beauty is not a composite of the three. When God creates beauty, for instance, in human form, the portrait painter has no chance to do more than to imitate, for he will be either forced to caricature or to 'sweeten' his model. And I know from experience how difficult a task it is to be true to the facts. p. 70: Actually, there is no difference between an ancient and a modern work of art as long as both are conceived by the eye in its creative capacity of seeing the three dimensions together, in contemplation. —To the rest of your letter I can only add—amen. Of course we will both miss the two or three hours of your personal presence, so plainly dear to us. You need not take this as a compliment to you, only as enjoying what you have received and are able to communicate humbly. But writing is still possible and will help out.

In Christ, our savior

Yours C + V

22. X. 65

Dear Tom: We miss your word since we are anxious to hear from you again. In fact you owe me a response to my last letter, though I do not ask for, I only would be delighted to hear from you again. This question of the 'ornament' is very important to me and I wish you would speak about it. It may even be that the word is translated carelessly and the difference between 'ornamentation' and 'decoration' not exactly considered. 'Ornament' is a very sincere matter and the idea of 'beauty' cannot simply be stated by the 3 words of St. Thomas. Perhaps no definition is possible at all, as one cannot 'define' God.—I send you essays on art by Huxley, hope you find interest in them. We are well and I can work; in fact a trip to Gethsamani would be possible if it would be permitted. Eremits could, I believe, always be consulted

Love, in Christ,

yours Victor

Nov. 2, 1965
Dear Victor:

Today I am sending you a copy of Chuang Tzu. J. certainly got this
one out fast. I have no doubt he will send you one too. You will see he
made a generous use of the books Carolyn lent us, for which I am very
grateful, and I hope they got back to you all right.

About "ornatus," I am afraid that I do not have much to offer in
the way of clear ideas. I know St. Thomas treats it somewhere as a
virtue, but I think only in connection with dress. More likely the
avenue to explore would be medieval metaphysics. For instance I
was reading a Cistercian of the 12th century who talks about the
accidental perfections of a being as being necessary to its full reality,
which is of course obvious in the case of anything created. My only
thought is that after all if we think of it, the mode which demands
an apparent absence of "ornatus" is itself in its own way a form of
ornamentation, i.e. an accidental style which adds a "character" of
some sort to the thing made. Ornatus in any case is not "ornament,"
hence I would say that strictly speaking even austere simplicity could
be classed as ornatus, for instance in Shaker work. However, I know
that this does not offer much light, and I must conclude that this is a
subject about which I know little. Whatever I may have to say about
it, if it makes sense, has already probably been said much better by
someone else: in this case you.

It would certainly be a great pleasure to see you and Carolyn, if you
could make the trip. I will see if something can be done to arrange it
at this end and will then tell you. Visits are supposed to have ceased in
principle, but of course some rare exceptions are still foreseen. If the
weather continues as it is now, November would be a good month. I
will try to let you know in a few days.

Meanwhile I will get the book in the mail. The hermit life seems
to agree with me. The complete isolation is a blessing, but it is also a
little difficult in some ways. However as I realize that this difficulty is

necessary for me, I do not mind it. And in any case, life among a large group of people has ceased to have any attraction for me whatever. Still less life in "the world."

Blessings to both you and Carolyn. Somehow I have had a hard time getting into the Eric Gill book and I think I must finally send it back without finishing it. But first let me see whether we will plan a visit.

With all affection, in Christ,
Tom

❀

Nov. 5, 1965
Dear Victor:

I spoke to Father Abbot yesterday about the possibility of his making an exception and permitting you and Carolyn to visit here as you did before. He said you could certainly come, so I am delighted. I do not know how much longer the good weather will hold out, so come as soon as you can. Probably you will want to stick to Saturdays as before, but any day is all right from my point of view. Perhaps next Saturday, the 13th[197] or the following one the 20th? The only day that would be not so good for me would be the 15th, Monday.

Please let me know if you are coming soon. I hope we will have good weather. If you come, just tell me the day and even if I do not reply at once, come that day because it will surely be all right unless I call you or send an urgent message. We will meet as usual at the gatehouse about 11.15. However, I will confirm the arrangements as soon as I can when you suggest a day.

How nice to think that we will continue to have our pleasant meetings out by the lakes or at the edge of the woods. I miss them.

With cordial good wishes always and blessings,
in Christ,
Tom

❀

Saturday [1965]
Dear Carolyn:

As I forgot to tell you the names of the two books on Rilke, I am
sending this along right away. It was so good to have you and Victor
here today and it was certainly as fine a visit as there has ever been. I
enjoyed it so much. It was good to see you both looking so well.

The Rilke books I need are:

W. Rose and G.C. Houston (eds) R.M. Rilke, Aspects of his mind
   and Poetry, 1938
H.M. Belmore, Rilke's Craftsmanship, Oxford, 1954

Also an idea occurred to me, for printing. Instead of my trying to
do a few more versions from Chuang Tzu, I thought I might send you
ten or fifteen pages from a notebook with material about the woods
and the solitude here. What do you think?

The lines from Goethe:

The True was found already long ago
It bound the noble spirits into one
Hold to the ancient Truth
Do not let go!

It really does say everything, doesn't it?

I do not know if Victor wanted that bill back, so I am enclosing it.

Again, thanks for coming. When you send the Rilke Victor could
also join to them the books he mentioned. I will be glad to have them.

With all blessings to you both,
Cordially in Christ,
Tom

Dec. 29, 1965
Dear Carolyn:

Today I am returning Peters, *Rilke, Masks and the Man.* As I
mentioned in my card I would like if possible to keep Mason *Rilke . . .
and the English Speaking world.*

Do you by any chance have the Leishman translation of the
Sonnets to Orpheus with the German text facing? I have no German
text of the sonnets. Even the plain German would be ok as I have a
translation.

Do you have E. Heller *The Disinherited Mind?*

Did the other Rilke books come back?

I would much appreciate any one of these if available.

Victor did not write or I did not get his "questions." Rilke is
interesting to me as the kind of solitude that should not be mine:
purely poetic. Not that it does not have a great importance, but it is
different from what I seek. Still, one must know Rilke. I wonder that
Victor does not like the Duino Elegies or the Sonnets to Orpheus:
they have a lot in common with the vision of the muses that is so
important in Victor's work.

Best wishes to you both for the New Year. I am kept busy
chopping wood to keep warm.

Cordially always in Christ,

Tom

PS. Could I please have a photo-copy of the last pages of the Peters
book—pp 185–194 inclusive—and let me know how much this is—
the abbey will take care of it. Many thanks.

10. II. 66

Dear Tom: Now it's warmer and I am happy that I have no longer to
think of you suffering the cold. Of course one can stand it when one is
younger. Thank you for the two mspts. you have sent, I began one but
was unable to finish for as you can see from the enclosed proofs that

I was not idle. I would like your frank criticism of the text. My main interest is still the typographic work. But this alone is not enough and so it has to be something worth printing. Is it worth it, or not? Today I am staying somewhat idle and will read what you have sent me. As to Rilke. He certainly was a poet and I have recently read a few lines of his which impressed me. But there is a certain funniness which you can't sense, not in his poetry but in the man which I cannot overcome. I will, next time tell one these stories about him. About your translation of the lines of Goethe there is that German tendency of making a noun of an adjective. Das Wahre instead of the truth, die Wharheit. In your translation you say 'the true' and then 'the truth.' I left it but Carolyn has printed it 'the truth' in both cases. Probably it makes no difference. Keep warm and you know that we love you.

Yours ever Victor

Feb 13, 1966
Dear Victor,

Not only do I like 'Pebbles'[198] very much but in many ways I think it is going to be your most attractive and articulate book and it must by all means be printed! Certainly continue with it. I am eager to be the next. I like the format as well as the idea.

When are you and Carolyn coming over? One of these next Saturdays might be good, don't you think? Just let me know in time. They are all good as far as I am concerned, though Lent would be a *less* good time.

As to Rilke—I know what you mean. He is a fine poet but I have grave reservations about him too. As prophet there is really something missing. One may however like the Duino Elegies in spite of these reservations. My reservations have been more seriously on the Orpheus Sonnets, and their 'Theogony.'

Best of wishes to you and Carolyn,
Cordially in Christ
Tom
What do you think of my French poem?!![199] For a broadside??

226

Mar 1, 66
Dear Victor

Many thanks for your letter. I would be glad to discuss the question
of your book and if it should go to J. (No harm in trying). The 12th,
19th and 26th are all right for me. 12th is the best. Let me know. I
will be ready any day you say, at usual time—11:15. All the best—
Tom

Dear Carolyn and Victor

I hope to get out of the hospital tomorrow (Saturday)[200]—The
operation was quite successful and though the first week was a bit
painful, things mended fast and I am feeling all right now. I am sorry
Victor had to go to the hospital again but I hope he is resting well and
improving now. Dr. Pellegrino did not come in—or if he did I missed
him. Don't worry I am doing well.

All blessings for Easter, in Christ
Tom
He stood in their midst and said PEACE

April 21, 1966
Dear Victor

I am returning your "pebbles" as you requested. Hope you are feeling
better again and can get along with them. J may come this way soon.
I am recovering, apparently, from the operation but all is not over yet
and I cannot do much work.

Do rest and keep well. Best wishes and blessings to you and
Carolyn, and warm regards always
in Christ
Tom

✿

May 6 [1966]
Dear Victor and Carolyn

I am sorry I could not come over with J and Nicanor Parra.[201] Too
much riding in a car is perhaps still to be avoided by me though the
back is slowly getting better. In fact J seems to have more pain with
his back now than I have with mine.

The weather is so beautiful it would have been wonderful to have
you here—perhaps we might think of some time in June. I will write
more about that at some other time.

So at this point I will leave J to bring you my very best wishes and
greetings—

as ever
In Christ
Tom

✿

May 20, 1966
Dear Carolyn

If you have in the library Walker Percy's new novel *The Last Gentleman*—
look at pages 26–28, a very funny comment on museums. Victor
might enjoy it though it might be hard to get into the crazy style
without an introduction. A good book. I have been meaning to write
but have bursitis in the elbow and my back is still sore so I don't write
much yet. How are you both? How is Victor? I think of you often,
maybe we can get together later in the summer.

My very best wishes and blessings to you both.
In Christ
Tom

✿

29. V. 66

Dear Tom we think of you and wonder how you really are. Perhaps still in the Infirmary? Let us know please. Would you like to have a dog in the hermitage? We have a very handsome charming one that we could give you.—I am still on my pebbles, now will finish that one on Henry Moore.[202] It is a mad world we live in and I am afraid you are not fully aware of it with the things you draw as an artist. Or are you? When could we come and see you?

In Christ yours Victor

June 6 [1966]
Dear Victor:

Many thanks for your good note. I was glad to hear from you and the news that you consider coming over is encouraging because it means you are feeling better. So am I. I am out of the infirmary for some time but still am limited in some activities, not however picnic by any means. How would June 18th[203] be? At the moment that is best for me as I may be caught with trips to the doctor on other possible dates. Or else we could think of July 2?? I am still not too sure about that but it is quite a good possibility. Let me know. As to the dog, much as I would like to have a dog I am afraid I am more occupied with keeping stray one away from here they make too much noise. But it is a nice thought. Best wishes to you both, hope to hear soon when you may come.

Yrs in Christ always,
Tom

21 June 1966

Dear Tom, the titles you wanted are being sent only in part—we have of Jean Grenier's work only:

L'Esprit de la peinture Contemporaine
Lexique

do either interest you?

Of the Briffault, there is another 3 vol. ed.—we are sending the
1-vol. ed. which is a 'condensed' version I gather.

Victor was so happy that he could come once again to see you; he
was very tired but this soon passed.

Sincerely,

Carolyn Hammer

22. VI. 66

Dear Tom: Here is a translation of Li Po's poem,[204] please send it back
when you are through.

We think of you and now it is our turn to pray for you and God
may heal you and give you the strength you need for overcoming this
attack. There is no other way

In Christ yours,

Victor

I wish that you had gone to Japan. Why not ask father Abbot to send
you now?

July 2 66
Dear Victor

As soon as I went to the book this morning it fell right open at—
our old favorite, the two elders who could not quarrel over the brick.
Erant duo seniores . . . Isn't that amazing?

So your letter is quickly answered. I am sending this special
delivery as you request and herewith 3 more call-slips for books—no
hurry I am still busy with the ones I have.

All blessings to you both—more later.

Faithfully in Christ

fr Louis

There were two men sitting together in a small apartment and they
had never had even the slightest fight with each other. One day one

said to the other: "Let's have a quarrel once like other people." The other man answered: "I don't know how to start a quarrel." Said the first: "Look, I put my body in the middle and say—this belongs to me—and you say—but no, it's not yours but mine—and that way we will get into a quarrel and strife."

When they had put the body in the middle, one of them said: "This is my property." The other one answered at first: "I hope, it belongs to me." The first one said again: "No, it is not yours, it is mine." The he finally answered: "If it is yours, carry it away." After having said this, they didn't find a way how to go on in the quarrel.[205]

July 11, 1966
Dear Victor

I am returning the "The Road to Shu is hard" after too long a delay. Forgive me. I have been behind with my mail and trying to catch up.

To my mind this reads well, my only criticism would be that often the word chosen is the weaker of alternatives. In line 12 for instance perhaps "bends" is a more usual and vivid word that "turns" for bends in a river. In 37 perhaps one should do more than just avoid tigers and snakes. I don't know of course what would exactly fit the Chinese original, but "watch out for" is a little more definite and concrete. Perhaps the whole text could be studied in the light of this, and the vocabulary could be tightened up, for the sake of the English reader. Reader of English I mean.

Everything is going all right with me, do not worry about me, except for details like bursitis and now a sprained ankle, I imagine I will survive and go on to other follies, and I am not disturbed.

When do you suppose you will be able to come back this way again? Should we plan something for August? It is a bit hot now, though we had a fine wild storm here last night.

Best wishes to you both, and God bless you,
Tom

Carolyn, thanks for the books. I would like to look at the two books you have of Jean Grenier[206] since he is important for Camus.

❧

18. VII. 66

Dear Tom, I was so happy to get your letter and am so glad to know that you are well and balanced.[207] We can come any Saturday, provided it is not too hot. But how to decide? It is really a problem.—I read your reviews of the Buddhist literature several times but cannot make sense of it at all.[208] It is probably my fault but I shall take the typescript with me and ask you specific questions.—I have sent about 45 pebbles, now *fragments,* to Laughlin. But Carolyn has started printing them and that is the 'ultimate reality' for me. Sometimes I am doubting still, but sometimes I think they are worth printing. At least they are a good pretext for printing.

 Always in Christ
 yours Victor

❧

July 25, 1966
Dear Victor:

Since the philosophical background of Buddhist thought is entirely different from our thought in the west, it is not surprising that the article on Buddhism seems strange, and it is certainly not "your fault." As to the Pebbles-Fragments, I don't see why you should wonder whether or not they are worth printing. Your views are just as much worth printing, I should think, as anybody else's, and the point is that they remind people that certain aspects and viewpoints are in danger of being overlooked. That they are being printed now is consoling to me as well as to you.

 As to your plans about "choosing a Saturday" suppose we do it this way. I need to know a couple of days ahead as I have to change the time of my Mass. If you call the gatehouse here on the Thursday and say you will be here the following Saturday (at usual time, about

11.15) then they can get a message to me and I will be ready. Can I expect a message this Thursday, saying you will be here the 30th? If not, how about the 7th? That will leave you the possibility of judging more or less what the weather might turn out to be. Perhaps a telegram to me on the Thursday would be even better. Messages are a bit erratic. But then everything is erratic.

In any case I will be glad to see you whenever you come.

With all my blessings and best wishes in Christ,

Tom

July 30, 1966

Dear Carolyn:

I will check down at the monastery to see if there was ever a message about you and Victor coming over today: it is certainly a lovely day. But one never knows what happens to messages around here. Since I have heard nothing I presume you are not coming.

Can you help me with some more books?

I have to review Edwin Muir's collected poems for Sewanee Review and I will need some background material: chiefly Muir's own *Autobiography*. Do you have this?

Also an important review of this book, Collected Poems in its earlier edition by Kathleen Raine in the New Statesman, April 23, 1960. If by any chance there has been anything about the book lately in magazines like the Kenyon Review and others of the same type, I would appreciate having access to them. Maybe you could obtain for me a Xerox of the Raine article, and the monastery of course would pay for it.

I just wanted to get this off while it was still fresh in my mind. Hope to see you and Victor soon on some such lovely day as this.

With warmest good wishes to you both,

in Christ,

Tom

I will return the Suzuki book soon.

Aug 5. 1966
Dear Carolyn

Thanks so much for your card. August 13[209] would be perfect for me, the 20th less so. Hence unless I hear otherwise I will be ready to meet you 11.15 Aug 13 as usual. Best regards to you and Victor

God bless you
Tom

Aug. 22, 1966
Dear Carolyn:

Many thanks for the Pavese books. I am well into one of them and he is a marvelous writer. I returned Suzuki on *Mysticism Christian and Buddhist.* I am not yet finished with Briffault, *The Mothers* which is marked for August 31. Could I perhaps have it a little longer? I notice that Muir's *Autobiography* seems to be marked for that date too, and I am still working on it.

Do you have these?

M. Harrington—The Accidental Century
E. Conze—Buddhist Meditation (I think I got that from you
	before).

If these are available I would be very happy to have them.

When would you and Victor like to come over again? I still do not know if there will be new arrangement about doctors, and perhaps it would be best to think of your coming here, say toward the end of September or the beginning of October. Please let me know what you think.

With all my best wishes and blessings to you both, in Christ,
Tom

23 Aug 66

If the Harrington and Conze titles are available, we will send them; also, please keep the Briffault and Muir as long as you need them. Victor is writing about dates to see when most convenient for you. He has also had a letter from Kolbsheim which he wants to tell you about: something a French priest wrote about the chapel.

Sincerely,
Carolyn Hammer

✿

Aug 23 [1966]
Dear Carolyn

In my letter yesterday I forgot to ask about books of, or criticism of René Char.[210]

I have his *Fureur et mystère* but anything else of his, or anything good about him, would be very helpful if you can get it to me. Thanks again

All the best always
Tom

✿

Aug 29, 1966
Dear Victor:

Many thanks for your note and for Lexi's good letter which I return herewith. Yes, I knew that Maritain was coming and I am delighted that he will be able to. I hope nothing gets in the way, as I look forward very much to being with him for a little while.

As to you, yes, by all means let us plan on something in September. The first Saturday is bad for me. The 10th, 17th and 24th are all right, and maybe the 17th would be the best. However, any of those three will do. Just drop me a line when, and I will expect to meet you at the usual time.

Have we ever spoken of Thomas Mann? I do not recall. I have

never really been able to get into him, but I see that I must quite probably read Dr Faustus. Do you know it? It is apparently a horrifying indictment of modern art and culture and probably a hair-raising book to read. I wonder if Carolyn could get it for me. If you want to look at it before she sends it on, fine. Or perhaps you would prefer to look it over in German.

Does she perhaps have in the library any poems of Miguel Hernandez?[211] A modern Spanish poet who died in one of Franco's jails. I am very impressed by him. Not to be confused with Menendez,—a Peruvian.

With all best wishes always and blessings in Christ,

Tom

As for my wasteland life, well a hermit is one who lives in the wasteland as an outsider but my cultural desolation is not total. There are books.

❀

Sept 20, 1966

Dear Victor:

I have tried my hand at translating the Goethe quotation: it is enclosed. I don't know if the result is very helpful, but it is about the best I can do. I suppose that you can adjust it to suit your needs if there is anything good in it.

Looking at the calendar I see October 22 will be quite a good day for me, as things are now shaping up. We might keep that in mind as the best date in that month, anyway. Otherwise perhaps the first Saturday in November.

Victor, I think that in all simplicity I owe you a few words of help and encouragement at this time when, as you said the other day,[212] "the last hour" cannot be very far away now. Since that is the most important part of a man's life in some ways, it is the duty of a friend and a priest to say something. Of course I know that there is a normal way of reconciliation with the Church—an official way. I am not going to talk about this as our relationship is not an official one in any case. But the fact of "reconciliation," however you look at it, is worth considering. When you are in fact a deeply Christian person and thinker (all your thought about art presupposes centuries of Christian thought on the subject it seems to me) it would be a pity for you to end your life in a kind of open rift with the Church, even though the Church has plenty of failings and limitations. It is as much a matter of you forgiving the Church as the Church forgiving you. However you look at it—and you may not for reasons of your own see fit to receive the Sacrament of the Sick and the other Sacraments,—I would say that there would be a definite point in affirming as well and as clearly as you can, in whatever way you can, your adherence to truths you have in fact lived by ("personal God" does not mean anthropomorphic God: but an ultimate Freedom which is infinitely creative and a source of all love and truth). In such a way as to say that you and the Church are not at odds on these truths and that it is your desire to leave this life as you have lived in it: with the total submission of your mind and heart and hands and all that you are, to the creative and loving source of all that you have ever loved, or admired, or striven for. I have no doubt that in fact you do this in your heart: if you can also do it in some more open expression—I leave you to think of this in your own way. I certainly think you have no obligation to do anything that would imply a repudiation of anything that has been of real value and meaning in your life. All that is good in our lives is from God. In any event, I will continue to pray for you as always and if you can in some way pray for yourself that is all to the good. With all my heart I ask God to bless you. Your friendship has been a great blessing, greater than I can say.

I did not mean to make this so long a letter, and I hope you do not think I have been officious about it. I just thought I ought to say what seemed to me important, and doubtless you have thought much of these things yourself.

All blessings to you and Carolyn.

Yours in Christ, always,

Tom

P.S. Turning to another question, that of Menendez: I think he and his work do not need to be discussed further in letters. I will clarify this next time we talk about the question.

> Long before truth has been known
> It has united the company of noble Spirits
> To ancient truth hold on
> Fast hold on to the ancient truth
> Truth long before has been known
> (German)

2. X. 66

Dear Tom, thank you for the translation, we will try it. In the meantime I have changed the word 'good taste' into 'good judgment.' Your letter moved me to tears, your friendship is so precious to me, it means so much. More I can hardly say and it took me a long time to say as much. I understand your anxiety. That I must leave Carolyn one day occupies my mind more than anything else. Meanwhile we are happy to have each other, and are working—for the higher glory of God—the best aim one can have

Love, yours Victor

Oct. 8, 1966
Dear Carolyn:

Many thanks for your note of the 3rd telling me of the exhibit of Stanbrook books there at the library.[213] I would very much like to get to see it, but as matters stand I think it is impossible for me to plan on it. If I were going to see a Doctor in Lexington it might come under consideration: but I am still seeing the man in Louisville, and it would not be possible for me to get permission to go to Lexington just to see the exhibit. I really wish I could. I presume it is not going to Louisville . . . ?? If it is, they perhaps I might catch it there.

Can you help me with the following books?

Any volume of verse by Laurie Lee
B. Rajan—Paradise Lost and the 17th Century Reader London 1947
E. M.W. Tillyard, Studies in Milton London 1951

I don't know if these are badly needed for courses, but if they are there and are available I would appreciate having them for a while.

Good, let's plan on some Saturday in November then. I think that October is now a bit crowded for me anyhow, and November would be better. So far all the Saturdays in Nov. are clear as far as I am concerned. If any hitch comes up I will let you know, but write me first which day you prefer when the time comes to prefer it.

All the best wishes to you and Victor, and blessings,

Tom

Oct 31, 1966
Dear Carolyn:

November is upon us. I wonder if Victor and you will be able to get over on the 12th, 19th or 26th. I am not too sure about the 26th for myself but the other two dates are wide open and the 26th remains a possibility. How about the 12th?

Under separate cover I send a few things. How Victor's portrait of me came to be reproduced in that magazine, I do not know. I hope he will not mind.

The other things I send—some of my own, and others for general interest. Continuum is worth the Library subscribing to if you do not already. The speech of my friend Ferry[214] is interesting: he is always quite good and anti-technological in a way that I think is fruitful.

Best wishes to you both, and do let me know if you plan to come—
which I hope you do soon.

Blessings and regards always,

Tom

Nov 17, 1966
Dear Carolyn:

I have jotted down some references to things I need: doubtless some
of them are in the library. Don't bother with the article in Accent, I
can catch that sometime in Louisville. Many thanks and best wishes
to you and Victor. I would be very grateful if you could send me one
or other of these items on loan—perhaps a loan extended beyond the
end of the year, or one that could be extended.

Again, thanks and best wishes,

Tom

Faulkner—The Bear (story)
W V O'Conner—Wilderness Themes in Faulkner
RWB Lewis—The American Adam. Chicago, Ill. 1955
John Muir—Story of my Boyhood and Youth, NY 1913
A Thousand Mile Walk NY 1916
Linnie Marsh Wolfe—Son of the Wilderness, NY 1945
H. Schultz—Milton and Forbidden Knowledge, NY 1955

ONE LIGHT/ONE RAY AND IT WILL BE THE ANGELS' SPRING:
ONE FLASH/ONE GLANCE UPON THE SHINY POND/AND THEN
ASPERGES ME! SWEET WILDERNESS/AND LO!
WE ARE REDEEMED!
—Thomas Merton—[215]

25. XI. 66

Dear Tom: may we use the lines of yours for a Christmas message?

Thank you. Got your several articles but have not started reading. When would it suit you that we come for a visit, it is mild outside and we may—this time—be favored by the weather. Next month—in two weeks I shall have lived 84 years and will start my 85th.

In Christ yours

Victor

Thank you for the German translation, now for the first time I get a feeling for your poetry. The translations seem to be excellent. I read that on solitude, it is perfect, she says in German what you said in English—not more, nor less. Professor (always stilted unpleasant in German) is now 'Lehrer,' so much more direct and pleasant.

Nov 26 [1966]

Dear Victor:

Certainly you may use my verse on your card. Delighted! Would it be possible to get a dozen cards or so for my own use? Or would that be too much trouble? I'd like them. And I do want to see you. Any Saturday in December is good for me. Shall we say Dec 10th? Or any other. Just let me know. But if it is the 3rd better let me know fast. I will wait to hear. When is your birthday? I will say Mass for you on that day if I can.

All best wishes and blessings always In Christ

Tom

Nov 27 1966

Dear Victor:

Yesterday I wrote you a note and then by mistake put it in the wrong box. It may have got lost, so I am writing another. Yes: by all means use the quote for your card. And would it be possible for me to have a few of the cards for my own use? Say a dozen? That would mean running off a dozen without your names on: no name at all. Would that be too much trouble? Then about coming: probably Dec. 10th would be the best. But any other Saturday is all right though the 3rd and 26th are less good. I hope you can make it the 10th. Will wait for a word from you. Best wishes always to both of you. in Christ

Tom

※

Dec 8. 1966
Dear Carolyn—

I was very sorry to hear Victor had to go to the hospital again. But I am glad he is recovering. Tomorrow, on his 85th birthday, I will say Mass for all his needs and I hope he will rapidly get back on his feet and be able to come over. So I hope all will be well. Many thanks for all the cards you will print up. I will be most grateful.

Meanwhile please give Victor all my blessing and best wishes and say I am praying for him to get well quickly.

All the best always—

Tom

I will put some books in the mail for the library.

※

21. XII. 66

Dear Tom: Yesterday I came back from the hospital, much improved by two pints of blood transfused into my veins. I am so sorry I missed to see you this month but we count on January now. When would it suit you? I have not read one of your papers it was such an interregnum, complete oblivion, could not remember even household words. I feel much better but am under Carolyn's orders for the doctor felt I should still stay in the hospital (to me an awful place).

All good wishes for the holidays
in Christ
Yours Victor

※

21.XII. 66

Dear Tom, when I wrote to you today I forgot to ask you to tell me the date on which you were operated on your neck.

This is part of a pebble:

1962 the picture of Merton finished

p. 50 of the pebbles has been set end of October 1966

Tom read p. 50 on Nov 5th 1966 and said: you straightened my neck before the doctor did

Tom was operated: when?

Don't you think this worth recording?

Yours Victor

Dec 24, 1966
Dear Victor:

Thanks very much for your two notes. I was very glad to hear from you and to know you were out of the hospital. I agree with you, a hospital is an awful place, and something that is good only for getting out of. I hope everything will go well at home, and that you will get the necessary rest and make a quick recovery.

Any Saturday in January except the 21st will be all right. Can we plan on the 7th or the 14th? Those would both be good. In fact if it seemed we were going to have nice weather on the 31st and you felt like coming over then, just call me the day before, in the morning. But make sure I get the message. In any event, drop me a note when you hope to come.

As to my operation, it was on March 25th. I do not know how much of an historic event it was, but that was the date, if you want it. I am glad to hear there are more pebbles being collected.

I don't remember if I thanked Carolyn for the cards: in any case I do so now, they are very nicely done.

My very best wishes to you both, with blessings: and of course I will be praying for you in the liturgy of these days.

With warm good wishes always,
Yours in Christ,
Tom

☙

Jan 3, 1967
Dear Carolyn:

I find I have kept that Hernandez book of poems beyond the end of the year. As I don't suppose too many people are wanting it, can I still hold on to it for a few months? I still have some translations I want to do. I think everything else that should be back is back now. Please let me know if not.

Could I please have (some of) the following at least for a short time (If they are badly needed please let me know and I will get them back fast).

Wm Faulkner Collected Stories
Irving Howe—William Faulkner
Kirk and Klotz Faulkner's People
Kobo Abe The Face of Another, (Knopf 1966)
L.A Govinda The Way of White Clouds.

I haven't heard from you or Victor: I hope Victor is all right. But I told you that I would not be free in the middle of January: now I have learned that the annual retreat will not be at that time, so *all* the Saturdays in January are free. I only hope Victor is well enough to come. Just let me know in time which day, and then come without further confirmation (I will try to confirm it).
Best wishes to you both, as ever,
Tom

☙

Jan 11, 1967
Dear Carolyn:

Thanks for your card and for the three books. Fine, they are very helpful. I will not keep them overlong.

Could I possibly have two more of Faulkner's?

Go down Moses
Wild Palms.[216]

These two would also, I hope, get back fast for I am engaged in a job on them now and hope to have it out of the way in a couple of weeks.

Do you have "Les Temps Modernes" in the library? There is an article in French on the Wild Palms in vol vii of that, the Jan. 1952 issue. Do you let out bound volumes of magazines like that? Or would I have to have a xerox if you had the volume? Could you please let me know about this?

I am sorry to hear Victor is recovering only slowly and is still a bit tired. But it is best to take things easy. It is a bit cold these days anyhow. I am free any Saturday except Feb. 11th, as far as I now can see. Hope things will improve, both in the weather, and for Victor. My best regards to both of you, and all blessings.

Tom

Have you heard anything from J? He has been very silent for a long while. I know his mother died, and that perhaps threw things out of joint for him for a while.

Jan 30, 1967
Dear Carolyn:

I think I had better get this longish list off to you in the hope that you may find one or two of the titles there. Otherwise it will just get longer and longer.

M. Coindreau—Apercus de la litterature americaine
E.W. Moseley—Pseudonyms of Christ in the Mod. Novel.

J. Hillis Miller—Poets of Reality

DH Lawerence—The Man Who Died.

Valery Larbaud—Ce vice impuni

R. Detweiler—Four spiritual crises in Mid-Century Amer.
   Fiction.

M. Foucault—Madness and Civilization

(This is new, sounds important, NY Review has some thing on it in November)

Hope to get some of the others back soon. I realize people must be needing the Faulkner volumes.

I keep thinking of you and Victor. How is he? I hope later as the weather gets better he can get over. Or perhaps if J finally gets down here later in spring we can get over there, but don't count on that. J. is busy and harassed in the office at the moment.

In any case, please give my very best regards to Victor. I keep you both in my prayers.

Gene Meatyard[217] was over here with a couple of poets and took some pictures that ought to be very interesting. I think you know him?

All the best, and blessings, in Xt
Tom

Feb 13, 1967
Dear Carolyn:

I address this to you as the ribbon is getting faint and Victor might not be able to read it easily. I was delighted to have a note from you both and especially happy that a visit may once again be possible. Here is how I think it ought to be arranged, so that we can communicate with a minimum of confusion.

First I can let you know ahead what would be a good week, or weeks.

Then when that week comes and you anticipate a good day, call the monastery the day before saying to leave a message for me that you are coming the next day. Then, if all goes well, just come at 12.30 the next day without further ado. Only call me if you are *not* coming. In my turn I will not do anything unless I send a wire or call you not to come, but I will try to take care to keep the whole week free once I have cleared it ahead of time.

It is impossible to expect them here to give a message promptly or correctly, and I doubt if it could ever be arranged for me to get a message and call in return on the same morning. Everything is too haphazard or too arbitrary to be dependable.

The last week in February is *not* good for me, I fear. This week seems nice, so if you get the urge to come later in the week, and think you can call a day ahead, do that and I will meet you next day at the gate at 12.30. (Unless you cancel it by another call). The last week of the month I have to get operated on for this bursitis and I am going to Louisville. Don't lets plan on a visit to the hospital, that would be too miserable, and we want to make the best of our chances. After that, any time from March 5th to 14th would be good. Maybe I'll call you from the hospital and we can talk of it some more.

Yes, I would like the Kobo Abe book.

My very best wishes to you and Victor. It is so nice now I wish you were coming today!!

All blessings, in Christ,

Tom

❧

15. IV. 67

Dear Tom: thank you for sending me the papers. I enjoyed several of them very much, especially that on technology. I have a friend in Germany, a writer, *Friedrich Georg Juenger,* and I wish you could send him: *Technology,*[218] *Preface to 'Lotus in the sea fire,'*[219] *Notes for a Statement on aid to Civilians,*[220] and *Ishi.*[221] His address is *Ueberlingen am Bodensee, Seepromenade 5, Germany* and adding a note that you send it on my instigation. Juenger has written a book: Failure of

Technology, which Regnery has published. The 'pebbles' will soon be ready, Carolyn is on the last section to be printed. We will send you a copy. Why can't the Trappists print books as we do? instead of making cheese?

Love from your friend

Victor

Perhaps you can send the papers air mail!

April 24, 1967

Dear Victor:

Thanks for your letter of the other day. I was very pleased to hear from you and to receive a letter in your own handwriting, which shows you are better. The papers are going off to Friedrich Georg Juenger but I have not been able to find exactly the ones you asked for. However the material I am sending is roughly equivalent—including for example the article that was recently in the *Saturday Review*,[222] which has a bearing on technology, at least indirectly.

In such lovely weather as we have now, I wish I could spend a few hours quietly picnicking with you and Carolyn. The spring has been perfect. However I shall probably have to be content with the hope of dropping in on you again in Lexington next time some friend of mine comes down with a car. I have been rather over visited lately—largely for business reasons—and that has held up both work and correspondence.

The other day I sent the new book,[223] and I want also to send you the little book (Cassiodorus) which they printed at Stanbrook. I like it in its splendor, but I prefer the simplicity of the Stamperia del Santuccio. But the nuns went to immense trouble to get paper and so on.

With my very best and warmest regards to both you and Carolyn, and all blessings, as ever, in Christ,

Tom

April 25
Dear Carolyn,

I already sealed my letter to Victor or I would have included this
note. Do they have at the library Georges Sorel—Reflexions sur
la Violence—or a book about Sorel? In a word can you find me
something of his or on him? Many thanks

All my best—

Tom

✿

May 28 1967
Dear Carolyn:

Bob Shepherd[224] had the kindness to write to me and let me know
that you not only have Victor in the hospital but your mother also. I
am very sorry to hear it, and I hope that since Bob wrote things may
have improved somewhat. At least, to judge from what he says, Victor
may be home again. But how difficult it is for you to have all this
happening at once. I wish there were something I could do besides say
"Courage" and assure you of my prayers.

I think often of you and Victor, and certainly things are much less
happy here than they were when you could come over regularly. We
can certainly be grateful for having had such wonderful times over
the years, and I hope will do so again. In any case, perhaps when my
lawyer, John Slate,[225] comes down this summer, we might be able to
get over there. But I will of course consult you first about it.

In a word, I do very much want to see you and Victor, if only
briefly. I hope he is able to do at least a few of the things he likes
to do, and that he is reasonably well. I am having a bout with food
allergies and the like, but nothing special. The back seems to be
holding up all right and in a word I have nothing to complain of.

Would it be more convenient for you if I sent requests for books
and things direct to someone at the library? I am most grateful for the
copy of the Ruthwell Cross[226] article and would like to follow that up

with a book that might be there. If you get a chance to drop me a note about this, I will do what you suggest.

With all my best to you and Victor, and thanks to Bob for his note, Cordially always,

Tom

2. VI. 67

Dear Tom: Do you know Herrigel's book on Zen? Gilbert Highet speaks about it in his book 'talents and geniuses.' —and today is the 14th! We read your good reply to the review of Carpenter's on Mumford's book.[227]—Maybe I will still be able to come to Gethsemani,—and bring a copy of the new finished book—the Fragments. But I am so weak. I wish you could come and see me.*— don't get old, old age is not easy—yet it has to be endured.

Love

Victor

*Perhaps Father Abbot would allow you to come.

June 16, 1967
Dear Victor:

It was good to hear from you again. Yes, I would very much like to come and see you and see the book too. I am not sure what I can plan just now, but I have a friend coming to visit and he will have a car. Perhaps then we will be able to drive over to Lexington. I am not sure when he will be coming. Perhaps next week. If he comes and I can get permission I will try to call you, but will come over to Lexington anyway.[228] If for some reason this will not work, send a note or a message.

It is rather hot now, and I suppose that is uncomfortable for you: it certainly is for me, as I do not get all the breeze in my cottage. However I can go out into a cool place in the woods. I am reading Mumford's new book, which the publisher sent me as a reward for writing that letter to the Times, more or less.

F. Juenger sent me a nice letter and I must reply some time. As to the Herrigel book on Zen: actually there are two, one of which is quite good. "Zen and the Art of Archery."

Yes, you are right about "getting old" I have more aches than I used to have and the machinery runs less well from year to year. Not having found the secret of arresting the process, I must accept it as you also do. Let us rejoice that things are not worse and go on as happily as we can. I hope to see you soon, if I possibly can. I will let you know as soon as I have more definite plans.

With all my best to you and Carolyn,

and God Bless you both,

Tom

※

July 10, 1967

Dear Carolyn:

This is just to let you know that word from Bob Shepherd reached me about Victor.[229] I offered Mass for Victor last Wednesday or Thursday as soon as I heard from Bob, and have been praying for him continually. I do think the help of the Church is a good thing, on his journey: I was not in a position to do much myself being out of my diocese there. But anyway I know that the mercy of God will be with Victor and he will find his way to where there is light and peace. I keep you both in my prayers. Blessings always,

Tom

※

July 11, 1967

Dear Carolyn:

After my note of yesterday had been mailed I received this morning the message from Lexington[230] and also a note from Bob Shepherd. Somehow it is just hard for me to believe that someone like Victor could possibly have left us. It is incredible, and will take an awful lot of getting used to. The fact that he does not now have to suffer and wait for the inevitable is something we can accept: but it does not help much with our own sense of loss. We will just have to get along with that as people do, and as we have tried to learn how to do in other bereavements. Yet this one is somehow different, because there was no one like Victor. Just no one. And for such a loss there are no compensations: except in our hope that he is where he should be, with God. A life like his, devoted to honesty and truth and good work, could not travel any other way but to God. I think it was most significant somehow that his last painting was of the Resurrection. And his last book, his best and his gift to you, will keep him present with us.

Today I offered Mass for the repose of his soul. He was also commemorated in the High Mass of the Community. I spoke to Bro Giles about the news and he too has been praying in a special way.

You have had a hard time of it, and I hope now you will be able to have a little rest and recuperation. And I hope in due course we will be able to get together again, here or there, and talk a little. I will write more later. For now, peace and God bless you.

Cordially as ever,
Tom

❀

15 July 1967

Please note clipping sent by Lexi and the last paragraph at foot of page (this letter came the day Victor died). What to do? I don't think V. ever wrote about his use of the Face on the cloth of Turin in the Crucifixus (and the same Face in the resurrected Christus— the painting unfinished on the easel; only the Christus is carefully and completely delineated). I have V.'s photographs from Turin and somewhere there are his notes on it. As you know, there are the three versions—the one at Gethsemani, the one here, the Kolbsheim one. If you would need a photo, I can provide one. All were painted during the years 1958–59 I believe. Were I a wealthy 'patron' I would send the Pope the Crucifixus here! Would the abbey?
CRH

❀

July 27, 1967
Dear Carolyn:

Victor's beautiful book—surely his most beautiful in every way—
arrived this morning and I have spent the afternoon reading it.[231] And
thinking of so many things. And looking over again at the catalogue
of the North Carolina exhibit. Remembering also the picnics at which
we had discussed this or that piece of the then "Pebbles" (I do think
the new title is better).

What can one say? How express gratitude for Victor, and that he
was with us as much as he was, longer no doubt that we deserved.
Or does such a statement make any sense? I suppose it can't. But you
know what I mean.

I am above all glad that he was able to really round it all out in
the form of these two testaments: the assembling of all his painting
and printing, and then this bringing together of his ideas in a more
effective way than any other, I think. It is a delightful book, and every
word tells. Besides, it is so beautifully made—and we have you largely
to thank for that.

It is so good to have this book, in which the very tone of Victor's
speech is actual. And of course he is with us, and we with him, not
only through the medium of the book. So significant, too, the fact
that all this really was ad majorem Dei gloriam, perhaps more so than
much that is professionally "religious."

Are you going to carry on with the press? I hope so, and I hope we
will find many more pretexts for printing. Also I have tried to suggest
to J. Laughlin the idea of a sort of collected works of Victor in one
volume, or a selection, or in any case a volume.

I suppose things must be tiresome for you now. I for my part have
been over visited and pulled this way and that, but the tide seems
to be going down now. Later when we are more free and ourselves,
perhaps we can get together again. I will keep it in mind. Bob could
take care of the transportation, one way or the other. It is of course

always much simpler for me when people come here: my going out is always a great and complex operation. But we'll see what comes up.

Meanwhile, I think of you often, and of course of Victor whom I remember always and especially in prayer. Blessings always, and my very best wishes.

Tom

❧

Dear Father Louis—a peace came to me while I rang the abbey the night of Victor's death and that kind voice assured me that you be told and that Victor would be commemorated in the High Mass of the Community. And that I now know you and Brother Giles prayed for him in your ways, that the Little Brothers of Jesus said for him a mass in his Chapel at Kolbsheim (Lexi cabled)—a deep peace is mine.

Today I found these words which Victor had written about his painting, the Resurrection, "Christ risen again has shed light over me for the remaining time of my life . . . Glory to him, the human image of the highest principle." I do not know just when he wrote that, in these last months I believe, for also there was his prayer for me.

If you can see me, Bob Shepherd will bring me on a convenient Saturday to you.

28 July 1967
Yours,
Carolyn R.H.

❧

July 31 [1967]
Dear Carolyn.

I was very glad to get your letter today—Certainly I would like to see you. August 12 would be the best for me now—could expect you at 11:30. And certainly I will send a photo of the crucifix to the Pope. We can discuss this when we meet. In a day or two I may send a note about some books.

All my best always
Tom

Aug 1. [1967]
Dear Carolyn:

As I mentioned in my note about you coming Aug 12—I am sending
a list of things I would be grateful if someone could look up for me in
the library, and am also enclosing some material for "the collection."
I was moved by the simple burial service and by the fact that my own
poem was included. With blessings and best wishes always,

Tom

2 Aug 1967
Dear Father Louis—

Bob Shepherd can bring me on August 12th at 11:30 (Eastern S.T.—
we did not go on day light saving time here in Lexington—I don't
believe you did at Gethsemani?). Mrs. Lowry will send you as many
of the books on your list as possible; I am not there until Sept. first.
Dr. Forth, our director will ask her, or someone in the Ref. Dept. to
provide a list from 1960 on.

Sincerely,
Carolyn R. Hammer

Dear Father Louis

I cannot find a photograph other than the Kolbsheim one above
the altar there and the two before the INRI was placed on the
one in Gethsemani, and the one we have here (which is to be sold
eventually). You can send all three of them should there really be
any meaning to this. If you do write to the Pope and send three
photographs, do you mind writing this to Lexi Grunelius as it was his
idea?

Carolyn R. H.
17 Aug.

August 22, 1967
Dear Carolyn:

Your note and the photos arrived today. I have to write to the Pope about some other business and so I will take advantage of the fact to send him the black and white photo and the transparency of the Kolbsheim chapel, which is very beautiful indeed.

Logically, I think that really it would have been smarter for Lexi himself to send all this because he could have explained in detail what he had in mind. I am sure that with an accompanying note from Maritain he would have had just as much chance of reaching the Pope directly as I have, if not more. However, I will do it, and I am sure that the Pope will be impressed.

As I said the other day, there are so many reasons why we should not send one of the crucifixes themselves. First, in that event that the Pope would probably never even see it. Second, there is no telling what would happen to it: but it would probably be just stored away somewhere. Third, there is all the problem of shipping. Fourth, the one here is a little chipped on one of the edges. There are so many little things like that to consider, beyond the fact that the Pope probably gets truckloads of paintings and other objects every day. I am sure he will appreciate the photograph and will keep you informed.

I received a couple of books from the library. They have put me on the regular interlibrary loan routine which is quite all right. I understand their predicament. It will perhaps mean less chance to get much work done on the books, but on the other hand I have got into the bad habit of just keeping them around until the six months were up. I am grateful to all concerned, anyhow.

It was good to have you over here with Bob and I hope we can continue. I am sure you can use a little outing once in a while, and for my part I very much enjoy having you come.

With all my best always, and blessings,
Tom

Are you going to continue printing? Can we think of "pretexts" for jobs?

✿

Aug 24, 1967
Dear Carolyn:

Bob wrote about coming Labor Day weekend sometime. I am tied up then. I will write to him about it. But J. is coming the following weekend and I thought he and I might drive over Saturday the 9th. How would that be for you? Could you let me know? It looks as thought I am going to have a few visitors in October, but you probably are going to be away then too, Bob said. We can work all that out later, but please let me know if the 9th is ok. Otherwise Bob could bring you over later in this month.

    In haste, with all my best,
    Tom

✿

Aug. 31, 1967
Dear Carolyn:

I just heard from Jay that he most likely will not come by here in September after all. So—unless there is another change—don't expect us on the 9th. I believe Bob is not around then, or I'd say both of you come over: but would you like to come on the 16th, 23rd or 30th? They are all free now, as far as I can see. Always 11.30 am good for me. I'll write for a book in a day or two—many thanks.

    All my best always, in haste (will write about printing also)
    Tom

✿

Dear Tom—

[Sir] Herbert Read has written and suggested that it might be possible for him to help in some way toward getting into print the translation of the Fiedler Aphorisms (done by Wayne with Victor's help) as a memorial to Victor. I would like to have you take a look at these things, and then I will write to James Laughlin (I too wish that he could have come this weekend). He (James) tried a Harvard reader and got a "well-sounding" negative report, but none of us: Wayne, Victor, me, thought much of his 'negatives.' Here we let it end though. J. offered to send the ms. to another friend for advice. If Read (and his letter may interest you) will write a foreword—then there is the NAME! Unhappy times. Bob cannot bring me on Saturday (the 9th) as he will be away. But I wonder if you could see me about this matter. My nephew[232] can bring me over this coming Saturday, the 9th? We would arrive at 11:30 if convenient. I am sure Bob can come later in the month but it is better for me if I can come sooner. However, the 16th would be all right if you prefer.

Sincerely

Carolyn Hammer

4th Sept 1967

❦

Tuesday [September] 5th [1967]

Dear Carolyn

By all means come Saturday 9th if that is convenient. I hope this will get out immediately and reach you by tomorrow or Thursday.

Anyway I will be looking for you at 11.30 Saturday.

All my best

Tom

❦

Sept 11, 1967

Dear Carolyn:

One thing I forgot to say the other day about Fiedler: perhaps still one of the best possibilities would be Helen Wolff at Harcourt Brace and World. She also might be interested in the other things of Victor's. Then, too, rethinking some of the things we spoke of, I believe that it would be best to stick to one idea in regard to the Niles songs: and see about them if and when J. comes.[233] I don't think the other project would be good right now. We can talk this over some more next time I see you.

I am really sorry I kept you so late the other day. It was inconsiderate of me.

There is one other book that I could use, if you have it there:
Norman Cohn: The Pursuit of the Millennium
I am glad the interlibrary loan dept will give me leeway with these books, but in my turn I will see to it that there is no unnecessary delay. I am grateful to all of you.

All my best
Tom

✿

18 Sept. 67
Dear Father Louis,

I think your idea to wait until James Laughlin comes to discuss the Niles songs is a good decision. I hope J. will be *able* to come. My dates for going to N.Y. are mid-October and perhaps I can see him then about the Fiedler *Aphorisms*. In the meantime, I have written to him that I am coming on Victor's estate affairs (the two trustees of the collection can both be in N.Y. on the 17th and 18th and I feel that I must go then though it is not a good time as I shall have to miss a class). James probably knows Helen Wolff. Victor knew her when she and her husband did the Peguy and V. designed and printed it. Due to the new set-up here, I will forward your request for the Norman Cohn, *Pursuit of the Millennium* to Mrs. Virginia Walker, Division of Interlibrary Loan. I will have no 'packager.' However, I will always be able to do a more involved request when you make it.

Sincerely,
Carolyn R. Hammer
Would you feel that you could 'introduce' me to Helen Wolff by a letter in advance? When I hear from James, I will write again.—crh

❧

Sept 22. [1967]
Dear Carolyn.

I am most grateful to the library for the xeroxes of articles. The
Oceania one has come quick first as you will see from the tape I am
sending you today. There is some Gregorian on it, some monastic
material (doubtless dull) and a largo epic.
    Best always
    Tom

❧

Oct 9, 1967
Dear Carolyn:

As a pretext for printing: I thought you might look at these early
poems of mine.[234] I just recently got copies of them, and had not seen
them myself for many years. I think a few of them are not too bad.
Perhaps five or six of them might make a small book or some kind of
document. In any case, I thought you might want to glance at them.
    I suppose you will soon be going to New York. Say hello to J. I still
hope he may come down, but I know he must be very busy.
    This is just a note. Incidentally, I am very grateful for all the
books which arrived safely on interlibrary loan, and for the xeroxes
especially. Perhaps I already mentioned that. I appreciate all this very
much.
    With all my best, as ever,
    Tom

❧

Monday [October] 23 [1967]
Dear Carolyn.

Sorry. I cannot manage Thursday, but I *can* get over to Lexington
Saturday 28[235] and hope it is possible to hear the songs at John J.

Niles's on that day. Will you please let me know—

1. if the songs can be heard then
2. if we can have lunch together somewhere with my friend Miss
   Dana who will drive me over (she is the literacy Executor of
   Gabriela Mistral).[236]

I have to be back about 5.30 or 6.
Hope to see you Saturday
Best always
Tom

2 Nov. 67

Dear Father Louis, the three titles requested: Du Bois, THE 1870
GHOST DANCE, Burridge, MAMBU, Barrera Vasquez, EL LIBRO . . . will
be sent on inter-library loan today. Fraenger, *The Millennium of
H. Bosch*, is here only in the German edition. If you should want this,
please ask for this call no.: *ART* Libr., 709.49313 and Mrs. Walker,
the Inter-Library Loan person, will get it for you. We had had some
mailing difficulties here—a temporary mix-up—but shipments should
go smoother now. I am very happy Doris Dana came my way—a very
intelligent and warm person. Perhaps you can tell me a little more
about her—her training, family background; in other words, how did
she come to know Mistral, be a god-daughter of Maritain, a friend of
the Manns? I will see her next when I am in N.Y. Denise Levertov[237]
is to be here on the campus in December (*ca.* 11th); I hope you can see
her. The very nice Wendell Berry[238] (lectures here and has published
two novels based on the life of his Ky. home town on the river) is in
charge.
    Sincerely,
    Carolyn R.H.

Nov 23, 1967
Dear Carolyn:

First of all, many thanks for the memorial book for Victor. It is as beautiful as anything you have ever done and I shall treasure it along with the others.

There are several things I have been meaning to write about. First of these is that there is a misprint in the *Selected Poems* version of the Responsory[239] which John Jacob Niles has set to music and which is to be sung in a few days at Transylvania. The misprint is in line 24 (right at the bottom of the page in the new edition). The line says wrongly "blooming" spheres. The word should be *booming*. (It might have given him a different idea!) As I don't have his address, may I entrust you with the mission of letting him know about it? Hope it is not too late. Also, J. said that any business with the publisher should go through New Directions (about rights etc). If his music publisher would contact J. in due time, that would be the way to do it.

Last Monday, 20th, I was in Lexington and called you a couple of times both at the library and at home, but failed to get to you.[240] As I was two and a half hours in a dentist's chair at the medical center and did not know in advance when I would return here, I could not plan on anything ahead of time. But I will be back next Wednesday morning, and hope to get to the library to do a little work. I'll call you or look you up then. I have a dentist's appointment at one, which doesn't leave time for lunch etc but at least it would be good to see you a moment. Later too I hope to see whoever it is in charge of the collection there, when we have worked out the "rules for use" that are being devised now. The Trust agreement is all signed and it seems workable.

In December I am going to have a seminar affair with some nuns here[241] and then other things will keep me tied up until Christmas. I hope that we can look forward to something later on, in January some time, if it is not too cold. As to Denise Levertov: Wendell Berry hopes to bring her over for a brief visit when she is here. I have met him and like his work. I hope in January or so we can plan a picnic with Bob, Jonathan, anyone you like.

Keep well. My best wishes always,
Tom

❀

Dear Father Louis—

Thurs., if you possibly can, do call me from 9–12 at the library—258-9000, ext. 2734; at home 254-3567 from 12:30 on.

I had dinner last night with the Niles—"blooming" was changed to "booming." A new song is on its way. "The Responsory" is so far the best, I think. Is not fragmented, but 'framed.'

Sincerely,
CR Hammer

❀

Dec 27 '67
Dear Carolyn.

More people are coming from Georgia[242] and I won't be able to get together with you all on Saturday. I sent Bob a couple of other dates, such as the 6th and 13th. Happy new year and all best wishes

Tom

❀

Jan 2, 1968
Dear Carolyn:

I'm very sorry. I have to change the signals again. At the end of this week a monk from Belgium[243] is coming and we have a lot of business to go into. And the higher superiors are to be here for pre-election flim flam. So Saturday 6th is just not possible for me. Besides with the weather as it is . . . Shall we let it wait and plan on a proper picnic in more springlike weather, or at least after the election and retreat i.e. end of January and beginning of February? Any reaction from Jonathan on the magazine?[244]

My best regards always,

Tom

I'll be over to dentist Jan 29th

Jan 21, 1968

Dear Carolyn,

I have been laid out with flu, had a bad case of it, and have been pretty much out of touch for a week. So I am behind with mail. One important thing: Teo Savory Brilliant (Mrs. Alan Brilliant) who published in California that poem of mine the Originators[245] of which you have a broadsheet, writes that her husband is doing an article on small presses for Paris Review and is also arranging an exhibit of work from same presses in Museum of Modern Art. She wants me to put her in touch with you as she has not seen any of Victor's work and wants to know about it and perhaps arrange to have some (books, etc.) to see and to exhibit. Write to:

Mrs. Alan Brilliant
317 East de la Guerra St
Santa Barbara, Cal.
93101

that is if you are interested. When I write to her next I will also give her your address.

Also. J. Laughlin says he wants to stop by here soon on his way back from the Rockies. I expect him this week or next. I don't know if I may be able to get over to Lexington with him, but will try, and perhaps he may come without me anyhow. But I do not know what the plans are and how much time he has. We do have to go to Louisville for one day over that Trust business.

Jonathan sent some poems I want to use in Monks Pond and I must write him soon and thank him. Happy to have them. The first issue is now all filled up and will go to press fairly soon I hope, depending on how close I can get to the press with all the liturgy people monopolizing it.

My very best. I'll write more soon. My next visit to dentist may be changed, but in any case, whether in Lexington or here, I hope to see you soon, with Bob and perhaps with all the ones who were hoping to picnic in January. Our election came off very well, we have a good solid, sober, open minded young Abbot.[246] He will not do anything revolutionary but I am sure things will look up in many ways. He was my candidate and being one of the other hermits is certainly pro-hermit. So that at least is very good.

My best wishes to all of you,

Warmly, as ever,

Tom

✿

23 Jan. 68

Dear Tom, it was indeed good to have word from you at long last, for your friends here worry—so very sorry that you had one of the severe flu attacks. I am most interested in publicity for the Hammers' press, for now I have to be, or at least I feel that I should be. Perhaps if Mrs. Brilliant (a fine if puzzling name) does want to write about the press or have some things for an exhibition, this would an opportunity for me to act in cooperation. Thank you for the suggestion. I will write, and try to do so soon. In the meantime, I should appreciate your sending my address to her. We read of the election in the paper (and rejoice in the non-revolutionary for I had wondered and worried again as a non-youth enthusiast-at-'helms'). I do hope James really comes and that he can bring you to Lexington. Await word from you. Now that the snow is melting, one's thoughts can turn before the next snow at least to picnics. We will scan the skies and look at the Farmer's Almanac when you say.

Yours,

Carolyn R.H.

✿

Jan 25, 1968
Dear Carolyn:

Thanks for your note. It turns out J. will not be here this week, but plans to try to get down the second week of February. I still do not feel very sure he and I will be able to get over to Lexington as there is business to be done in Louisville. Also I have cancelled my dental appointment in Lexington because I don't think that big fancy renewal job is worth the bother.

But the weather is looking better. Do you think we might gamble a picnic on Saturday February 3rd?[247] At least you and Bob and his wife might be able to get away at short notice. It is a long time since we have had a chance to do this, and if the weather holds it would be worth trying as Lent might not be so good.

Let me know if you think the Farmers' Almanac will be benign for Feb 3rd, and if the stars are in the right conjunctions. If all is OK I could meet you out in front avenue around 11.15.

My very best, to all of you,
Tom
Or another Saturday in February if the 3rd doesn't work?

March 2 [1968]
Dear Carolyn:

Here at least is the first splash of the Pond.[248] It is quite an education trying to edit a magazine, for many reasons!

We can talk of all this when we next meet, which I hope will be next Saturday. And I hope it is as nice as today is turning out to be. I look forward to it. (If you have any New Yorkers saved—I can use the ads etc. for my long poem)

Thanks for the card from Florida. Yes, a nice big pond, but the picnics there cannot equal those on the shores of Monks Pond.

My best always
Tom

19 March 1968
Dear Father Louis,

The articles for the library were received and will be turned over to
the proper places after Bob and I have read them. I am pleased that
you answered the McCarthy piece.[249] Enclosed are poems of Jonathan
Greene's that I was supposed to hand to you when we were last over; J.
thought you might be interested in seeing them. As he has never been
over, would you be able to see him and me on Saturday, 27th April?
(I am leaving the following week for Ireland and then on to Italy
circuitously.) We could come in time for lunch, or just for an hour or
so in the afternoon? The 20th would also be a possible earlier date.

Sincerely,
Carolyn Hammer

Mar 22 1968
Dear Carolyn:

Thanks for sending the J. Greene material. Glad to have it. And of
course I do want to have a talk with you and him—and a picnic if not
too much trouble! The 27th of April is out, but the 20th is open, and
I'd be happy to meet you out in the avenue about 11.15.[250] By that
time too I hope this weather will be better than it is today with this
blizzard. Thanks for the mouscatcher picture. Maybe I can use it—it
is the kind of thing, exactly. And maybe we'll all have to go on the
mouse standard when gold fails us.

Best always,
Tom

20 May 1968

I am just back from Callow-End and our long grilled talks with

Dame Hildelith—a really charming woman.[251] The trip progresses well enough. Sister Joan and Sister Marcella[252] and Dame H. send greetings to you. As do I. Tomorrow I am to Amsterdam, then the Grunelius.

Sinc. Yours,

C. Hammer

❀

June 30 1968

Dear Carolyn:

Many thanks for your card from Stanbrook. I hope you enjoyed the whole trip, notwithstanding turmoil in France etc. J. said he saw you in New York. My own trip to California was a great success and I hope to tell you about it.[253]

When I got back I was so submerged in meetings,[254] visits and so on that I am trying to catch my breath by taking July as a more or less retreat—only exceptions being two engagements I had promised before this decision. Hope I can see you all later.

Here is the clipping about H. Read. The curious emphasis is due to the fact that it comes from a pacifist paper.

I am still very much engrossed in Levi Strauss and also some of the other structuralists, like Roland Barthes, on whom I am to write an article.[255] If you have occasion to run across anything about them, article or such like, and if you can save it, please do. Sometime I'd like to know what UK has in the library of Roland Barthes and Michel Foucault. Maybe I can get over there in August some time.

My best wishes to all of you

Cordially always,

Tom

❀

July 31 1968

Dear Carolyn:

I was glad to get your note. I was thinking about the possibility of getting together in August. How is Saturday 10th for you? It looks like the best day for me so far—and it is the earliest available one. Let me know if that is all right, and I will expect to meet you and Bob etc at the gate around 11.30, as usual.

I am in the midst of getting shots, working on visas and so on. The Bangkok meeting[256] is definite and also another one in Darjeeling planned for October,[257] so I will leave earlier than I expected.

Does the library have a book by Clifford Geertz, the Religions of Indonesia? If so, I'd be grateful for a look at it, I need to do this as I am going to our monastery there.

Eager to hear about your European trip!

Best always,

Tom

❀

Aug 5, '68

Dear Carolyn,

Fine—I'll expect you the 10th about 11.30—and maybe the 31st but I am not too sure about that one myself. I'm sure the mistake about *Religions of Java* is mine. Thanks for sending the book.

My very best

Tom

❀

Sept 6 1968

Dear Carolyn:

I have been lucky with gifts: yours, the kit for keeping ones toothbrush, shaving things and so on, is just fine. I was needing that. Thanks much.

Thanks too for your letter. The nun you refer to might have been Dame Marcella,[258] the one who translated Raïssa Maritain? Sounds like her. I think often of them and know they must be having it hard in some ways, as they are more sensitive to the traditional values. The recent Liturgical Conference in Washington[259] was pretty awful, from what I hear.

Yes, I am naturally expecting a great deal from the trip. But I am not determining in advance what I intend to get out of it. I just hope to let things arrange themselves, and to work with them. It is too big and too sudden a thing to have been planned, or to be totally planned by anyone even now. I just know that I have an itinerary, a passport, some visas and tickets on the way. I start next week, but will be in the U.S. until mid-October.

Sorry I was not able to get over to the Niles' but the date kept moving up on me.

With warm regards to all of you,

Tom

Could you please pass on the enclosed to the library?

☙

Dear Carolyn—

Here is a nice picnic space—though there are at present no picnics. Delhi is fine, and tonight[260] I take a train up to the Himalayas. The mountains looked marvelous from the plane in the distance, the other day. My best wishes to all especially to JJN[261] for the Bellarmine occasion

Tom

☙

WESTERN UNION
TELEGRAM
659 EST DEC 10 68 CTA400
CT LVA443 RX PD TDLV NEW HAVEN KY 10 547P EST
MRS VICTOR HAMMER, FONE AND MAIL
220 MARKET ST LEXINGTON KY
WE REGRET TO INFORM YOU OF THE DEATH OF
FATHER THOMAS MERTON IN BANGKOK
BROTHER PATRICK HART SECRETARY.

Afterword

With your words you have silently embraced me, I feel the touch of your hand on my shoulder, so kind. We are tools in the hands of God, we have to remain sharp and true. It is a fine duty and is the only rewarding turn for what we do. You have sensed this and said it. However much or little we can give or rend, we ought to be content with the fact that we did not cheat and this too is no merit but grace.
—Victor Hammer to Thomas Merton, February 3, 1965, after receiving Merton's essay for the North Carolina Museum of Art exhibition catalogue of Hammer's works

The exchanges included in this collection of letters provide the reader with insights into the shared interests and concerns of very sophisticated and deeply spiritual individuals, offering a glimpse of their lives and times, ranging from mundane concerns—the coordination of timing for a visit, given the difference in time zones between Lexington and the Abbey of Gethsemani, for example—to sublime reflection and thoughtful attention to aesthetic and spiritual truths. Merton and the Hammers took great nourishment from their ongoing dialogue and evolving friendship. It is hoped that the readers of these letters will have been able to share in the friendship of these polymaths and, from their exchanges, to have extracted nourishment for themselves. Toward that end, the editors offer this afterword, highlighting what seem to us the most valuable facets of their dialogue. There are four major foci of this correspondence to be considered here: art and spirituality, the collaborative publications, Merton's reading lists, and mutual friends.

A substantial portion of the evolving friendship between Merton and the Hammers, vividly revealed in their letters, is focused on the interrelationship of art and spirituality. These letters involve a discussion of their individual perspectives on art, a critique of "modern art," and a discussion of the importance of "ornament" as the tool that binds a work of art into a whole.

Indeed, the first letter from Victor Hammer to Thomas Merton, of November 8, 1955, is a condensation of his entire philosophy of art. This letter and Merton's response to it provide the backdrop for their ongoing dialogue of the next decade, fundamental to their exchanges about "classic art" and "cave art." Here Hammer and Merton delineate very clearly the vantage points from which each sees and understands the world and argues for the validity of his perspective.

Victor Hammer's understanding of art was greatly influenced by the not well-known German neo-Kantian Conrad Fiedler (1841–1895), whom Hammer considered to be the most important nineteenth-century art theorist. Hammer had assisted in the translation of *Three Fragments from the Postumous Papers of Conrad Fiedler*, which he printed in 1951. He summarizes Fiedler's ideas in this first letter, which bears quoting:

> It took me almost thirty years of reading Fiedler in order to realize what he was talking about. If now I would try to word Fiedler's theory in my own terms I would, in brief, say: our apparatus of vision, the eyes, can perceive only in the manner of flat or curved planes, that is, in two dimensions. Visual actuality, i.e. three-dimensional seeing can only be realized in and through works of classic art. Primitive art does not go beyond two-dimensional perception; it states its facts on uninterrupted, as it were unframed, planes. Classic art sees and produces three-dimensionally. In order to achieve this it has turned deliberately away from the uninterrupted planes, from the fields, from the environment of earth and water, setting up a man-made enclosure, the frame of the agora, the market place, the polis. Art becomes spiritual, intellectual, human; classic art is civilized art.

Within a definite frame (of inorganic, crystalline, i.e. spiritual character) it creates a foreground that pushed the onlooker somewhat outside the frame, preparing him to realize depth visually, as a third dimension; then, behind the foreground the main plane rises, acting against a background. These three planes, so interrelated that in the elevation the ground plan can be sensed, permit the onlooker to perceive all three dimensions in a single act of contemplation. This is the visibility of civilized man who turns his eyes toward the dwelling place of the gods. No aesthetic pleasure is involved, he is lifted above animal vision. The secret of art then, to Fiedler, its essence, consists in the creation of three-dimensional space with two-dimensional means.

This applies to sculpture and architecture as well as to painting. The artist who creates classic works of art does not need focused perspective, to him overlapping forms suffice. However, these individual overlapping forms must be so proportioned that one form cannot be confused with the other within the frame. Spiritually active, the artist conceives his work as pure form which is strong enough to hold any content, such as beauty, emotion, and even aesthetic pleasure. Woe to the artist who does not conceive in pure form or neglects it altogether.

Merton responded on November 26, 1955, from the poverty of the desert solitude:

I was very interested in your remarks on Fiedler's theory, and they tend to entrench me in my own prejudice *against* classicism. Not as art, but as *sacred* art. It is quite true that primitive and two dimensional art is intellectually poor and limited. Precisely. Less human also—just that! It is the poverty of primitive art that makes it more able to serve as "matter" so to speak for a sacramental and religious form.

It seems to me that the self-assurance with which the classical eye accepts the "man-made enclosure" tends, at least in most cases, to exclude the transcendental in the sense of the "Holy"—das ganz Andere. Precisely, in the polis, everything is familiar. In the agora we trade our own opinions and our own vegetables too: and this is right and fitting. There must be humanism, and Christianity is humanistic. And it certainly speaks up in the market place—where else? But it brings the desert into the market place too, and the desert is vast, empty, and poor, and has no frame . . .

I do not argue that three dimensional art cannot be holy—(Fra Angelico!)—only that it grows up in a context where in fact holiness is not encouraged: the academic context.

All these letters between Merton and the Hammers reveal both views shared together as well as disagreements—but always each was respectful of the other's position. These two initial letters establish a basis for a dialogue—a dialectic—that evolved over their entire friendship. As our introduction to this volume explains, Victor Hammer was committed to classical art and architecture—a commitment he traced to his childhood experiences in the oldest quarter of Vienna, which formed his vision as an artist; he had no chance or capacity as a little boy to realize that the world with which he was contemporaneous was already two hundred years old. The well-ordered space of the Universitätsplatz in front of the Jesuit church was the womb that nurtured Victor Hammer's art throughout his life, later to be articulated and clarified for him by Conrad Fiedler's theories.

Thomas Merton, on the other hand, after his dramatic introduction and conversion to the Byzantine aesthetic, with its stress on otherworldliness, at the Church of Sts. Cosmas and Damian in Rome, was provided with a basis for his view that art can only be a vehicle to higher spiritual ends and aims. The Byzantine aesthetic was for him the foremost mode to those ends, informing his interior dialogue regarding art and spirituality.

Victor Hammer sent Thomas Merton a copy of his 1951 publication of Fiedler's fragments. Merton reported on December 17, 1955:

> It is intensely interesting and thought provoking. As I had suspected, the arguments I tentatively put forth in my last letter had little really to do with Fiedler whom I see to be just as "anti-academic" as I am. . . . I find many of his intuitions very powerful and right. . . . But how on earth are we ever to get anyone to see these things? It is enough to reduce one to despair. But the world is being punished for its sins—*all* its sins. The depravation of human nature, even for instance of human techniques of work, is also a sin against God the Author of nature. Is it not part of the natural law that man should work humanly and taste joy in creating, and work for something else besides money? . . . PS I fully understand what you mean about cities. If I had seen more of Vienna and less of London and New York, I would have less prejudice. In fact, I sent to the Ky U. library a page or two I once wrote about Havana which shows that we agree too about the *polis* after all.

Accompanying his letter of September 10, 1959, Merton sent the Hammers an offprint from *CrossCurrents*. Victor Hammer responded on September 18, 1959: "I liked your article on Christianity and don't you see this is exactly what the classic artist must do—not heading for beauty or anything else, only trying to open the eyes of those who might be able to see. But woe to him who tries to fake a work of classic art by trying to use their recipe for making one, he would fail as much as the Pharisees failed. Humility at least can prevent one from making a fool of oneself."

As he prepared to print Thomas Merton's manuscript of *The Solitary Life* in 1960, Victor Hammer wrote on January 7, 1960, about his hand-cut uncial type: "I know quite well how difficult it is for most persons—including you—to get used to it. You may even regret that the

Desert Fathers have been set up in this unusual, and uncompromising type. It is the same with almost everything I am doing—conservative as I am, it takes people years and decades to see the reason why I am so severe, so uncommitting. And you will understand why I dedicate my work to God, not to man, and why I don't care for immediate reward."

Thomas Merton seems to have been receptive to Victor Hammer's clarifications of his perspective, when he wrote on February 19, 1960: "I will break this off, with no more than a word to say that I am becoming very *classical minded* since reading F. M. Cornford. . . . I will talk more about my conversion to classicism later. Victor's good angel must have been working on me."

Victor Hammer responded on February 22, 1960, as he prepared to print *The Solitary Life:* "You are entitled to any change in your text, without any charge, our time has no monetary value, we want the book to be written as good as you can do it and we will print it accordingly." Victor Hammer and Thomas Merton were in agreement that the *Opus Manuum* is the *Opus Dei,* and that we human beings are all "tools in the hands of God."

Both Merton and the Hammers viewed modern abstract art as somehow an aberration—the Hammers more so than Merton. Making the point, Victor Hammer wrote on August 7, 1960:

But when I say: In order to understand modern art we must cast off all the strange notions of the artist as a genius, a prophet, a redeemer—I should have been readily understood. And are we not saying the same thing when I talk about the emptiness of all space-relations which constitute the core of classic art, or when I insist that all "art work" (what a word!) should be undertaken for the higher glory of God? And it was Fiedler who, more than 80 years ago in the last fragment said that the subject-object relation may be a necessary crutch for establishing scientific method, but that in all other human endeavors where truth is either created or revealed, it makes no sense nor has it any value, on the contrary—and Suzuki makes that very clear too. Not being a child of my age or society, I may bluntly add that I consider Picasso an able experimenter but in no ways an artist.

Merton had as one of his dearest Columbia friends Ad Reinhardt, who was a well-respected abstract painter. Merton defended Reinhardt on numerous occasions against observations by Hammer about Reinhardt and abstract painting in general. Merton remarked in an April 1959 letter: "Though Reinhardt is a very abstract painter, he is perhaps the most severe painter in the world and I am sure you would agree basically on classicism—though his painting is very two dimensional. I don't know why. But austere." Though Merton argued that Reinhardt and Hammer would agree on classicism, the Hammers were not so persuaded that they quite agreed. Indeed, on the basis of their understanding of Fiedler's theories and what they perceived the true nature of art to be, abstraction and, especially, abstract expressionism fell far short of classical art, or what Victor Hammer referred to as "civilized" art. Hammer completed his essay *On Classic Art* in 1959. Merton's March 6, 1959, response to the proof says: "I may say that I am really in agreement with all that you say, and that I heartily approve of your distinction between city art and cave art: but then at last we come to my incorrigible preference for cave art. I cannot do otherwise, because I think that city art is in itself less capable of being sacred."

On May 2, 1959 Hammer wrote:

I am very sorry we missed your friends Lax and Reinhardt. I would have liked to talk to Reinhardt as I am still unable to see anything in abstract art or understand it. These triangles, squares, dashes and moving lines ought to *underlie* a work of art (as it is the case in all classic art), they ought to be hidden and *not to be shown*. They are the hard core, the skeleton of a work of art.—If we were insects with the hard crust outside, abstract art would be appropriate. Characteristically enough we depict death as a skeleton. To me abstract art is pure perversion. Reinhardt may be sincere, but as an abstractionist he is a sinner against the Holy Ghost. It is a travesty on creation Carolyn said.

It is apparent that at this point Merton had not yet quite understood Hammer's "requirements for a work of civilized art," which forms the penultimate section of his essay *Concern for the Art of Civilized Man*, which he printed in 1963. The Hammers' remarks prompted a defense of his colleague and friend from Merton on May 14, 1959. He suggested again that Hammer and Reinhardt would be in agreement on some of the features of art—regardless of styles and approach to painting: "When Reinhardt was here he was discussing art too. His approach is very austere and aesthetic. It is a kind of exaggerated reticence, a kind of fear of self expression. All his paintings are very formal and black. I certainly do not think he is a quack like so many others, on the contrary he is in strong reaction against them. I think you and he would be in fundamental agreement. It is a pity he was not able to get over there. He is certainly not a brilliant success (like so many of the others who are making fortunes with their stuff.)" He continued this theme and provided a kind of concluding remark in his letter of November 9, 1963:

As to saying "what is art," well, I don't think there is much chance of making any sense out of the question if one is looking for a pure essence. On the other hand the question is not without *meaning*. It is a matter of communication, not of discovery: not of defining the thing and getting command over it, but of clarifying one's own concepts and conveying what one means, or does not mean.

After all, one has to be able to say that abstract expression is *not* art, and I think that clarifies most of what needs to be said about it, both for and against. That is precisely what is "for" it: that it is not art, though it seems to be. I know this statement is scandalous, and I think the ambiguities are bad ones in the long run (it should not pretend to be art, which in fact it does). I do not think that throwing paint on canvas and saying "this is not art" merits twenty thousand dollars. It is too obvious. However, even the obvious has its place.

Despite the differences between their aesthetic preferences—Merton's Byzantine and Hammer's classical—they were in substantial agreement about art that adorns churches, and art done to edify and lift the spirit of those who worship in places where art is an important part of the liturgical life. Victor Hammer happily assisted Brother Giles's efforts to improve the aesthetics of the abbey with the positioning of Peter Watts's Stations of the Cross, which occasioned Hammer's first meeting with Merton. But his most important contribution was the *Crucifixus* requested by Merton for the novitiate chapel, which currently hangs in the infirmary chapel. Victor Hammer had initially painted this crucifix—depicting Jesus on the cross, his face modeled on the image on the Shroud of Turin, with Saint Mary and Saint John on either side—for the chapel he was commissioned to build at Kolbsheim in Alsace. When Hammer took it to be positioned in this chapel, he realized it looked too small above the altar, and so he painted a larger version. The smaller one was completed after Hammer added "INRI" ("Jesus of Nazareth, King of the Jews") above the cross and entrusted it to the abbey's care. Hammer made a third version, which now hangs in the Chapel of Our Lady at the Newman Center in Lexington. After Merton completed his tour of duty as master of novices and became a hermit, he lamented the fact that he was no longer able to say Mass in front of Hammer's *Crucifixus.* The Hammers completed several other small projects for the abbey, altar cards and other small printing jobs, yet Merton had hoped for other substantial collaborations, which never came to fruition, including a tabernacle and candlesticks for the novitiate chapel, modeled on those Hammer had crafted for the chapel at Kolbsheim.

During his European years, Victor Hammer had made his living as a society portrait painter; he had had a number of important patrons in Austria, France, Germany, and Italy. Although he worked on several versions of his depiction of the story of Christ and the adulteress from St. John's Gospel, his other religious and mythological works were the result of his freedom from portrait commissions that his teaching positions in the United States afforded him, first at Wells College and later at Transylvania College. Here he was able to choose his own subject matter. By the time of his exhibition at the North Carolina Museum of Art in 1965, several examples were included. Merton, in his essay for the exhibition catalogue (included in appendix B), went to the heart of the matter:

> The content of Victor Hammer's religious paintings is at once concrete, spiritual, and individual. And though he generally uses traditional iconographic styles and patterns, his religious art is not *Art d'Eglise*. His rood Cross painted for the chapel of Alexandre and Antoinette de Grunelius at Kolbsheim, in Alsace (a replica of the same Rood hangs in the chapel of the novitiate at the Abbey of Gethsemani), is simple, noble and even in some sense mysterious, though this judgment might surprise the artist himself. But the adjective is chosen by one who worships daily before this Rood, and he has the right if not the duty to make the impression known.

Though Merton specifically focused on the rood in his essay, another religious painting inspired much discussion and then collaboration: the triptych painting *Hagia Sophia Crowning the Young Christ,* the source of Merton's meditative poem and its printing as *Hagia Sophia.* The letters regarding the triptych and the poem reveal one of the most inspirational illustrations of the synergy of idea and image these friends shared. A careful exegesis of the letters of Hammer (May 2, 1959) and of Merton (May 14, 1959) is key to understanding the influence of religious art on Merton, and the way Hammer influenced many of Merton's religious reflections.

Hammer provided a backdrop for his religious paintings in a letter to Merton of September 29, 1963, focusing on five versions of the story of Christ and the adulteress, a narrative that he thought could be conveyed purely visually. He traced the development of the painting, and the number of attempts to assure verisimilitude to the biblical message of that work. He attached to the letter an essay composed in 1950 defining in detail his reflections as he went about the preparation of nearly a lifetime of work. With the fifth version Hammer felt he had finally achieved the desired result: "I feel that I cannot go further, that the visual part of the theme [a circle amid uprights] is definitely stated, and that only now I understand my own work."

As our introduction to this collection suggests, Victor Hammer's most important contribution to religious art is the chapel at the Château de Kolbsheim in Alsace. As his patron Alexandre de Grunelius said, it is "Victor's greatest offering to god, and the place where all of his gifts as an artist were united: architecture, sculpture, stone-carved letters, painting, the gold-smith's craft."[1] Its unity and completeness demonstrate Victor Hammer's belief that all forms of art are really architecture in disguise. He once remarked: "I am aware that I have always painted with a sculptor's eye . . . yet my sculpted figures at the portals of the chapel in Kolbsheim are as a painter saw them to be."[2] And this is so for him because architecture necessarily and clearly bears the marks of the unifying spiritual gesture—a religious principle that is sensed in all works of classical, civilized art. In his essay for the North Carolina Museum of Art exhibition catalogue (see Hammer's letter of March 21, 1965), Jacques Maritain writes of the chapel: "Everything in this chapel built of grey native stone promotes a spirit of meditation (and what a relief it is to be delivered from reinforced concrete, the hideous ruins of which, in centuries to come, will be a desecration to the earth). And the total effect corresponds to the three notes which, according to St. Thomas, constitute beauty and which are so typical of the house and garden at Kolbsheim: Integritas, Consonantia, Claritas. I especially like those moving groups, carved in rose-colored sandstone, which form the tympanum above the chapel door. It is a perfect sculptural melody."

Victor Hammer contrasted the contemporary state of religious art with that of earlier times in his September 29, 1963, letter, observing:

> The priests of the religious orders defined exactly what they wanted and needed as painted stories on the walls of their churches, in order to teach the believers who could not read but were able to see. Though the wishes of the clerics (laymen too regarding the arts) were set down exactly in writing and contracts with the artists made, no patron, as the Church was, would have expected the artists to "express themselves." Yet the artists were free to strive after artistic truth as they saw fit.
>
> This kind of layman no longer exists, and church art became as poor as it is. The churchmen do not know what they want and actually they don't want anything specific; they wait for what the artist offers and meekly accept it, or after a while reject it for the wrong reasons. As the Abbot of Scheyern, when I asked him when the frescoes on the barrel vault of their Romanesque church were painted, said: Oh, that was when we had too much money. . . . Sad world in which we live and involuntarily take part of the spirit that reigns in it.

A full statement of Victor Hammer's critique of the modern era is appended to his letter to Merton of January 20, 1965. But Hammer's own perspective on art can be seen as an antidote to the state of affairs he addressed. Indeed, his dialogue on art and spirituality with Merton was an attempt to explain to Merton the liberation his own views on genuine art allowed. Nowhere in their exchanges is this more clear and compelling than in their discussion of *ornatus*, focused on in letters of the summer and fall of 1965. Victor Hammer wrote on October 22, 1965: "This question of the 'ornament' is very important to me and I wish you would speak about it. It may even be that the word is translated carelessly and the difference between 'ornamentation' and 'decoration' not exactly considered. 'Ornament' is a very sincere matter and the idea of 'beauty' cannot simply be stated by the 3 words of St. Thomas. Perhaps no definition is possible at all, as one cannot 'define' God." Merton replied on November 2, 1965: "My only thought is that after all if we think of it, the mode which demands an apparent absence of 'ornatus' is itself in its own way a form of ornamentation, i.e. an accidental style which adds a 'character' of some sort to the thing made. Ornatus in any case is not 'ornament,' hence I would say that strictly speaking even austere simplicity could be classed as ornatus, for instance in Shaker work." It is precisely the "'character' of some sort [added] to the thing made" with which Hammer is concerned. His extensive discussion of this can be found in chapter 2 of his 1956 book, *Memory and Her Nine Daughters the Muses: A Pretext for Printing Cast into the Mould of a Dialogue in Four Chapters*. Here, in a discussion about the construction of the chapel at Kolbsheim, Hammer meditates on architectural styles, but his thoughts can be extended to address all forms of the visual arts:

> We . . . have become conscious of the fact that architecture is coexistent with light . . . without light it ceases, in a very real sense, to exist. Building and architecture are intimately connected, yet are not the same; building would satisfy the needs and wants of a blind man, while architecture exists only for those able to see. . . . what can the masterbuilder do in order to make the seeing see? . . . only by using a spiritual gesture can he hope to unify and immortalize what by its nature is transitory. This gesture, being of essentially magic character, and powerful enough to leave its mark on the raw construction, is actual (or real), because what the gesture effects remains visible. . . .
>
> This is what makes the finished work a living organism. . . . Cutting grooves into the stones—grooves that create shadows and intensify lights—is like speaking to the spectator with a gesture, saying: this is now a coherent whole, a living organism covered with a fitting skin of lights and

shadows under which structure is distinctly visible. . . . The gesture of unification is a religious principle because it aims at life in the future, or, more precisely, it aims at the spiritual life in the future, since it appeals to the eye alone. . . .

The principle from which all architectural styles rose has found a terse formulation in the Greek word "Kosmos" which, in all its derivatives means either order, array or ornament. Architecture is founded on order, as well as on ornament: a means to the end of making order evident. Order in art is an order of visibility, or to be more precise: of evidence, because it is dependent upon the characteristics and limitations of human vision and understanding. . . . This order of visibility needs brute matter as a medium of execution. Having no life, brute matter disintegrates but does not pass away; man however, can endow it with life. He can use ornament as a gesture and our eyes will understand, and will grasp its meaning. . . . To the Greeks, aware of the spiritual nature of ornament, the idea of cosmos in the sense of order must have meant order of any kind. . . . We know that Greek stonecutters referred to ornamentation by using the word "kosmopoiein" which means literally "to create order," and Greek temples were not naked structures. They were adorned as Greek women were.[3]

Reflecting on his own work in creating the chapel at Kolbsheim, Hammer continued:

Thus ornament was not prepared before hand and then plastered on the structure, here, there and yonder . . . rather it was the expression of an act of humility. . . . Since ornament sustains the life of buildings as long as their substratum (even in ruins) lasts, the use of ornament in architecture is a confession of human weakness, and as such, a religious act. As long as ornament is understood and used in this sense, it will appear on buildings like flowers on a hillside, but when ornament appears on the structure as pretentious or confused display it will be mere decoration and lose its religious meaning.

It was in the chapel at Kolbsheim where Victor Hammer was able to demonstrate his understanding of *ornatus*. The chapel's unity and compeleteness clearly bear those visible marks of the unifying spiritual gesture—a religious principle that he felt present in all true works of art. The wholeness, the work, and its harmony, its rhythm, combine to reveal a radiance that arrests the eye, stills the mind, and enchants the heart. True art, genuine art, is the vehicle of transformation for spiritual growth. Because it is made whole through an integrating spiritual gesture, it lifts up those who observe to apprehend the sublime. Our consciousness is therein forever altered. Victor Hammer's work shows the task of the artist—his responsibility and vocation—is to produce visible order, to give stability of form, which can be visually remembered and understood for what otherwise are only fleeting perceptions. The artist gives us through the work, in which the trace of the human hand lingers, a vision of the whole; he or she sees for us the radiant whole of things in one particular form, within the harmonic unity of the individual work. The artist tells us his truth, not with words, but with gestures, forms, symbols. The proper work of art, the genuine work, opens the eye of the beholder to see reality unfolded, undivided and whole, prepared for contemplation.

A second major portion of the correspondence between Merton and the Hammers is also of great interest and concerns the publication of works by Merton that the Hammers set in type and printed by hand. These publications included essays, poems, commentary, and translations. (A bibliographic listing of these works appears in appendix C. A synopsis of the several presses with which the Hammers were associated is included in our introduction.) Though their mutual collaboration produced several beautiful printed works, there are other ideas discussed in the letters that did not come to fruition for various reasons, including works by A. K. Coomaraswamy and Nicholas of Cusa. Some works by Merton were also printed by other presses, such as the *Christmas Sermons of Bl. Guerric,* printed by the Abbey of Gethsemani.

As we have indicated earlier, perhaps the most remarkable collaboration of Hammer and Merton was Merton's *Hagia Sophia,* printed at the Stamperia del Santuccio in 1962. The story of this poem is well known by most Merton scholars but rarely understood in its entirety; it is clearly enunciated here in these letters. Victor Hammer related the background of the triptych painting to Merton in his letter of May 2, 1959, after Merton had visited them for lunch in April. Merton responded on May 14, attempting to define and clarify the feminine principle in the Godhead, the wisdom of God. Merton's poem encompasses their thoughts, reflected and documented in their letters. He sent Hammer the manuscript in May 1961, and it was published in 1962; the letters of that summer document the details of the printing and publication. Hammer had intended to use an image derived from the painted triptych as a frontispiece for the edition. Toward that end, he produced two woodcuts and a criblé engraving in brass. He was unable to complete the engraving because a cataract had compromised his vision. No frontispiece was used in the 1962 edition. The edition had a distinctive wrapper on which was printed a passage about holy wisdom from Proverbs in Latin, with the English translation interlinear. The quotation begins with a two-color initial *S* cut from brass by Hammer. When Carolyn Hammer printed a second edition in 1978, the frontispiece engraving was included. This was the last book bearing the Stamperia del Santuccio imprint.

In 1964 Victor Hammer had surgery to remove the cataract in Louisville. At the time, this was a significant piece of surgery, but it was successful. Hammer was overjoyed at the recovery of some of his sight, and he asked Merton to write a brief poem in Latin and English to celebrate this recovery. Hammer's father had been blind at the time of his death, and he had resigned himself to the same fate. Merton complied with Hammer's request and wrote the brief poem, which Hammer inscribed on the verso of his last painting, *The Resurrection,* which he was never able to complete. The poem is appended to the letter of November 3, 1964.

There were two publications of Merton's work by the Stamperia del Santuccio before the collaboration of 1962. The first, *What Ought I to Do? Sayings of the Desert Fathers from the Collection in Migne's Latin Patrology*, was printed in 1959. It is a translation by Thomas Merton of sayings of early monks living in the Egyptian desert. The discussions of the publication are contained in the letters from the fall of 1958 through the early spring of 1959. On the wrapper for this volume appears a printed selection in Latin, beginning with a two-color initial *E* whose background depicts a monk holding a scroll.

The second volume of this trilogy of Merton's work is *The Solitary Life*, published in 1960. Merton first mentioned the text to Hammer in January 1960. A reading of the subsequent letters early that year shows that Hammer envisioned this second volume as a "companion" to the first, again using his American Uncial typeface, and its being of the same dimensions. This book also has a beautiful wrapper, printed with Merton's poem "I, Solitude," composed especially for this wrapper, beginning with a long initial *I* cut from brass by Hammer. This book was subsequently published by James Laughlin at New Directions. There were several other collaborations between Merton and the Hammers, though not necessarily authored by Merton. In 1958 the Stamperia del Santuccio published *The Unquiet Conscience* by Piero Bargellini. It was a small book translated by Merton from the Latin. Apparently, Merton used it for some of his classes for his novices, as he referred to their wanting copies of the text in the correspondence.

Merton's affection for and interest in Zen Buddhism is well documented. He read its literature extensively and wrote several pieces about Zen. There are numerous references regarding Zen in the letters, and the number of books on the topic, which he asked Carolyn Hammer to provide from the King Library, are requested early and often. In 1960 *Ox Mountain Parable* by Meng Tzu was printed as the second broadside issued by the Stamperia del Santuccio, with an introduction by Thomas Merton.

In addition to Stamperia del Santuccio publications of Merton's work, others were printed by other hand-press operations with which the Hammers were involved. In October 1967, following Victor Hammer's death in July, Merton shared a series of poems he had written following his entrance into the abbey. These were printed in 1971 as *Early Poems 1941–42*, and it was the one of two of Merton's works printed at The Anvil Press. The King Library Press printed Merton's *Prometheus, A Meditation*, first mentioned in his letter of August 8, 1957, and occasionally mentioned in letters through 1958, when it was published.

The correspondence between Thomas Merton and Boris Pasternak is well known to Merton scholars. Merton wrote to Pasternak in 1958, even before he was awarded the Nobel Prize for Literature. This correspondence continued for two years, until Pasternak's death in 1960. Early on in his correspondence with Merton, Dr. Lawrence Thompson had asked that Merton share with the University of Kentucky Library materials that the library could archive and make available to scholars who wished to study them. Among the items Merton provided were the letters he exchanged with Pasternak. These letters form the basis of a book printed at the King Library Press, Thomas Merton and Boris Pasternak, *Six Letters*. In a July 1958 letter to Hammer, Merton mentioned his intent to write to Pasternak and send him a copy of *Prometheus, A Meditation*, which the King Library Press had just published. Merton also shared with Hammer an article he had written about Pasternak in 1959, an article that had caused difficulties with censors of his order.

Needless to say, in his vocation as a writer, Merton often experienced difficulties with the censors. He was vocal about the problems of the censorship of his writing with the Hammers. While there are several letters dealing with these difficulties, one of his clearest descriptions is from August 24, 1957, regarding *Prometheus, A Meditation*. He observes:

> If you sell copies of the meditation, it will have to be censored. And this is such an inordinate amount of trouble, that

for a small thing of this sort, and particularly for a small edition, it is hardly worth while. The censors begin by keeping every manuscript for three or four months if not more. Then, if they don't lose it, they find an excuse for causing all kinds of trouble over the slightest things. Then the Abbot General gets up in the air about it, and in the end we end up where we started, because there is usually nothing wrong anyway. In order not to have to spend the next five months in a teapot tempest over something that is for all practical purposes a manuscript, I think it would just be best for *us* to pay the costs, and distribute the work, leaving you of course as many copies as you want for yourselves.

The Hammers were not, apparently, familiar with the necessity of censorship of Merton's work by the Church, and they asked about the terms *nihil obstat* and *imprimatur*. In a letter of July 4, 1958, Merton details for Carolyn exactly what is involved in obtaining those designations, which would allow Merton's work to be published. Merton, of course, knew the ins and outs of the process and in some cases—notably the *Cold War Letters*—how to circumvent it.

A third substantial selection of letters, specifically from Thomas Merton to Carolyn Hammer, reveal and document Merton's requests for books, which he was otherwise unable to obtain at the abbey, from the library of the University of Kentucky. Though he borrowed books from other libraries, he certainly used the King Library extensively. Dr. Lawrence Thompson, the director of the library at the University of Kentucky after Margaret I. King, began a correspondence with Merton in 1950 and established a relationship with him. Thompson obviously knew the potential interest of scholars in Merton's work, for by then *The Seven Storey Mountain* had been published, and Thompson was eager to establish the University of Kentucky as a base for archival material that Merton was producing, including early typescripts of his books. In at least one letter he asked Merton for early typescripts of *The Seven Storey Mountain*. The Merton Archives in the Special Collections at the University of Kentucky are not extensive but do contain important pieces that Merton gave the library, including the Pasternak letters. There was no doubt some disappointment when Merton decided to establish a permanent site for his archives at Bellarmine University. Nevertheless, as a result of the relationships that Merton had with both Lawrence Thompson and Carolyn Hammer, his correspondence is filled with book requests, requests to hold on to books longer, lists of library slips, et alia. We have not attempted to carefully compile the requests that Merton made for books, but it is obvious from the letters that the selection of titles he requested was extensive both in breadth and depth. His reading habits are well known, and his consumption of books on topics of interest to him is remarkable.

A quick glance through the requests reflects his varied interests, from his early reading in Buddhism, especially Zen, as well as oriental and eastern literature, to his interest in Russia and Russian history, including Marxism-Leninism and communism. The period of time when he seriously considered relocating to a monastery in Central or South America is also represented in his book requests. There is no doubt that Carolyn Hammer worked hard to ensure that he had what he needed, and she looked beyond his immediate requests to identify books of the same genre about which he had inquired to share with him. The correspondence is filled with information about books and articles that the Hammers felt would be of interest to Merton and probably formed the basis of some of their picnic conversations.

Another dimension of this collection of letters is the many exchanges regarding friends of Merton and of the Hammers, several of whom they shared. A number of these friendships are notable, and a brief survey may further clarify these relationships.

James Laughlin, the founder of New Directions, published a substantial amount of Merton's writing, Laughlin having been a close friend since Merton's days at Columbia. Laughlin also became a friend of the Hammers, having lunch in their home on Market Street in Lexington, and visiting and picnicking with Merton and the Hammers at the abbey. Many of the pieces that were printed by hand and published by the Hammers were subsequently published by New Directions. There are many references in the letters to "J.," as Laughlin was often called in Merton's correspondence. Laughlin traveled back and forth to the abbey fairly often to arrange details of the publication of Merton's work

Jacques Maritain, the noted Roman Catholic philosopher, theologian, humanist, and aesthetician, was a close friend of both the Hammers and Merton. Alexandre de Grunelius (1890–1977) and his wife, Antoinette Slumberger (1908–1994), were early patrons of Victor Hammer. Alexandre de Grunelius, referred to as "Lexi" in some of the correspondence, was the administrator of Dietrich Enterprises, and he had inherited his family château in the village of Kolbsheim in Alsace. They were very good friends of Jacques and Raïssa Maritain, and through their efforts the Maritain Center and its archive is located close by the château. The Gruneliuses' children were godchildren of Jacques and Raïssa Maritain, who often stayed for long periods with the Grunelius family. The Maritains lie buried in the Grunelius plot in the cemetery at Kolbsheim. As our introduction notes, Victor Hammer came to know the Maritains when he was completing the construction of the chapel at the château.

Jacques Maritain taught at a number of American universities, including Columbia, Notre Dame, and Princeton. Merton had made use of Maritain's *Art and Scholasticism* when working on his Blake thesis at Columbia. He first met Maritain when Maritain lectured in New York in 1939, after which he began a correspondence with Maritain that has subsequently been published. Maritain and Merton were interested in each other's work. When Merton was having problems with censorship, Maritain assisted in getting *The Sign of Jonas* published. After Vatican II, Maritain wrote suggesting that Merton's essay on Suzuki might be included in a collection including works by Fromm, Tillich, and Eliade. This time the censors said no. Merton was unable to travel abroad while in the abbey. But since the Hammers visited Europe periodically, including Kolbsheim, their letters to Merton from abroad recounted news about and their conversations with Maritain and his wife, Raïssa.

In addition to these mutual friends, the Hammers introduced Merton to some of the Lexington artistic and intellectual community. There is reference in the letters to Clay Lancaster, a longtime friend of Carolyn Hammer, who was a nationally renowned architectural historian, the preeminent authority on Kentucky architecture, and a native of Lexington. Lancaster lectured in architecture and Far Asian art at Cooper Union, Columbia, New York University, and the Metropolitan Museum of Art. He was the author of numerous important books about the architectural history of Brooklyn Heights, Nantucket Island, Lexington, and the Bluegrass.

The Hammers also introduced Merton to George Headley and his wife, Barbara. Headley was a talented jewelry designer and the creator of miniature sculptures he called "bibelots," which formed the heart of the collection of the Headley-Whitney Museum in Lexington, which he founded.

One of the most productive introductions the Hammers afforded Merton was to John Jacob Niles and his wife, Rena, also longtime friends. In addition to George Headley, the Nileses, along with the Bob and Hanna Shepherd, were occasionally part of the Hammers' picnics with Merton. Eventually Niles, a respected composer and compiler of folk music, began to set a series of Merton's poems to music, around the time of Victor's death. Before his Asian journey began, Merton went to the Nileses' farm, called Boot Hill, to hear part of the song-cycle being performed, and to enjoy lunch. Carolyn Hammer assumed responsibility for much of the communication between the Nileses and Merton at this time, as some of the letters reflect.

We hope the readers of these letters have been nourished by this aliquot of the correspondence between the Hammers and Merton, as their friendships nourished each other through their disciplined, principled, and creative lives, sharing their common aim and bond. To underscore this, we leave you with Victor Hammer's short explanation of its meaning, in his letter to his friend and patron Norman Strouse, April 1965: "There is for you great hope in your attitude . . . your attitude shows much self-criticism, and you will need that when you work on your own. From this angle you will understand the four words 'AD MAJOREM DEI GLORIAM' better. If this is the aim one must give one's best, however small that may be. It is not nice to cheat men, but one cannot cheat God."

Appendix A

Letters between Veronica (Moni) Hammer and Thomas Merton

The two letters that this appendix comprises are between and Merton and Victor Hammer's daughter, Veronica, nicknamed Moni. Much of Moni's letter reflects her and her mother's (Rosl) difficulties with Victor; however, her major concern was Victor's state of grace and standing with the Church. Victor's state of grace was a source of continuing concern; in the section of his journal published as *Learning to Love*, in March 1966 Merton described his concern for Victor's religious beliefs, as he said, referring to "Apologies to an Unbeliever," subsequently published in *Harper's Weekly*, "Why did I write it? I don't know. Compassion for Victor Hammer, who is after all a very believing 'unbeliever' and for so many others who have to be alone and confused, penalized for the sincerity which prohibits facile options." This anxiety about Victor's state of relationship with the Church is reiterated in his letter of September 20, 1966, in which Merton, writing as a priest, expressed concerns to Victor about his relations with the Church and hopes that he would reconcile with it. Although Victor's exact religious convictions are never further discussed in the correspondence, there exists a continuing worry. Anyone familiar with Victor's feelings, however, knows that his work was *ad majorem Dei gloriam*, a paean to God and thus a religious expression that reflected his underlying belief in God.

Dec. 21, 1965
Dear Moni Hammer:

I am sorry not to have answered your letter before this, but I have very little opportunity to take care of correspondence. Still, I appreciate your concern and will answer you as best I can.

Victor and Carolyn were over here last month, in fact your letter came just a few days after their visit. Victor was looking better than I have seen him for a long time, and just coming over here was quite an achievement. Fortunately a new road has just been built and the driving is much quicker and easier, and it puts less strain on him as the distance has been shortened somewhat. I was glad to see him looking so well. But of course at his age, we cannot expect him to go on for many more years and God might take him from us at any time.

You ask how he stands with the Church. I do not think he is what one would call a really steady "practising Catholic" and I think it will be a great grace if he dies with the sacraments of the Church. I hope he will and pray for this. But on the other hand, if I know anything about people, I know that he is a very sincere believer and that in his heart he certainly loves God and Christ. The question of the Church is one which I think he has settled in some way of his own, as so many modern men do, and as far as I am concerned he is living according to his conscience and is I feel in the friendship of God and basically a Catholic. I know that he is willing to respect and accept the Church much more because I do not try to get him to do certain things externally which would signify his religious commitment as a Catholic, and I think he would be hurt if I seemed to press him in any way, with regard to these things. How shall I explain it? I think that a priest owes modern man a certain respect and trust for his own personal decisions, even in such matters as these, when he is obviously a good person, honest and sincerely Christian. However, if you ask me to speak to him about these matters I will do so, saying that you asked me to. Would this be a wise thing? I leave you to judge. But I assure you that I have personally no fears about his salvation. He is living sincerely according to his conscience as a product of a certain type of society and in his own way he is certainly a child of the Church. This is something one simply accepts with trust and one prays for him. However I agree with you that it could be much better if he would actually go to the Church regularly and receive the sacraments, if he could do so while remaining true and consistent with himself (that is to say not simply pushed by someone else).

It was good to hear from you. Are you the daughter whose portrait he painted? If so, then I feel that I know you. I have seen the portrait often in his house and I think it is one of his best. All blessings and a holy Christmas to you.

Cordially in Christ

1150 Wien—Witzelsbergergasse 4/18
Monday
Grüss Gott!!

Dear Father Louis—It is exactly two years ago,* that I received your kind letter—Excuse that I never answered—but it was hard for me to answer, because I had not the same opinion as you—But now I must write to you, to tell you, why I asked you how father thinks about the sacraments of penance—You are right when you say that a priest owes modern men a certain respect and that everyone has to be less-minded against his next—But, I, as a member of the family have seen all the years of my childhood and youth that father was really not too nice to my mother. He was not faithful to her and so many other things—But she loved him so much, that she would stand everything—and it was her who really made that out of him what he is—with her intelligence and her adaptability—and her absolute faithfulness—she had a very hard life—and she was a martyr—but never complained—I don't want to tell you details—its no use—but I want to make you understand why I am troubled about father—All the years I can remember, except the last year of mother's life—father was not as nice to her, as he is to Carolyn—I am not blaming him being nice to Carolyn, I am really happy that he has Carolyn, and she is a good and charming woman—But what troubles me is, if he ever thinks that he hurt my mother so after—and if he ever regrets it—I never could talk about similar subject with father, as I always was the little girl in his eyes—the little child, which has no own mind and has only to be instructed and advised—Therefore I asked you, to tell me if fathers actions catholic faith is so strong that he will be able to be ready for a contrition—Dear Father Louis—I hope you don't think I am narrow-minded, but please try to understand what I mean and feel—I put this affair completely in your hands—and whatever you do and say will be right—right for fathers peace with God—This last news I got from Carolyn don't sound too nice—but at that age of fathers—each day is a gift given by God—Whatever happens in the next time to father, please do write to me, what you think or did about my troubles—You ask if I am the daughter whose portrait was painted—yes that's me—

Best wishes for Christmas—we say in Austria blessed wishes or blessed Christmas—

Yours

Moni Hammer

*[Editors' note: Moni Hammer's letter to Thomas Merton is not dated but cannot have been written two years after he wrote her in December 1965, as this would date her reply to December 1967, five months after Victor Hammer's death. It is possible that she misremembered the date on which Merton's letter actually arrived and perhaps did not have it at hand when she replied.]

Appendix B

Foreword to the Hammer Exhibition Catalogue, North Carolina Museum of Art

This piece is the foreword to the retrospective exhibition of Victor Hammer's work at the North Carolina Museum of Art. This foreword is discussed in several letters in early 1965, as the exhibition was taking shape. It represents Merton's appreciation and understanding of Victor Hammer's art and his feelings regarding his artistry.

Victor Hammer
A Retrospective Exhibition
April 4–25, 1965
North Carolina Museum of Art, Raleigh

FOREWORD

George Seferis, the Greek poet and Nobel prize winner recently wrote of Delphi that it was precisely the place of purest illumination in ancient Greece because it was the place where the obscure forces of the earth dragon, Python, had been vanquished by Apollo. The understanding of this myth is the test of authentic classicism. For if it is interpreted merely as the destruction of darkness by light, as the suppression of instinct by reason, we do not arrive at classic light but only at a classicist and academic "enlightenment." What is important, and Seferis brings it out, is that from the body of the Python slain by light emanates a living force

299

of prophecy. And this prophetic force is powerful in proportion as the drive of darkness was so mighty and so threatening as to summon against it the discipline of the strongest light.

Pursuing the myth further, then, we can observe that the error of eighteenth century academicism was to assume that Python had to be altogether destroyed and done away with, not a trace being left, while there is a certain Dionysian romanticism abroad at the present time which asserts, on the contrary, that Python must be left entirely alone to do as he pleases. Both errors of perspective are quite understandable in their historical contexts, but both are errors. And as a result of them, says Seferis, in a quotation which he does not identify,

> The rich dwelling has fallen down
> Phoibos no longer has a hearth
> No prophetic laurel tree
> No singing fountain
> For the water has ceased to speak.

The art of Victor Hammer has in it not only the luminosity of classic technique but the eloquence of classic myth, and though he is concerned with the universal human measure in art, and does not seek merely to "express himself," he turns out to be as individual as anyone you please. This is simply another manifestation of the truth that one does not acquire an identity by subjective election in a void of undetermined liberty, whether in art or in anything else. One must first accept the tools and materials with which to become oneself quite real in choosing to do an authentic, honest, and humble work, properly understood in a context that is not only possible and reasonable, but above all actual.

Now the context in which Victor Hammer has chosen to work as an artist is not that of the current art market or of ephemeral fashion. Nor is it, of course, a completely imaginary context in which no thought of any market could possibly be relevant. His is the classic and traditional ambient of the patron who commissions and an artist who executes the commission.

His art is then to be seen in this classic and human relationship (alas no longer "actual" as it was in the Renaissance), which limits and defines it to a certain predictable content. Python, in other words, is not expected to be turned loose to devour both artist and patron and then proceed on his way to fresh adventures. But, slain and disciplined by light, Python still speaks in his prophetic laurel tree, or the eloquent spring flowing from the Delphian rock. For Victor Hammer, Muses are not conventional figures for a Masque in the park of Versailles. They are real, because myth is real. There are certain realities which can only be expressed in terms of myth. Such are in fact the deeper realities of life.

The content of Victor Hammer's religious paintings is at once concrete, spiritual, and individual. And though he generally uses traditional inconographic styles and patterns, his religious art is not *Art d'Eglise*. His rood Cross painted for the chapel of Alexandre and Antoinette de Grunelius at Kolbsheim, in Alsace (a replica of the same Rood hangs in the chapel of the novitiate at the Abbey of Gethsemani), is simple, noble and even in some sense mysterious, though this judgment might surprise the artist himself. But the adjective is chosen by one who worships daily before this Rood, and he has the right if not the duty to make the impression known.

Aelred of Rievaulx wrote in the twelfth century that the Rood Cross was the proper kind to have in the chapel of an anchorage, that is to say in the chapel where a recluse (his sister) was to spend her life of prayer. The rood, with the figures of Mary and John by the Crucified, is in fact a cosmic as well as redemptive symbol, and it has the deepest eschatological significance (the "recapitulation of all in Christ"). The anchorage needs to contain in its heart this picture of the World not as it is in itself, but as it is in Christ. Aelred was not familiar with the modern concept of psychological archetypes, though he was deeply imbued, as were all his contemporaries, with Biblical typology. It is the archetypal and typological quality of Victor Hammer's religious paintings that makes them so arresting and, I might add, sometimes so enigmatic. For though he has devoted himself to making *explicit* the content of his paintings, I must confess that I still find more that is implicit and therefore mysterious, and in fact I think he is sometimes more enigmatic, at least to me, than much abstract painting.

All this is simply to say that it would be foolish for one who might recognize at a glance (and surely that is not difficult) that these paintings are not the kind that are currently in fashion, to turn away without giving them his full attention. To begin with, there is the peculiar excellence of the portraits. Then there is the classic and archetypal realm of these religious and mythical paintings which not only illumine with purity of universal form but also disconcert with the force of individual expression. Victor Hammer's world of spiritual imagery is personal, concrete, non-eccentric, in many ways deceptively prosaic. Though he uses and defends a style that intends above all else to make content accessible, I am afraid that in his paintings as in those of all other true artists, whether traditional or anti-traditional, there are certain unavoidable demands made on the viewer. Not only, in the case of Victor Hammer especially, are the paintings difficult to locate in the first place: but when you have found them you still have to work and reach for the content, and the fact that the subject matter is obvious does not dispense one from this effort.

It is fortunate that this exhibition has brought these rare paintings together in one place where they can, at least temporarily, be found and seen.

Thomas Merton
Abbey of Gethsemani
1965

Thomas Merton–Related Books Printed at the Stamperia del Santuccio, The Anvil Press, and the King Library Press, Lexington, Kentucky

1. Bargellini, Piero
The Unquiet Conscience, Stamperia del Santuccio, 1958
4 pages; *leaf:* 20.5 x 14 cm.; *type:* American Uncial; *edition:* 50 copies on Magnani paper. Translated from the Latin by Thomas Merton. Printed by C. R. Hammer. Sewn in paper wrappers.

2. Meng Tzu
Ox Mountain Parable, Stamperia del Santuccio, 1960
8 pages; *leaf:* 27.5 x 19.5 cm.; *type:* American Uncial printed in black, red, and blue; *edition:* 100 copies on Magnani paper numbered at the press. Introduction by Thomas Merton. Broadside II. Designed and printed by C. R. Hammer. Binding varies.

3. Merton, Thomas
Hagia Sophia, Stamperia del Santuccio, 1962
10 pages; *leaf:* 24.5 x 15.5 cm.; *type:* American Uncial printed in black and red, title page in Andromaque Uncial printed in black; *edition:* 69 copies on Whatman paper, numbered at the press. On the wrapper (Magnani paper) is printed a passage from Proverbs beginning with a two-color ini-

tial letter *S* cut from brass by Victor Hammer. The English translation of this Latin passage is interlinear in red. Opus XVII (see also variant edition no. 3, 1978). Printed by C. R. Hammer. Case-bound by Lucy Crump.

4. Merton, Thomas
Hagia Sophia, Stamperia del Santuccio, 1978
18 pages; *leaf:* 28 x 19 cm.; *type:* American Uncial printed in black and red; *edition:* 50 copies on Magnani paper with an unfinished engraving on brass of *Hagia Sophia Crowning the Young Christ* by Victor Hammer (see also no. 2, Opus XVII). Binding varies.
Note: The text pages were composed and printed by Victor Hammer in 1962, but the book was not completed. In 1978 Carolyn Hammer printed the frontispiece and title page for this edition. This book was the last one to bear the imprint of the Stamperia del Santuccio.

5. Merton, Thomas
The Solitary Life, Stamperia del Santuccio, 1960
28 pages; *leaf:* 24.5 x 15.5 cm.; *type:* American Uncial printed in black and red; title page in Andromaque Uncial printed in black; *edition:* 60 copies on Whatman paper numbered at the press. On the wrapper (Magnani paper) is printed a poem by Thomas Merton beginning with the initial letter *I* cut from brass by Victor Hammer. Opus XVI. Printed by Victor Hammer, with the assistance of C. R. Hammer. Case-bound by Lucy Crump.

6. Merton, Thomas
What Ought I to Do? Sayings of the Desert Fathers from the Collection in Migne's Latin Patrology, Stamperia del Santuccio, 1959
40 pages; "Sayings" numbered I–C; *leaf:* 24.5 x 15.5 cm.; *type:* American Uncial printed in black and red; *edition:* 50 copies on Japanese Hosho paper numbered at the press. On the wrapper (Magnani paper) is printed a selection in Latin beginning with a two-color initial *E* (printed in blue) cut from brass by Victor Hammer; the background (printed

in red) depicts a monk with a scroll. Opus XV. Printed by C. R. Hammer. Case-bound by Lucy Crump.

7. Merton, Thomas
Early Poems 1941–42, The Anvil Press, 1971
28 pages; *leaf:* 24.5 x 15 cm.; *type:* American Uncial; *edition:* 150 copies on Hosho paper. Foreword by Jonathan Greene. Designed by C. R. Hammer and printed with the assistance of W. Gay Reading. Binding varies.

8. Merton, Thomas
Prometheus, A Meditation, King Library Press, 1958
10 pages; *leaf:* 24 x 15 cm.; *type:* American Uncial printed in black and red; *edition:* 150 copies on Hosho paper. Printed by Nancy Chambers, Stokley Gribble, C. R. Hammer, and Mary Vorhees. Binding varies.

9. Merton, Thomas, and Boris Pasternak
Six Letters, King Library Press, 1973
28 pages; *leaf:* 21 x 15 cm.; *type:* Caslon Old Style printed in black and red; *edition:* 150 copies on Hosho paper. Designed by C. R. Hammer. Printed by Gray Zeitz, Mabel and Travis DuPriest, Margaret Williams, Christopher Meatyard, Ida Nieves-Collazo, and Paul Holbrook, apprentices. Case-bound in paste papers.

10. Merton, Thomas
Thomas Merton's Four Poems in French, with translations into English by Rupert E. Pickins and an afterword by Robert E. Daggy, The Anvil Press, 1966
54 pages; *leaf:* 31 x 32 cm.; *type;* American Uncial printed in black and red; *edition:* 100 copies on Iyo Glazed paper. Composition by Carolyn R. Hammer. Printed by Paul E. Holbrook. Case-bound in blue paper with a linecut illustration of Merton's birthplace, Number 1, rue du 4 Septembre, Pardes, France.

Notes

Foreword

1. Many other potential visits crop up in Merton's correspondence with the Hammers, but this number is just the actual number of visits that can be verified from Thomas Merton's journals. I owe a word of thanks here to Patricia A. Burton for her assistance in locating many of these references.

2. The Abbey of Gethsemani paid Jaime Andrade $1,100 for the statue of the Virgin Mary and child Jesus that he carved at Merton's request. Merton to Jaime Andrade, February 6, 1959, Thomas Merton Center, Bellarmine University, Louisville, Ky.

3. Thomas Merton, *Run to the Mountain: The Story of a Vocation* (San Francisco: HarperCollins, 1995), 128–29.

4. Victor Hammer to Merton, May 2, 1959.

5. Merton to Victor Hammer, May 14, 1959.

6. Thomas Merton, *Dancing in the Water of Life: Seeking Peace in the Hermitage,* ed. Robert E. Daggy (San Francisco: HarperCollins, 1997), 162.

7. Merton to Victor Hammer, November 3, 1964.

8. Victor Hammer died in July 1967 and Ad Reinhardt soon after, on August 30.

Preface

1. *Ad maiorem Dei gloriam* or *ad majorem Dei gloriam* was a popular Christian phrase when it became the motto of the Society of Jesus, a religious order of the Roman Catholic Church, also known as the Jesuits. Ignatius Loyola, founder of the order, used it as the focus of human endeavor, his full phrase as he wrote it being *"Ad maiorem Dei gloriam inque hominum salutem"* (To the greater glory of God and salvation of humankind). Victor Hammer became aware of this idea in his childhood, playing in sight of the portico of the Jesuitkirche in Vienna, into which was carved AD MAJOREM DEI GLORIAM in Roman capitals. Hammer's interest in what he referred to as "the classical order of the city", as it mirrored the order of the universe, and his conviction that the highest purpose of human art

and craft was to God's greater glory, led him to adopt the phrase for the colophon of his hand-printed books. Throughout the correspondence between the Hammers and Thomas Merton, "maiorem" is spelled with the classical *i*, not the later *j*, although this collection of their letters uses the latter spelling. When *i* functions as a consonant in Latin, it is often represented by *j*, because it proved inconvenient for *i* to be both vowel and consonant as the Latin alphabet was adapted to the Germanic and Romance languages. The first English book to distinguish between the *i* and *j* was published in 1634. *J* was the last of the twenty-six letters to be added to the English alphabet, beginning as a typographical flourish or swash form of a word-final *i*. Eventually *j* came to be used for the consonant and *i* was restricted to vowel use. *J* was not universally considered a distinct letter in the alphabet until the nineteenth century.

Introduction

1. Thomas Merton, *Figures for an Apocalypse* (Norfolk, Conn: New Directions, 1948), 101.

2. Arthur W. Biddle, ed., *When Prophecy Still Had a Voice: The Letters of Thomas Merton & Robert Lax* (Lexington: University Press of Kentucky, 2001).

3. Letters of Merton to the Hammers have been quoted in numerous books and essays, including Michael Mott, *The Seven Mountains of Thomas Merton* (Boston: Houghton Mifflin, 1984), and David D. Cooper, *Thomas Merton's Art of Denial: The Evolution of a Radical Humanist* (Athens: University of Georgia Press, 1989).

4. Cooper, *Thomas Merton's Art of Denial*, 93.

5. Thomas Merton, *The Seven Storey Mountain* (New York: Harcourt Brace, 1948), 108.

6. Mott, *The Seven Mountains of Thomas Merton*, 214.

7. Ibid., 550.

8. Victor Hammer, *Fragments for CRH* (Lexington, Ky.: Stamperia del Santuccio, 1967), 1–4.

9. Victor Hammer, *Four Dialogues* (Lexington, Ky.: Stamperia del Santuccio, 1956), 101.

10. Paul Evans Holbrook, comp., *Introduction to Victor and Carolyn Hammer* (Lexington, Ky.: Anvil Press, 1995), 22, 32.

11. Ibid., 32.

The Letters

1. *The Christmas Sermons of Bl. Guerric of Igny* had an introduction by Merton and was translated by Sister Rose of Lima. It was published with the copyright of the Abbey of Gethsemani in 1959 and not by any of the Hammers' presses.

2. J. P. Migne, ed., *Patrologia Cursus Completus,* Series Latina, 221 vols. (Paris: Garnier, 1844–1865).

3. Peter Watts (1916–2002) was a British sculptor.

4. Dr. Lawrence Thompson (1916–1986), a classics scholar, was the director of the Margaret I. King Library at the University of Kentucky; he carried on an active correspondence with Merton from the early 1950s.

5. Hugo von Hofmannsthal (1874–1929) was a Viennese dramatist and playwright whose bust was sculpted by Victor Hammer.

6. Victor published *Three Fragments from the Posthumous Papers of Conrad Fiedler, MDCCCXLI–MDCCCXCV,* trans. Thornton Sinclair and Victor Hammer (Lexington, Ky.: Stamperia del Santuccio, 1951).

7. Conrad Fiedler (1841–1895), a philosopher of art, is little known. Victor Hammer thought he was the most important art theorist of the nineteenth century and translated some of his work into English.

8. Alexander de Grunelius (1890–1977) and his wife, Antoinette Slumberger (1908–1994), were patrons of Victor Hammer. He was the administrator of Dietrich Enterprises and inherited Le Château de Kolbsheim, where Victor Hammer built their chapel. The Grunelius children were godchildren of Jacques and Raïssa Maritain.

9. Jacques Maritain (1882–1973) was a Thomist theologian, philosopher, and aesthetician. He served as the French ambassador to the Vatican in 1945 and later taught at Princeton. His library and archives are in Kolbsheim. He and his wife, Raïssa (1883–1960), are buried with their Grunelius friends. He was familiar to Merton, as well, and they met and maintained a correspondence from the time that Merton was a student at Columbia.

10. The phrase "das ganz Andere" is German for "the very different."

11. Brother Giles was responsible for the physical structure of the abbey at Gethsemani and was the person who asked Victor to assist with the placement of the sculptor Peter Watts's Stations of the Cross in the abbey, the occasion of the Hammers' first meeting with Merton.

12. *Tower of Babel* was published in a limited edition (250 copies) on a hand press by Richard von Sichowoky of Hamburg, for New Directions; see William H. Shannon, Christine M. Bochen, and Patrick F. O'Connell, *The Thomas Merton Encyclopedia* (Maryknoll, N.Y.: Orbis Books, 2002), 490, for details.

13. These materials are not available.

14. The triptychon was later named *Hagia Sophia Crowning the Young Christ.*

15. Ulrich Middeldorf (1901–1983) was a prominent art historian and sometime director of the Kunsthistorische Institut in Florence and a professor at the University of Chicago. He was responsible for the art exhibit of Hammer's that resulted in the invitation for Victor be "in residence" at Transylvania University.

16. James Laughlin (1914–1997) was the founding publisher of New Directions. Merton published a great deal of his work with New Directions, and he and Laughlin became friends, as did the Hammers.

17. Merton visited Cuba in 1940, and he wrote in *The Seven Storey Mountain* (279) that he had gone to Cuba "to make a pilgrimage to Our Lady of Cobre." This resulted in his poem "Song for Our Lady of Cobre."

18. Merton served as novice master at the Abbey of Gethsemani from June 1955 through August 1965; see Shannon et al., *Thomas Merton Encyclopedia,* 288–89, for details.

19. Bernard Craplet, *Auvergne Romane* (Yonne: Zodiaque, 1958).

20. In spite of this agreement, the Guerric book was not published by any of the Hammers' presses.

21. Daisete T. Suzuki (1870–1966) was a scholar of Zen with whom Merton later entered into correspondence and visited in New York in June 1964.

22. There are several references to the possible publication of translations of Flavius Magnus Aurelius Cassiodorus (485–585), a Roman statesman, religious writer, and Christian educator. It was published by Stamperia del Santuccio as *Of Scribes* (from *De Antiquariis*) by the Hammers in 1958. This was the first occasion Victor and Carolyn Hammer shared the Stamperia del Santuccio imprint.

23. Paul Hindemith (1895–1963) was a German-American composer with whom Merton became involved in a collaboration for a musical version of *The Tower of Babel,* which was never performed.

24. D. T. Suzuki, *Manual of Zen Buddhism* (1935; repr., London: Rider, 1950).

25. Presumably the sixth set of Merton's *Monastic Orientation* conference notes, given to the scholastics in 1954–1955, just before he became novice master.

26. Prayer to the Sacred Heart; see Merton to Hammer, July 19, 1956.

27. This is the first reference to one of Merton's favorite books, *What Ought I to Do? Sayings of the Desert Fathers from the Collection in Migne's Latin Patrology,* trans. Thomas Merton, which was published by Stamperia del Santuccio in 1959.

28. Merton did in fact do a Cassiodorus translation for the Stanbrook nuns in 1967.

29. Albert B. ("Happy") Chandler (1898–1991) was governor of Kentucky 1935–1939 and 1955–1959; for his visit to Gethsemani, see Merton's journal entry for May 14, 1957.

30. Victor Hammer, *Memory and Her Nine Daughters the Muses: A Pretext for Printing Cast into the Mould of a Dialogue in Four Chapters* (Lexington, Ky.: Stamperia del Santuccio, 1957).

31. Thomas Merton, *Prometheus, A Meditation* (Lexington, Ky.: King Library Press, 1958).

32. The visit took place on February 27—see his journal entries for February 28, 1958, and March 6, 1958.

33. Victor Hammer painted three versions of his *Crucifixus*, depicting Jesus on the cross, with the face modeled on the Shroud of Turin. Saint Mary and Saint John are depicted on either side of the Cross. The *Crucifixus* was made for the chapel at Kolbsheim. One version is in the Kolbsheim Chapel, one at Gethsemani, and one in the Newman Center at the University of Kentucky, where it was given by John Gaines.

34. *The Unquiet Conscience* by Piero Bargellini, later translated by Thomas Merton (see Merton to Hammer, July 29, 1958).

35. Presumably proverbs for *Prometheus*—see the following letter.

36. See his journal entry for July 9, 1958, for an account of this visit.

37. Saint Notburga was praying the Angelus when her overlord demanded she work. She threw her sickle up in the air as an act of defiance, where it remained suspended above her head. *Saint Notburga* was a painting by Victor Hammer of the thirteenth-century patron saint of peasants and servants.

38. This refers to "Art and Worship," never published.

39. Numa Denis Fustel de Coulanges (1830–1889) was a French historian.

40. "Letter to an Innocent Bystander"; see Merton to Carolyn Hammer, July 4, 1958.

41. "Liturgical Feasts and Sessions," two sets of novitiate conference notes.

42. Merton did succeed in sending Pasternak a copy of *Prometheus, A Meditation*. See his journal entry for October 18, 1958, for details.

43. *Inside Russia*, by John Gunther, was published in 1958.

44. "Letter to an Innocent Bystander" was published in Merton, *Behavior of Titans* (New York: New Directions, 1961), 51–64, and Merton, *Raids on the Unspeakable* (New York: New Directions, 1966), 53–62.

45. Merton never published a book on sacred art.

46. *The Unquiet Conscience* (originally written in Latin by Piero Bargel-

lini) was published by the Stamperia del Santuccio, Lexington, Ky., in 1958. It was translated from the Latin by Thomas Merton and printed by Carolyn Hammer.

47. "That which pleases when seen"—Thomas Aquinas's definition of beauty (*Summa Theologica*, I–II, q. 27, a.1, ad 3).

48. *The Unquiet Conscience* (see note 46, above).

49. Sacred spring.

50. Victor Hammer, *On Classic Art* (Lexington, Ky.: Hammer Press, 1959).

51. For an account of this visit, see his journal entry for April 4, 1959.

52. See his journal entry for April 23, 1959, for an account of this visit to the Hammers' home.

53. Victor Hammer made three beaten silver plates for Merton and the Hammers to eat from when they were together. They were inscribed with a quotation chosen by Merton, "The tongue of the righteous is choice silver."

54. "Silver has its origins in veins."

55. Ad Reinhardt and Robert Lax were both close friends of Merton's from his days at Columbia. Reinhardt was a respected abstract painter and Robert Lax was a poet.

56. This is a reference to "A Signed Confession of Crimes against the State," first published in *Carleton Miscellany* (Fall 1960): 21–23 and reprinted in *Behavior of Titans*, 65–71.

57. Shortly before this letter was written, Merton had visited the Hammers in their home. While he was there, he noticed the triptych that Victor was painting, a painting that had been commissioned by Carolyn Reading before she and Victor were married. The triptych shows a woman crowning a young Christ, who stands in front of her. Merton asked Victor who she was, and Victor explained that she had started as a Madonna and Child, but he now did not know who she was. Merton quickly replied, "I know who she is; I have always known her. She is Hagia Sophia." From this observation and the exchange of the next two letters came one of Merton's most famous poems, *Hagia Sophia*, which was published by Stamperia del Santuccio. The triptych is portrayed in several other media, including two woodcuts, a linecut, a criblé engraving on brass, many drawings, and the finished tempera and gilt triptych entitled *Hagia Sophia Crowning the Young Christ*.

58. See Shannon et al., *Thomas Merton Encyclopedia*, 30, for details.

59. Constantine Cavarnos, *Anchored in God: Life, Art, and Thought on the Holy Mountain of Athos* (Athens: Astir Publishing, 1959).

60. Probably Sister Therese Lentfoehr, SDS (1902–1981).

61. Giovanni Mardersteig (1892–1977) was a prominent printer in Vero-

na, Italy. He did the printing for Clement of Alexandria, *Selections from the Protreptikos,* an essay and translation by Thomas Merton (New York: New Directions, 1962). Evidently at this point there was some idea that he would do the printing for the expanded version of the Desert Fathers mentioned in *The Wisdom of the Desert* (New York: New Directions, 1961).

62. Victor Hammer crafted a two-color initial *E* with a monk in the background. It was used in Cassiodorus's *Of Scribes,* as well as Merton's *What Ought I to Do.*

63. "There was a certain brother, a nonentity having for his own resources only the Gospels, which he sold for the nourishment of the poor, saying:

Now too the Word itself has been sold, because it commands, 'Sell all and give to the poor!'"

64. Kurt (1887–1963) and Helen (1906–1994) Wolff were German publishers who immigrated to the United States and founded Pantheon Books in 1941. She later worked for Harcourt, Brace.

65. See his journal entry for August 9, 1959, for a description of their visit the previous day.

66. Harry Duncan was the printer at the Cummington Press in Cummington, Mass., who had originally been commissioned by James Laughlin to do the limited-edition version of Merton's *The Tower of Babel,* but he had to withdraw when Paul Williams, his partner at the press, was killed in an automobile accident. See *Thomas Merton and James Laughlin: Selected Letters,* ed. David D. Cooper (New York: W. W. Norton, 1997), 105, 107.

67. See *When Prophecy Still Had a Voice: The Letters of Thomas Merton and Robert Lax,* ed. Arthur W. Biddle (Lexington: University Press of Kentucky, 2001), 174–75.

68. Frank Dell'Isola was the compiler of *Thomas Merton: A Bibliography* (New York: Farrar, Straus and Cudahy, 1956).

69. The magazine is *Sponsa Regis,* published at St. John's University, Collegeville, Minn., and edited by Merton's friend and correspondent Kilian McDonnell, OSB. Merton wrote a series of articles for *Sponsa Regis* on spiritual direction, published in the June, July, and November 1959 issues, so the manuscript in question could have been for any (or all) of them, or it might have been for upcoming articles on art and worship published in the December 1959 and January 1960 issues. The spiritual direction material from the February, March, April, May, and June issues of *Sponsa Regis* would subsequently be published as *Spiritual Directions and Meditation* (Collegeville, Minn.: Liturgical Press, 1960). The January 1960 article on art would be published in Merton, *Disputed Questions* (New York: Farrar, Straus and Cudahy, 1960), 151–64.

70. Raymond Léopold Bruckberger (1907–1998) was a French Dominican and friend of Albert Camus.

71. Guerric of Igny, *The Christmas Sermons of Bl. Guerric of Igny: An Essay by Thomas Merton,* trans Sister Rose of Lima (Trappist, Ky.: Abbey of Gethsemani, 1959).

72. The Hammers (though not J. Laughlin) came to Gethsemani on December 19, 1959; see the account of the visit in his journal entry for December 20, 1959.

73. On December 22, 1959, Merton went to Lexington to pick up these crucifixes and had lunch with the Hammers; see his journal entry for December 26, 1959.

74. See his journal entry for December 26, 1959, for a description of the visit; see also his journal entry for June 7, 1959, for Merton's first visit to Shakertown.

75. See "Pleasant Hill: A Shaker Village in Kentucky," in Thomas Merton, *Mystics and Zen Masters* (New York: Farrar, Straus and Giroux, 1967), 193–202, originally published as "The Shadows: American Celibates Who Danced to the Glory of God," *Jubilee* (January 1964): 36–41. "Pleasant Hill" also appears in Thomas Merton, *Seeking Paradise: The Spirit of the Shakers,* ed. Paul M. Pearson (Maryknoll, N.Y.: Orbis, 2003), 54–71.

76. Thomas Merton, *The Solitary Life* (Lexington, Ky.: Stamperia del Santuccio, 1960).

77. There was discussion of a tabernacle and candlesticks to be made by Victor for the novitiate chapel at Gethsemani, but they were never made.

78. This was done: the Shakertown at Pleasant Hill Historic District is today a National Historic Landmark.

79. See Thomas Merton, *Emblems of a Season of Fury* (Norfolk, Conn.: J. Laughlin, 1963), 125–34, which includes an introduction and five poems by Carrera Andrade, and *The Collected Poems of Thomas Merton* (New York: New Directions, 1977), 841–46, which includes these five translations and one additional translated poem.

80. The Hammers went to Gethsemani on January 13, 1960, when James Laughlin was also visiting; see his journal entry for January 14, 1960.

81. Shirley Burden was the photographer for *God Is My Life: The Story of Our Lady of Gethsemani,* introduction by Thomas Merton (New York: Reynal, 1960). The collaboration on the Shakers never resulted in a book.

82. Robert Giroux (1914–2008), editor and publisher with Farrar, Straus and Cudahy (later Giroux), was a friend of Merton's.

83. Thomas Merton, "Notes for a Philosophy of Solitude," in *Disputed Questions,* 177–207.

84. For an account of this visit, see his April 3, 1960, journal entry.

85. For an account of this visit, see his May 16, 1960, journal entry.

86. George W. Headley (1908–1985), a jewelry designer and collector, was a friend of the Hammers and Merton.

87. Attached to this letter was the cover for *The Solitary Life*, the poem "I, Solitude," subsequently published as "Song: If You Seek" in *Emblems of a Season of Fury*, 38–39, and *Collected Poems*, 340–41, and used as Christmas cards by Merton and the Hammers.

88. Ananda Kentish Coomeraswamy (1877–1947) was a Ceylonese philosopher, metaphysician, and art historian. He was the pioneering interpreter of Indian art and symbolism to the West. He served as a curator for many years at the Museum of Fine Arts, Boston.

89. For the July 30 visit, see his journal entry for this day.

90. Thomas Merton, "Theology of Creativity," *American Benedictine Review* (September 1960): 191–213, published as part of a symposium, and reprinted in Merton, *Literary Essays of Thomas Merton*, ed. Patrick Hart (New York: New Directions, 1981), 355–70. See *Thomas Merton: Selected Essays*, ed. Patrick F. O'Connell (Maryknoll, N.Y.: Orbis Books, 2013), 86, for details.

91. "The nature of beauty is not ontological but axiological."

92. Merton was working on an introduction to Meng Tzu, *Ox Mountain Parable* (see note 105, below).

93. He refers to the text of *Ox Mountain Parable;* see his journal entry for July 10, 1960.

94. Clay Lancaster (1917–2000) was a native Lexingtonian and a noted architectural historian of the Bluegrass, Nantucket, and Brooklyn, N.Y. He was a longtime friend of Carolyn Reading Hammer and an ardent preservationist.

95. Merton's visit took place on October 8, 1960; see his journal entry for October 9 for details.

96. Mahatma Gandhi, *Non-Violence in Peace and War,* from which Merton was getting texts for *Gandhi on Non-Violence* (New York: New Directions, 1965). See his November 12, 1960, journal entry for more details.

97. Merton's *Wisdom of the Desert* was designed by Giovanni Mardersteig.

98. "Herakleitos: A Study," *Jubilee* 8 (September 1960): 24–31, reprinted in *Behavior of Titans*, 75–84.

99. Merton refers to what will become the hermitage; see Shannon et al., *Thomas Merton Encyclopedia*, 197–200, for details.

100. See his October 25, 1960, journal entry, in which Merton stops for supper at the Hammers' on the way back from Cincinnati and is told of someone (i.e., David Rowland) who can make a copy of Victor's table.

101. "As you heard a musical chord with heavenly reverberation."

102. Charles Journet (1891–1975), a Swiss theologian, was eventually made a cardinal.

103. He refers to "Notes for a Philosophy of Solitude."

104. Dr. James Wygal was Merton's psychiatrist. He and his wife went with the Hammers and Merton on a visit to Shakertown.

105. Mencius [Meng Tzu], *The Ox Mountain Parable,* trans. I. A. Richards, ed. Thomas Merton (Lexington, Ky.: Stamperia del Santuccio, 1960).

106. The Sisters of Loretto are in Nerinx, Ky., about sixty miles south of Louisville and close to Gethsemani. For Merton's close relations with Loretto and its dynamic superior, Mary Luke Tobin, see Bonnie Thurston, ed., *Hidden in the Same Mystery: Thomas Merton and Loretto* (Louisville: Fons Vitae, 2010).

107. Frank Dell'Isola compiled *Thomas Merton: A Bibliography,* rev. ed. (Kent, Ohio: Kent State University Press, 1975).

108. I. A. Richards (1893–1979) was a Harvard philosopher, literary critic, and rhetorician. He had taught earlier at Cambridge.

109. For a Guggenheim fellowship.

110. Sir Herbert Read (1893–1968) was a British poet and literary writer.

111. Princeton University Press's Bollingen Series had its beginnings in the Bollingen Foundation, a 1943 project of Paul Mellon's Old Dominion Foundation. From 1945 the foundation had independent status, publishing and providing fellowships and grants in several areas of study including, archaeology, poetry, and psychology. The Bollingen Series was given to the university in 1969.

112. His letters to Doña Luisa Runstein, Coomaraswamy's widow, appear in *The Hidden Ground of Love: The Letters of Thomas Merton on Religious Experience and Social Concerns,* ed. William H. Shannon (New York: Farrar, Straus and Giroux, 1985), 125–33.

113. Though there was a discussion between Merton and Hammer about a piece on Coomaraswamy, it never came to fruition.

114. INRI are the Latin initials for "Jesus of Nazareth, King of the Jews," which Pilate had written above the cross. Victor added it to the one at Gethsemani and the one now at the Newman Center in Lexington.

115. Thomas Merton eventually wrote this book, but not for the Hammers. See Nicholas de Cusa, *Dialogue about the Hidden God,* trans. Thomas Merton (New York: Dim Gray Bar Press, 1989), and Shannon et al., *Thomas Merton Encyclopedia,* 326, for details.

116. J. J. Bachofen (1815–1887), *Walls: Res Sanctae, Res Sacrae,* trans. B. Q. Morgan (Lexington, Ky.: Stamperia del Santuccio, 1961). He was a Swiss antiquarian and jurist.

117. Thomas McDonnell was coming to discuss *A Thomas Merton Reader* (New York: Harcourt, Brace & World, 1962), which he edited. See Merton's journal entry for May 27, 1961.

118. Wayne Williams was a graduate student in philosophy and friend of the Hammers. He translated Conrad Fiedler's aphorisms (never published). He was later head of medical illustration at the University of Kentucky, Duke University, and the University of North Carolina.

119. Jean Danielson; see his July 18, 1961, journal entry.

120. Vladimir Lossky, *Théologie négative et connaissance de Dieu chez Maître Eckhart* (Paris: J. Vrin, 1960).

121. A poem by Merton, "Chant to Be Used in Processions around a Site with Furnaces," was published in 1961 by Lawrence Ferlinghetti in the inaugural edition of the *Journal for the Protection of All Beings.*

122. Merton was much taken by the Shakers and Shakertown, as evidenced by his correspondence. He took numerous photos of buildings and corresponded with Victor and Carolyn about restoration of the buildings. His correspondence about Shakertown, along with many of his Shakertown photos, is in *A Meeting of Angels: The Correspondence of Thomas Merton with Edward Deming and Faith Andrews,* ed. Paul M. Pearson (Frankfort, Ky.: Broadstone Books, 2008).

123. See these articles in Thomas Merton, *Passion for Peace: The Social Essays,* ed. William H. Shannon (New York: Crossroad, 1995); see also Shannon et al., *Thomas Merton Encyclopedia,* 352.

124. For an account of this visit, including Merton on Victor Hammer's first sketch for his portrait of Merton, see his journal entry for November 17, 1961.

125. Thomas Merton et al., *Breakthrough to Peace* (Norfolk, Conn.: J. Laughlin, 1962); see Shannon et al., *Thomas Merton Encyclopedia,* 32–33, for details.

126. William Congdon (1912–1998) was an abstract expressionist painter, a Catholic convert who visited Gethsemani on May 27, 1961; Merton wrote an endorsement of his work for a book, William Congdon, *In My Disc of Gold: Itinerary to Christ* (New York: Reynal, 1962) (see his journal entry for June 10, 1961), which appeared on the volume's cover (see journal entry for February 20, 1962) and was also published in *Liturgical Arts* 20 (February 1962).

127. Attached to a previous letter was a copy of Merton's poem "Original Child Bomb," the name given by the Japanese to the atomic bomb that exploded over Japan; it was published as *Original Child Bomb: Points for Meditation to Be Scratched on the Walls of a Cave* by New Directions in 1962. See

precise publication details in Shannon et al., *Thomas Merton Encyclopedia*, 342.

128. Hilaire Belloc, *The Path to Rome* (New York: Longmans, Green, 1902), was the title of the book that Victor Hammer was asking for.

129. This is another version of *Hagia Sophia Crowning the Young Christ*, a criblé engraving in brass; previous discussions concerning the frontispiece were about a woodcut that was never used, and the brass was never finished. The unfinished engraving was used as a frontispiece for the second edition of Merton's essay *Hagia Sophia*, published as the last issue of the Stamperia del Santuccio, in 1978.

130. "Tender poem, like a rainbow, is drawn only on a dark background."

131. Jonathan Greene was a poet and the publisher of the Gnomon Press and a friend of both Merton and the Hammers. See *On the Banks of Monks Pond: The Thomas Merton/Jonathan Greene Correspondence* (Frankfort, Ky.: Bardstown Books, 2004).

132. Thomas Merton, ed., *Peace in the Post-Christian Era*, was not published until 2004, by Orbis Books.

133. Congressman Frank Kowalski of Connecticut. The prayer was published in Thomas Merton, *The Nonviolent Alternative*, ed. Gordon C. Zahn (New York: Farrar, Straus and Giroux, 1980), 268–70. It was first published in the *U.S. Congressional Record* 108 (April 18, 1962), 5:6937.

134. Leo Szilard (1898–1964) was a physicist and inventor who was responsible for the development of nuclear reactions and was involved in efforts during the 1960s to warn the president of the consequences of nuclear war and advocate for nuclear disarmament. See Merton's April 12, 1962, letter to him in Thomas Merton, *Witness to Freedom: The Letters of Thomas Merton in Times of Crisis*, ed. William H. Shannon (New York: Farrar, Straus and Giroux, 1994), 49–50.

135. This is an acronym for the Committee for Non-Violent Action.

136. See Merton's June 3, 1962, journal entry for details of this visit, when Victor Hammer brought his drawing and portrait of Merton.

137. See Merton's journal entry for July 8, 1962, for his comments on this visit.

138. See Merton's journal entry for June 7, 1962, on this prayer, and the one for July 3, 1962, on his translation. It was eventually printed in 1967 as *A Prayer from the Treatise "De Anima,"* by the Benedictine nuns of Stanbrook Abbey in England. See Shannon et al., *Thomas Merton Encyclopedia*, 366–67, for details.

139. Merton refers to works by Notker Balbulus ("The Stammerer") (ca. 840–912), a poet and Benedictine monk at the Abbey of Saint Gall in Switzerland, that the Hammers had brought to him on July 7.

140. With this letter, Merton signed his first name, Tom, and the Hammers addressed him by that name.

141. Thomas Merton, "Grace's House," in *Emblems of a Season of Fury*, 28–29, and *Collected Poems*, 330–31.

142. See his journal entry for August 27, 1962, for an account of this visit.

143. Victor Hammer had been encouraging Merton to translate some of the poems of Giacomo Leopardi (1798–1837); see his journal entry for September 20, 1963.

144. For an account of the Hammers' visit on March 23, see Merton's journal entry for March 27, 1963.

145. See his journal entry for June 5, 1963.

146. Frank Dickey was president of the University of Kentucky when Merton was awarded the honorary doctor of letters degree.

147. *Chapters on Writing and Printing* (Lexington, Ky.: Anvil Press, 1963) included four essays from Paul Standard, Victor Hammer, R. Hunter, and Carolyn R. Hammer.

148. The Benedictines were Dom Burkhard Neunheuser and Dom Adrien Nocent; see his journal entry for August 13, 1963.

149. Apparently, the Hammers did not go to Gethsemani that day; in his September 8 journal entry Merton mentions Fr. Bernard Haring being there, but not the Hammers.

150. Merton was in the hospital from September 12 through 25, 1963. See his journal entries for September 19, 20, 23, and 28, 1963, for details.

151. Victor Hammer, *Concern for the Art of Civilized Man* (Lexington, Ky.: Stamperia del Santuccio, 1963).

152. The work Merton is referring to is "Art and Worship," which was never published.

153. Iris Origo, *Leopardi: A Study of Solitude* (London: Oxford University Press, 1935).

154. What follows is Victor's efforts to provide Merton with additional information regarding the woman taken in adultery, which Merton could then use for his foreword to the catalogue for an exhibition of Victor's work at the North Carolina Museum of Art. Victor painted five versions of the painting in his long life, *John VIII: Christ and the Adulteress*, first in 1930, in 1939 (unfinished), 1948, 1961, and the fifth version in 1962–1963.

155. This is the beginning of the collection of Merton's works that resulted in the creation of the Thomas Merton Center at Bellarmine University.

156. See information in note 122, above.

157. Stanley Morison (1889–1967) was a British typographer, designer, and historian of printing.

158. Thomas Merton, "To Each His Darkness: Notes on a Novel of Julien Green," *Charlatan* 1 (Spring 1964), n.p., reprinted in *Raids on the Unspeakable* (New York: New Directions, 1966), 27–33.

159. For more details about this visit, see his journal entry for January 13, 1964.

160. Edmund Pellegrino, M.D. (1920–2013), professor of medicine at the University of Kentucky, later of medicine and medical ethics at the Kennedy Institute of Ethics, Georgetown University, was a friend of the Hammers.

161. For this visit see his journal entry of April 20, 1964.

162. See Merton's comments on this primitive painter in Thomas Merton, *An Introduction to Christian Mysticism: Initiation into the Monastic Tradition,* ed. Patrick F. O'Connell (Kalamazoo: Cistercian Publications, 2008), 134–35.

163. When used together, "schluss" and "grüss gott" mean "in closing and farewell."

164. The Hancock Shaker Village is near Pittsfield, Mass.

165. On this topic, see Paul M. Pearson, "Merton and the Celtic Monastic Tradition: Search for the Promised Land," *Merton Annual* 5 (1992): 263–77.

166. Clyde Kennard (1927–1963) was a civil rights pioneer who tried to desegregate Mississippi Southern College and was framed and imprisoned.

167. Marco Pallis (1895–1989) was a British musician and author. He wrote extensively regarding Tibet and was a connoisseur of early Baroque music.

168. See his journal entry for October 25, 1964, for details.

169. Thomas Merton, *Seeds of Destruction* (New York: Farrar, Straus and Giroux, 1964).

170. Eugene Ionesco is the subject of one of Merton's most celebrated essays, "Rain and the Rhinoceros," *Holiday* 37 (May 1965): 8, 10, 12, 15–16; reprinted in Merton, *Raids on the Unspeakable,* 9–23.

171. An exhibition of Merton's calligraphies was held at Catherine Spalding College in Louisville. For information on this exhibition, see Roger Lipsey, *Angelic Mistakes: The Art of Thomas Merton* (Boston: New Seeds, 2006), 28–29.

172. For the occasion of Carolyn Reading Hammer's ninetieth birthday, in 2001, this poem was reprinted in her honor at the King Library Press. It is also included in Merton, *Collected Poems* (New York: New Directions, 1977), 1005.

173. Stanbrook Abbey Press was at the time the oldest press in England. It was at an abbey built especially for Benedictine nuns. The press published limited editions of Merton's *The Solitary Life: A Letter of Guigo* (1963) and *A Prayer of Cassiodorus* (1967).

174. For an account of the visit see his journal entry for December 20, 1964.

175. Thomas Merton, "From Pilgrimage to Crusade," was first published in *Cithara* 4 (November 1964): 3–21, and reprinted in *Mystics and Zen Masters*, 91–112.

176. "From Pilgrimage to Crusade" also appeared in *Tomorrow* 13 (Spring 1965): 90–102.

177. Edmund Waller was an English poet (1606–1687) and author of "Go, Lovely Rose," about which Merton made a presentation at a conference on January 7, 1965.

178. Dr. Justus Bier (1899–1990) was chair of the Art Department at the University of Louisville, and later director of the North Carolina Museum of Art.

179. Merton prepared a foreword for the catalogue of Victor's art exhibit at the North Carolina Museum of Art; it is reproduced in appendix B.

180. He refers to his essay *Concern for the Art of Civilized Man*.

181. What follows are Victor's reflections that he provided to Merton as Merton considered writing the foreword to the exhibition catalogue for the show at the North Carolina Museum of Art. Like his previous reflections on the nature of art and artists, these are intended to inform Merton as he crafts his foreword.

182. Edgar Kaufmann Jr. (1910–1989), an art collector and art historian, was a student of Victor Hammer in Florence. He purchased Hammer's portrait of Merton, along with several other commissions.

183. *Dépouillement* (French): restraint.

184. *Recueillement* (French): meditation.

185. The following was a reflection by Jacques Maritain on the chapel at Kolbsheim, which was designed and furnished by Victor Hammer; it appeared in the catalogue that accompanied Victor's exhibition at the North Carolina Museum of Art. Maritain had suggested to Victor that he carve the words INTEGRITAS, CONSONANTIA, CLARITAS into the library mantel at the château at Kolbsheim while he was at work on the chapel.

186. Thomas Merton, "For a Renewal of Eremitism in the Monastic State," *Collection Cisterciensia* 27 (1965): 121–49, reprinted in *Contemplation in a World of Action* (Garden City, N.Y.: Doubleday, 1970), 284–327.

187. Merton and James Laughlin visited the Hammers in Lexington on May 4, 1965; see his journal entry for May 10, 1965, for details.

188. Thomas Merton, *The Way of Chuang Tzu* (New York: New Directions, 1965). For details see Shannon et al., *Thomas Merton Encyclopedia*, 521–23.

189. Lewis Mumford (1895–1990) was a historian, sociologist, and philosopher of urban life. He and Victor Hammer had an extensive correspondence.

190. For this visit see his journal entry for June 6, 1965.

191. Mai-mai Sze, *The Tao of Painting,* 2nd ed. (New York: Pantheon, 1963), which Merton borrowed on his June 6 visit.

192. Eric Gill, *Clothes: An Essay upon the Nature and Significance of the Natural and Artificial Integuments Worn by Men and Women* (London: J. Cape, 1931). For Merton's negative comments on this work see his journal entry for October 13, 1965.

193. "Anthology of Irish Poetry," a twenty-three-page mimeograph of poems taken from Kuno Meyer's translations, in *Selections from Ancient Irish Poetry* (London: Constable, 1911).

194. Thomas Merton, *Gethsemani: A Life of Praise* (Trappist, Ky.: Abbey of Gethsemani, 1966); see Shannon et al., *Thomas Merton Encyclopedia,* 175–76, for details.

195. Thomas Merton, "Symbolism: Communication or Communion," *Mountain Parables* 3 (October 1966): 339–48; reprinted in Merton, *Love and Living,* ed. Naomi Burton Stone and Patrick Hart (New York: Farrar, Straus and Giroux, 1979), 54–79.

196. Merton moved to the hermitage permanently on August 20, 1965, the feast of St. Bernard.

197. For this visit see his journal entry for November 13, 1965.

198. "Pebbles" was the working title that Victor used for a book that was subsequently published as *Some Fragments for C.R.H.* (Lexington, Ky.: Stamperia del Santuccio, 1967).

199. "Le Secret" was originally published in *Table Ronde* (July–August 1966): 88–90, and reprinted in *Collected Poems,* 635–37. Eventually this was included in *Thomas Merton's Four Poems in French* (Lexington, Ky.: Anvil Press, 1996), the final "collaboration" between Merton and the Hammers.

200. April 9 (Holy Saturday), 1966.

201. Nicanor Parra (b. 1914) is a Chilean mathematician and poet. James Laughlin and Nicanor Parra went to Gethsemani on May 4, 1966, and traveled with Merton to Louisville on May 5; see journal entries for May 4 and 7, 1966. For Merton's translations of eight of Parra's poems, see *Collected Poems,* 972–81; for his letters to Parra, see Thomas Merton, *The Courage for Truth: The Letters of Thomas Merton to Writers,* ed. Christine M. Bochen (New York: Farrar, Straus and Giroux, 1993), 212–14.

202. Henry Moore (1898–1986) was a British sculptor.

203. For this visit see his journal entries for June 18 and 19, 1966.

204. Li-Po (701–762) was a Chinese poet.

205. A "revised" version of the Desert Father story is included as #88 in *What Ought I to Do?* and as #112 in *Wisdom of the Desert.*

206. Jean Grenier (1898–1971) was a French philosopher who was Camus's professor at the University of Algiers.

207. This is apparently a covert reference to Merton's relationship with the student nurse he met after his surgery in March. See his journal entry for August 15, 1966, for the Hammers' concern about this.

208. Merton, "The Zen Koan," *Lugano Review* 1 (1966): 126–39, reprinted in *Mystics and Zen Masters*, 235–54, and "Buddhism and the Modern World," *Cross Currents* 16 (Fall 1966): 495–99, reprinted in *Mystics and Zen Masters*, 281–88.

209. For this visit see his journal entry for August 15, 1966.

210. For Merton's translation of Char's poem "Thatch of the Vosges," see *Merton Seasonal* 30.4 (Winter 2005).

211. See Merton's poem "For the Spanish Poet Miguel Hernandez," in *Collected Poems*, 641–42. For Merton's translation of a poem by Miguel Hernandez, see *Collected Poems*, 958. Seven more translations were published in the *Merton Seasonal* 28.2 (Summer 2003): 7–12; 28.3 (Fall 2003): 12–14; and 28.4 (Winter 2003): 6–8.

212. See Merton's comments on the Hammers' visit and "*Die Letzte Stunde*" in his journal entry for September 17, 1966.

213. See Merton's letter of December 28, 1964, to Carolyn Hammer for his inquiry about the University of Kentucky library's hosting this exhibit.

214. Wilbur H. (Ping) Ferry (1910–1995) was an American activist and vice president of the Center for the Study of Democratic Institutions and a close friend of Merton. See Merton's letters to him in *The Hidden Ground of Love*, 201–45.

215. This appears to be attached to the preceding letter from Merton; the Hammers asked if they might use it on their Christmas card in the following letter, dated November 25, 1966.

216. Merton, "'Baptism in the Forest': Wisdom and Initiation in William Faulkner," in *Mansions of the Spirit: Essays in Literature and Religion*, ed. George A. Panichas (New York: Hawthorn Books, 1967), 15–44, and reprinted in *Literary Essays*, 92–116.

217. Ralph Eugene Meatyard (1925–1972) was an optician and accomplished photographer who encouraged Merton's photographic efforts. For the January 17, 1967, visit of Meatyard with Jonathan Williams and Guy Davenport, see Merton's January 18, 1967, journal entry. Meatyard's photographs of Merton were published in Ralph Eugene Meatyard, *Father Louie: Photographs of Thomas Merton*, ed. Barry Magid (New York: Timken, 1991), and in *Meatyard/Merton: Merton/Meatyard: Photographing Thomas Merton* (Louisville: Fons Vitae, 2013).

218. Unpublished mimeograph in the twenty-four-volume "Merton: Collected Essays," assembled after Merton's death and available at the Thomas Merton Center, Bellarmine University, Louisville, Ky., 6:53–59.

219. Merton wrote the foreword to Thich Nhat Hanh, *Vietnam: Lotus in a Sea of Fire* (New York: Hill and Wang, 1967), vii–x.

220. Thomas Merton, "Notes for a Statement on Aid to Civilian War Victims in Vietnam," *Fellowships* 1 (January 1968): 15, 29, reprinted in *Nonviolent Alternative*, 265–67.

221. Thomas Merton, "Ishi: A Meditation," *Catholic Worker* 33 (March 1967): 5–6, reprinted in Merton, *Ishi Means Man: Essays on Native Americans* (Greensboro, N.C.: Unicorn Press, 1976), 25–32.

222. Thomas Merton, "Prophetic Ambiguities: Milton and Camus," was first published in shortened form as "Can We Survive Nihilism? Seton, Milton and Camus," *Saturday Review*, April 15, 1967, 16–19, and reprinted in Merton, *Literary Essays*, 252–60.

223. Merton, *Mystics and Zen Masters*.

224. Robert Marshall Shepherd, a watercolorist, bookbinder, and designer (1922–2002), and his wife, Hanna de Döry Shepherd (b. 1923), were friends of the Hammers and of Merton, and were part of the many picnics at Gethsemani. Bob Shepherd was with Victor at the hospital when he died.

225. John Slate (1913–1967) was a Columbia friend of Thomas Merton whom Merton selected to do the legal work in establishing the Merton Legacy Trust to oversee his literary affairs. For Slate's initial visit to Gethsemani, see Merton's April 6, 1965, journal entry. Slate died of a heart attack on September 19, 1967, before he could make a return visit to the monastery to work out details for the trust. See Merton's journal entry for September 22, 1967.

226. The Ruthwell Cross was a monumental Anglo-Saxon cross carved in runes with verses from the old English poem "The Dream of the Rood." See Merton's brief review of John Fleming, "'The Dream of the Rood' and Anglo-Saxon Monasticism," *Tradition* 22 (1966): 43–72, in *Collectanea Cisterciensia* 29 (1967), reprinted in *Cistercian Studies* 3 (1968): [120].

227. See his June 25, 1967, journal entry for details of Mumford's letter to Merton after Merton wrote a letter to the editor of the *New York Times Book Review* in response to his review.

228. For Merton's June 24, 1967, visit to the Hammers, see his journal entry for June 25, 1967.

229. See his July 8, 1967, journal entry on learning of Victor Hammer's critical illness.

230. The message was that Hammer had died on Monday, July 10; see Merton's reflection in his journal entry for July 14, 1967.

231. See his journal entry for July 27, 1967, for comments.

232. Gay Reading.

233. The Hammers introduced Merton to their friend John Jacob Niles, who set some of Merton's poems to music. The story is described in more detail in Ron Pen, *I Wonder as I Wander: The Life of John Jacob Niles* (Lexington: University Press of Kentucky, 2010). John Jacob Niles (1892–1980) was an American singer, composer, and collector of ballads. He and his wife, Rena, were friends of the Hammers and the Shepherds.

234. They were later published as Merton, *Early Poems 1941–42* (Lexington, Ky.: Anvil Press, 1971).

235. For this visit see his journal entry for October 29, 1967.

236. Gabriela Mistral (1889–1957) was the pen name of the Chilean poet Lucila Godoy Alcayaga, recipient of the Nobel Prize for Literature in 1945.

237. Denise Levertov (1923–1997) was a British-born American poet who converted to Catholicism in the last part of her life. Her poem "I learned that her name was Proverb" was based on Merton's dream as related in his October 23, 1958, letter to Boris Pasternak (see *Courage for Truth*, 90); see Denise Levertov, *The Stream and the Sapphire: Selected Poems on Religious Themes* (New York: New Directions, 1997), 8.

238. Wendell Berry (b. 1934) is a Kentucky poet, novelist, essayist, farmer, and environmental activist.

239. Thomas Merton, "A Responsory, 1948," in *Selected Poems of Thomas Merton*, enlarged ed. (New York: New Directions, 1967), 219–20.

240. See his journal entry for November 21, 1967, for this trip.

241. See his journal entries for December 7 and 8, 1967, for details of this first retreat with contemplative prioresses. Transcripts of Merton's resolved controversies for this retreat have been published in Thomas Merton, *The Springs of Contemplation: A Retreat at the Abbey of Gethsemani*, ed. Jane Marie Richardson (New York: Farrar, Straus and Giroux, 1992).

242. They were from Gethsemani's daughter house, the monastery of the Holy Spirit in Conyers, Ga., coming to Gethsemani for an election of a new abbot.

243. Father Charles Dumont was the editor of *Collectanea Cisterciensia;* see Merton's journal entries for January 6, 8, 10, and 18, 1968.

244. The poet Jonathan Greene had submitted a poem to Merton's new (four-issue) poetry magazine, *Monks Pond;* see Robert E. Daggy, ed., *Thomas Merton's Little Magazine* (Lexington: University Press of Kentucky, 1989). For details see Shannon et al., *Thomas Merton Encyclopedia*, 309–11.

245. Thomas Merton, "The Originators," broadside (Santa Barbara: Unicorn Press, 1967), reprinted in *Collected Poems*, 613.

246. Fr. Flavian Burns was elected abbot of Gethsemani on January 13, 1968; he resigned on January 31, 1973. For details see Merton, *Other Side of the Mountain: The End of the Journey,* ed. Patrick Hart (San Francisco: HarperCollins, 1998), 34–43, and Shannon et al., *Thomas Merton Encyclopedia,* 35.

247. For this visit, which included Bob and Hanna Shepherd and John and Rena Niles, see his journal entry for February 4, 1968.

248. He refers to the first of four issues of *Monk's Pond.*

249. Thomas Merton, "Regain the Old Monastery Clericalism," *National Catholic Reporter* 4 (January 11, 1968); this was a reply to an article by Colman McCarthy on monasticism. See his journal entry for December 19, 1967.

250. For this visit, made with Jonathan Greene on April 18, see his journal entry for April 18, 1968.

251. Dame Hildelith Cumming, OSB (1909–1991), was a Benedictine nun in charge of the printing press at Stanbrook Abbey, Callow End, Worcester, U.K., which printed Merton's *The Solitary Life: A Letter of Guigo* and *A Prayer of Cassiodorus.* For Merton's letters to her see Thomas Merton, *The School of Charity: The Letters of Thomas Merton on Religious Renewal and Spiritual Direction,* ed. Patrick Hart (New York: Farrar, Straus and Giroux, 1990), 161–62, 168, 170–72, 175–76, 177–78, 203–4, 216–17, 222–23, 234, 251–52, 268–69, 289, 318, and 330–31. The nuns spoke to visitors through a grille.

252. Dame Marcella van Bruyn, OSB; for Merton's letters to her see *School of Charity,* 160–61, 182–83, 190–91, 205–6, 249–50, 270–71, 284–85, 298–300, 302, and 311–12.

253. Merton visited California and New Mexico May 6–20, 1968; see "Woods, Shore, Desert: A Notebook, May 1968," in *Other Side of the Mountain,* 89–113, and his journal entries for May 21 and 24, 1968.

254. He refers to the second retreat for contemplative prioresses (see his journal entries for May 28 and June 4, 1968) and for Cistercian novice masters (see his journal entries for June 4 and 17, 1968).

255. Thomas Merton, "Roland Barthes—Writing as Temperature," *Sewanee Review* 77 (Summer 1969): 535–42, reprinted in *Literary Essays,* 140–46.

256. This was the Conference for Monastic Superiors of the Far East, held December 9–15, 1968, at the Red Cross Conference Center outside Bangkok, Thailand, at which Merton gave a presentation on Marxism and monastic perspectives on December 10 and accidentally died by electrocution from a faulty fan shortly thereafter. See Thomas Merton, *The Asian Journal of Thomas Merton,* ed. Naomi Burton, Patrick Hart, and James Laughlin (New York: New Directions, 1973), 326–43.

257. The Spiritual Summit Conference, sponsored by the Temple of Un-

derstanding and held in Calcutta in October 1968, was relocated from Darjeeling because of flooding. See his journal entries for October 19–27, 1968, for Merton's time in Calcutta and *Asian Journal*, 305–19, for Merton's informal presentation, formal prepared paper, and closing prayer at the conference.

258. Dame Marcella Van Bruyn (see note 252, above).

259. The conference was held in Washington, D.C., in August 1968, at which four of Merton's "Eight French Songs," with settings by Alexander Peloquin, were performed as a memorial for Martin Luther King by a choir from Ebenezer Baptist Church in Atlanta (King's own choir) and members of Peloquin's choir from Providence, R.I.; see his journal entry for April 26, 1968.

260. October 31, 1968; see his journal entry for October 31, 1968.

261. John Jacob Niles.

Afterword

1. Alexandre de Grunelius, "Requiem for Victor Hammer (9.XII.1882–10.VII.1967.)," in *Victor Hammer: An Artist's Testament* (Lexington, Ky.: Anvil Press, 1988), 298.

2. John Rothenstein, *Victor Hammer: Artist and Craftsman* (Boston: David Godine, 1987).

3. Victor Hammer, *Memory and Her Nine Daughters the Muses: A Pretext for Printing Cast into the Mould of a Dialogue in Four Chapters* (Lexington, Ky.: Stamperia del Santuccio, 1956), 49–54.

Index